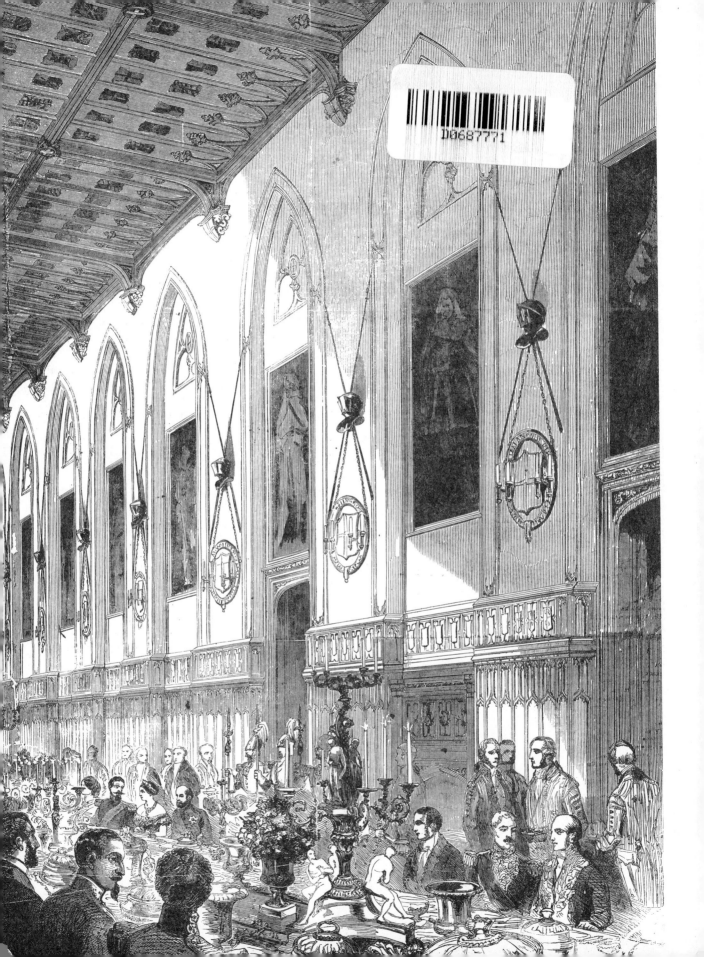

Lady Maclean's

Second Helpings

and More Diplomatic Dishes

Collins

By the same author

LADY MACLEAN'S COOK BOOK
LADY MACLEAN'S SAUCES AND SURPRISES
LADY MACLEAN'S DIPLOMATIC DISHES

William Collins Sons & Co Ltd

London * Glasgow * Sydney * Auckland

Toronto * Johannesburg

First published 1984
© Veronica Maclean 1984

ISBN 0 00 217356/5

For Fitz
who only asks
for more
when it's
good

Contents

Foreword

Diplomacy is the art of conciliating enemies, influencing friends, and establishing an ascendancy over rivals.

It often goes hand in hand with Gastronomy, which is apt to have similar aims; and where else can these two serious occupations be so agreeably practised as at an impeccably planned and furnished dinner table?

Talleyrand understood this, and was a Grand Master of both arts; and so did Thomas Jefferson, William Hamilton, George Curzon, Duff Cooper, and Christopher Soames .... the list is long and the tradition endless.

I have always admired 'embassy food', and the skills of my kindly diplomatic hostesses in manipulating the produce and cuisines of the countries to which they are accredited. I have often pleaded for their recipes and have even, on occasion, been allowed into embassy kitchens to learn from embassy cooks.

So many of the recipes in this book come from diplomatic gastronomes (or the other way round) in France, Belgium, Holland, Spain, Italy, Jugoslavia, Austria, Germany, Sweden, Greece, Brazil, Turkey, Russia, Iran, the United States, Canada and Tibet. Some have been revised and improved since their first appearance in 'Diplomatic Dishes', and I have now added to them a large number of other foreign and family favourites, begged, borrowed or stolen from good cooks and cookery writers, young and old, the world over. I thank them all for their generous and positive contribution to International harmony, and gastronomy, and this book.

Acknowledgements

I would particularly like to thank the following
who have all helped me get this book out of
the oven and on to the table - it could not have
been done without them.

Mrs Cockerill, Mrs Rob MacPherson
Mrs Donald Campbell, Coralie Dorman,
Alison Cochrane and Mary Cohen,
Les Lawrence and Elizabeth Bowes-Lyon.

Soups

GEORGE NATHANIEL CURZON, MARQUESS CURZON OF KEDLESTON
1859–1925
Viceroy of India, 1898–1905
Secretary of State for Foreign Affairs, 1919–1924

WINTER WARM SOUP

1 large leek	salt and pepper
1 large potato	water
2 celery sticks	2 oz (50 g) butter
2-4 medium Jerusalem artichokes	1 pint (600 ml) milk, or less
1 large onion	¼ pint (150 ml) cream
1 garlic clove	

Trim all the vegetables and place them in a saucepan with salt and
pepper and enough water to cover.   Bring to the boil and simmer
until they are quite mushy.   Pass through a sieve or blender.
Return to a saucepan and re-heat, blending in the butter and
diluting with milk.   Correct seasoning and stir in the cream just
before serving.

Lady Lovat

DALMATION CHICK PEA SOUP

about 8 oz (225 g) chick peas	salt and pepper
water	1 garlic clove, halved
1 tbs olive oil	1 lemon, thinly sliced

Soak the peas in water overnight.   Drain.   Boil the peas in
about 2 pints (1.2 litres) of fresh water to which you have added
a spoonful of good olive oil.   Season well with salt and pepper.
When just soft, or 'al dente', pour into a hot bowl or tureen you
have rubbed lightly with the garlic, and float a few thin lemon
rounds on top.
This is an ultra simple soup, but very comforting after a bout of
rich food.

Madame Rafo Ivancevic   -8-   Korčula

GAME SOUP

This recipe is adapted from Major Hugh Pollard's "The Sportsman's Cookery Book" published by Country Life in 1926, in the days of large shoots and shooting parties.   It starts: "Unlike boiled pheasant, which requires a young bird, pheasant soup is the Cook's provision for dealing with a very old one."

Cut from your pheasant the breast and winged portions and put aside. Hack up the remainder and put into the Stockpot with:

2½ pints (1.5 litres) Marrow Bone Stock	A Crushed Clove of Garlic
A small Celery Heart, chopped	A Bouquet Garni
2-3 Carrots, chopped	A Bayleaf

And if you have a Bacon Bone to hand, throw that in too.
Boil up, then simmer together gently for as long as you can - 4 hours minimum, - adding more water or Stock when necessary.   Sauté 2 finely chopped Onions in 1 Tablespoonful of Butter till they are soft and golden brown. Emulsify the saved Pheasant Meat with a little of the Stock in a blender: add to it breadcrumbs or a broken-up French Roll which you have steeped in Stock and the Yolk of an Egg.   Blend together to a creamy purée.   Strain the Stock into a clean pan, pressing down hard on the debris with a wooden spoon, then skim carefully.   Add the Pheasant Purée and the sautéed Onions to the strained Stock and bring it once to the boil.   Finally, add Sherry to taste, correct seasoning, and just before serving stir in ¼ Pint (150 ml) of Cream.   Croûtons, sautéed in butter and drained on kitchen paper, should be served with the Soup.
This recipe can be used for any old bird, including Grouse, but then a little Port should be substituted for the Sherry.

LA SOUPE DE SANTÉ AUX LAITUES

A traditional light Spring Soup for purifying the system, and dispersing the Rheums of Winter.

2-3 Spring Lettuces	A Little Chervil (or Parsley)
3-4 Leaves of Spinach Beet, with their Spines	3 Carrots
	2 Cloves of Garlic
A Handful of Sorrel	Pinch of Salt
2 Leeks	Pinch of Brown Sugar

Chop up the Vegetables quite roughly and wash them well in several waters. Throw them into 1¾ Pints (1 litre) of boiling water and add a little Salt and a pinch of Sugar, but no Pepper.   Simmer for 45 minutes.   Leave the vegetables in the Soup and make a meal of it alone, or toast thin water biscuits to eat with it.

LEYLA SOUP FROM ANKARA

2 tbs Butter
2 tbs Flour
2 Pints (1.2 Litres) Chicken Stock
2 Eggs

Juice of 1½ Lemons
Salt and Pepper
1 tbs Chopped Mint
1 Pint (600 ml) Thick Plain Yoghurt

Melt the Butter in a pan and stir in the Flour to make a Roux. Slowly add the Stock. Bring to the boil, stirring all the time. In a warm bowl beat the Eggs until they froth and add the Lemon Juice. Pour into a double boiler and add the cooled Stock Mixture. Bring to the boil then quickly remove from heat. Add Salt, Pepper and Chopped Mint to taste and the Yoghurt. On no account let the Yoghurt boil but bring back to serving heat, if you wish the Soup to be hot.

It is also very good served cold.

Derek Hill

GARLIC SOUP

"Soupe à l'ail" is very good for you, but unlike most things in this category it is also very good.

One Large Head of Garlic
2½ Pints (1.5 Litres) of Water
Salt
2 Egg Yolks

Approximately ¼ Pint (150 ml)
  Mixed Olive and Corn Oil
Pepper
Bread/Butter

Crush the unpeeled Garlic in a mortar, then put it on to boil for 30 minutes in slightly salted water.

In a lukewarm bowl make a Mayonnaise in the usual way with the 2 Egg Yolks and 2 Oils (this is a matter of taste; the Corn Oil merely lightens the stronger flavour of the Olive Oil).

Give it a twist or two of Pepper from the Pepper-Mill but do not add Salt or Vinegar.

Spoon it into an earthenware Soup Tureen, which you have warmed, and pour the strained Garlic Bouillon slowly over it, stirring vigorously, till you reach the right consistency.

It will produce a creamy soup that does not overpower, but has a rather delicate and non-garlicky flavour - You can serve it with fingers of thin buttered toast or make rounds of dried Toast and float these on top of each serving.

Marie et Louis Philippe

CHICKEN CREAM

In this soup you really taste the chicken. It is from an old French recipe book, c. 1775. Use all chicken stock if liked.

6½ oz (190 g) butter
3 tbs flour
1¼ pints (750 ml) blond de veau stock
1¼ pints (750 ml) chicken stock
1 boiling fowl
8 oz (225 g) lean veal, chopped
2 carrots

1 small slice turnip
2 celery sticks, with leaves
2 leeks, white part only
¼ pint (150 ml) single cream
2 egg yolks
salt and pepper
croûtons

Make a roux with 1½ oz (40 g) of the butter and the flour and cook it in a large soup pan for a few minutes without colouring, then add the boiling stock to it. Blend well. Put in the trussed fowl, veal, carrots, turnip, celery and leeks. Bring the soup back to the boil and simmer gently for about 2 hours.
Take out the fowl, bone and skin it and emulsify the white flesh with the veal in a blender, adding some of the remaining butter and cream, a little at a time. Strain the stock through a muslin cloth or nylon sieve, add the equally sieved purée of fowl, mix all together and give it a boil up.
Take the pan off the heat and bind the soup with the egg yolks beaten up with a little more butter and cream. Correct seasoning and serve in very hot soup plates with croûtons.

A Very Rich Lobster Bisque

If you wish to make a specially rich lobster bisque use the chicken cream soup recipe as above, substituting lobster butter for the ordinary butter. Just at the end, put in the meat of a small lobster and a few bits of the fowl. Season to taste. For the lobster butter, pound the spawn and coral of a small hen lobster with double the amount of butter. Sieve and refrigerate until wanted.

The Duchess of Portland

SPANISH ALMOND SOUP

½ pint (300 ml) milk

5 tbs chopped blanched almonds, fresh if possible

2 oz (50 g) butter

1 small onion, finely sliced

1½ tbs flour

1½ pints (900 ml) chicken stock

salt and pepper

1-2 celery sticks, sliced

2 egg yolks

3 tbs cream

Bring the milk to scalding point, add the almonds, cover the
saucepan and leave to infuse for 10 minutes, on very low heat.
Melt the butter in another saucepan, and add the onion.   Cook
slowly until soft.   Do not let it colour.   Blend in the flour
and then add the chicken stock slowly.   Season well and stir
until boiling.   Add the celery and simmer for 15 minutes.
Now emulsify the almonds and the milk, that have been keeping
warm in the first pan, using an electric blender, or pass them
through a fine nylon sieve.   Strain the chicken broth and
combine the two liquids.
Re-heat the soup and adjust seasoning and thicken, off the heat,
with a liaison of egg yolks and cream beaten together.   This
soup can also be served cold, in which case, add a few peeled
and halved green grapes, at the last moment.

Matilda, Duchess of Argyll

BLACK MUSHROOM SOUP

This is best made with flat dark-gilled mushrooms or better still, field mushrooms.

$\frac{3}{4}$ lb (350g) Mushrooms
Milk
1 large Onion
1 garlic Clove
2oz (50g) Clarified Butter
Salt and Pepper

2 pints (1.2 litres) bone stock
A Bouquet Garni
1 Bay leaf
$\frac{1}{2}$ pint (300ml) Double Cream
$\frac{1}{4}$ pint (150ml) Dry Sherry, warmed (optional)

Wipe the mushrooms with a damp cloth. Put $\frac{1}{2}$ lb (225g) into a blender with enough milk to blend. Blend medium fast to a creamy purée.

Cut the remaining mushrooms into thin slices. Chop the onion and garlic finely, then sauté them till soft in the butter. Add the sliced mushrooms, sprinkle them with a little salt to bring out their juices and sauté them too, till cooked. Put aside, but keep hot. Bring the stock with the herbs and seasonings to a slow boil, add the blended mushroom purée and simmer for 20 minutes.

Take the herbs out of the soup and stir into it the sautéed mushroom ragôut; mix well together, then remove from the heat and add the cream. Gently re-heat - don't boil - and just before serving add sherry, if you like it.

FISH CHORBA

1 lb (500 g) filleted fresh haddock or
  cat fish, or any white fish which flakes
1¾ pints (1 litre) water
bouquet garni
salt and pepper
1 large onion, chopped
3 oz (75 g) butter
1 large tomato, chopped

1 tbs flour
4 oz (100 g) fresh peeled shrimps
  prawns or canned shrimps
8 oz (225 g) white grapes,
  peeled and pips removed
½ pint (300 ml) double cream
fennel or basil, chopped

Simmer the fish in the water with a bouquet garni, and salt and pepper, for 10 minutes only. Remove skin from the fish and flake. Sauté the onion in butter, add the chopped tomato and flour; stir in some of the strained stock, then add all the stock, the flaked fish, the prawns or shrimps with their juice, and the grapes. Simmer a little longer. Add the cream just before serving, re-heat but do not boil. Sprinkle each serving with a little chopped fennel or basil.

H.E. Lady Wilson

LADY CLARK of TILLYPRONIE'S

PARTAN BREE

An Aberdeenshire crab soup that may owe something to Lady Clark's very high standards of good food. Her husband's long diplomatic career and their family Chef's training, which could be traced back to Second Empire Paris, make most of her recipes 'hors concours'.

2 large fresh crabs (or lobsters)
salt and white pepper
5 oz (150 g) rice
1 pint (600 ml) milk

3 pints (1.75 litres) clear fish stock
1 tsp anchovy sauce
7 fl oz (200 ml) double cream
1 egg

Boil 2 large crabs (or lobsters) in salted water; when cold remove the meat from the bodies and put it in a basin. Boil the rice in milk until tender, then drain and pass it, together with the crab meat, through a food mill or blender.
  Stir, gradually, into the resulting purée, the clear fish stock made without vegetables, and season with salt, pepper and the anchovy sauce.
  Put this into a casserole and heat it up, stirring all the time; then add the meat from the large claws, but first cut it into small pieces.
  Remove from heat and stir in the cream.
  If the soup is not thick enough add an egg whipped up before serving.

BLACK BEAN SOUP

2 pints (1.2 litres) Rich Marrow Bone Stock   2 oz (50 g) Bacon Fat
Bouquet Garni   1 Garlic Clove, crushed
Bay Leaf   1¾ lb (750 g) Canned Black Beans
Salt and Pepper   ¼ Pint (150 ml) Dry Sherry
1 Large Onion, chopped   ½ Pint (300 ml) Cream

Put Stock, Herbs and Seasoning to taste into a large pan and simmer while preparing the other ingredients. Sauté the Onion in the Bacon Fat. Add the Garlic to the Stock. Add half the Beans to the Stock and simmer this mixture until the Beans begin to split. This will make them easier to blend. Strain the Beans from the Stock, continue to simmer the Stock, and blend or sieve the Beans until creamy. Return the Bean Purée to the Stock. Simmer this for 10 minutes, then add the remaining whole beans to the soup. Cook until these are hot, stir in the Sherry and, lastly, the Cream. Serve very hot, as this is a fairly thick soup.

Joy Rainbird

HARE SOUP

½ Hare   1 oz (25 g) Butter
6 oz (175 g) Veal, chopped   Lemon Juice
3 Carrots, chopped   1 tbs Flour
2 Onions, chopped   2 fl oz (50 ml) Port
A bunch of Herbs   Pinch of mixed ground Spice
Salt and Pepper   4 tbs Cream
8 oz (225 g) Mushrooms   Croûtons

Put part of a Hare, a bit of Veal, Carrots, Onions and Herbs in salted water. Bring slowly to the boil. Skim the Stock and simmer it till it is well reduced.
Strain off the Stock and then purée the Meat, together with the Stock and Vegetables, in a food mill or blender.
Sauté the Mushrooms in some of the Butter with a little Lemon Juice. When they are cooked, purée them and then thicken the purée with a roux made with the rest of the Butter and Flour, moistening it with some of the Stock.
Add the game purée, the strained Stock, the Port, Salt and Pepper and Spice to the Mushroom Purée. Simmer together for 15 minutes, then bind the Soup with Cream. Do not reboil. Serve with Croûtons.

Mrs. Rob MacPherson

RICH RUSSIAN BORTSCH (for 8-10 people)

2 lb (1 kg) vegetables, including 1 small cabbage, a little
  white turnip, celery, leeks, onions and potatoes

4-5 pints (2.25-2.75 litres) good veal or beef stock

2½ tbs vinegar

14 oz (400 g) canned Italian whole tomatoes

bay leaf

salt and pepper

3 tbs good lard

8 oz (225 g) smoked lean ham and bacon, diced

4 oz (100 g) raw steak, diced

1 raw beetroot, shredded

9 fl oz (250 ml) sour cream

2½ tbs chopped fresh dill

Cut the washed vegetables into julienne strips. Cover with
the stock, vinegar and tomatoes, and bring to the boil. Add
the seasonings, the lard, bacon and ham and steak, and cook
until tender. Then add the raw, shredded beetroot. Remove
from the heat and blend in the sour cream. Sprinkle a little
chopped dill on to each serving.

NB This is a wonderfully satisfying peasant soup - practically
a meal in itself - but don't serve it at an elegant dinner party
where there is rich food to follow.

Mrs. Joe Dobbs

SPINACH SOUP FROM WILLIAMSBURG

1 lb (500 g) frozen spinach
¼ pint (150 ml) chicken stock
1 oz (25 g) butter
½ pint (300 ml) sour cream
4 oz (100 g) canned minced oysters
milk
salt
grated nutmeg
½ tbs lemon juice
dash of Worcester sauce
whipped cream, to serve

Put the spinach in a pan with the chicken stock and the butter. Cook until thawed through and then cool a little. Put into a blender with the sour cream and oysters and whirl until smooth, then thin down with milk until it is of the right consistency. Re-heat gently, but do not boil. Season with salt and nutmeg. Lastly, stir in the lemon juice and a dash of Worcester sauce.

Put a teaspoon of whipped fresh cream on top of each serving.

N.B. This soup is also delicious when chilled.

Fitzgerald Bemiss

RUSSIAN SORREL SOUP

1 onion, chopped
1 carrot, chopped
1½ tbs butter
2 tbs flour
2 pints (1.2 litres) stock
  (chicken or beef)

1 potato, finely chopped
salt and pepper
about 8 oz (225 g) French
  or garden sorrel, washed
  and finely chopped
3 hard-boiled eggs
sour cream, to serve

Fry the onion and carrot in butter until soft. Add the
flour, make a roux, then add the hot stock. Add the potato
to the stock and cook for 10 minutes or so. Season to
taste. Add the finely chopped sorrel leaves, and boil for
5 minutes more. Put half a hard-boiled egg (cut lengthways)
on each soup plate and ladle out boiling soup on to it.
Serve with a little sour cream.

This soup may also be put through a blender, but I prefer
it the way it is.

H.E. Lady Wilson

SHELLFISH SOUP

for 10

$2\frac{1}{2}$ tbs butter
$2\frac{1}{2}$ rounded tbs flour
6 fl oz (175 ml) unsweetened evaporated milk
2 pints (1.2 litres) canned clam juice
1 large onion, grated
8 oz (225 g) crab meat
8 oz (225 g) lobster meat
1 lb (500 g) peeled shrimps
2 sole fillets (or any good white fish that flakes well)
$\frac{1}{4}$ pint (150 ml) milk
$\frac{1}{2}$ pint (300 ml) milk mixed with $\frac{1}{2}$ pint (300 ml) double cream
$1\frac{1}{2}$ oz (40 g) capers, drained
4 fl oz (100 ml) white wine
salt and pepper
a little chopped parsley

Make a roux with the butter and flour, then slowly add the
evaporated milk, and, when you have a smooth sauce, the clam
juice. Bring again to the boil, add the grated onion and
boil a minute or two longer, then add the crab, lobster meat
and shrimps, cut in pieces. Poach the sole fillets in the
milk, mash and add these also to the soup. Just before
serving add the thinned down cream, capers and white wine.
Do not boil again, just keep very hot. Season to taste and
add a little chopped parsley just before serving.

Mrs. John Ryan

OTTAWA

NOVA SCOTIAN CLAM CHOWDER

4 oz (100 g) bacon rashers or salt belly of pork, diced
1 onion, chopped
3-4 potatoes, diced
½ pint (300 ml) boiling water
1¼ lb (600 g) canned clams
milk
¼ pint (150 ml) single cream
½ oz (15 g) butter
salt and pepper
celery salt
parsley or paprika to garnish

In a large, heavy saucepan fry the salt pork or bacon.
Remove them from the pan and fry the onion in the pork fat
until transparent.   Add diced potatoes and water and boil
until the potatoes are just tender, about 10 minutes.
Drain the clams, reserving the liquid, and add to it enough
milk to make 1¾ pints (1 litre).   Add this liquid to the
cooked potatoes and heat slowly.   Then stir in the clams,
pork (or bacon), cream, butter and seasonings.   Heat again
but do not boil, and serve garnished with parsley or paprika.

H.E. Lady Hayman

TOMATO SOUP À LA CRÈME DORÉE

This is a clear Tomato Soup with a whipped Cream and Sesame Seed topping.

14 oz (400 g) canned Italian Tomatoes	Worcester Sauce
1 Beef Shin	Salt, Black and Red (Paprika) Pepper
3 Pints (1.75 litres) Water	1 tbs Brown Sugar
A Large Bunch of Herbs	½ Pint (300 ml) Double Cream
(or 2-3 tsp Dried Herbs)	1 tbs Sesame Seeds

Boil the Tomatoes, Beef Shin, Water and Herbs together for several hours until the Meat is in shreds, then strain through a sieve, and add a little Worcester Sauce, Salt, the Peppers and Sugar, all to taste.

Whip the Cream in a bowl till it forms peaks. Pour the hot soup into individual small earthenware casseroles till they are nearly full and make sure they too are hot.

Spread one large tablespoon of Cream carefully over the top of each serving, so that no Soup shows, and sprinkle the surface with a little Sesame Seeds.

Flash under a hot grill for a moment or two, to just gild the surface, but be quick about it, and serve at once.

Mrs. Rob MacPherson

TOMATO AND YOGHURT SOUP

A very refreshing uncooked Summer Soup.

4 lb (1.75 kg) Ripe Tomatoes	1 tbs Icing Sugar
1¼ Pints (750 ml) Plain Yoghurt	Salt and Pepper
2 Garlic Cloves, crushed	1 tbs Worcester Sauce (optional)
The Juice of 1 Small Lemon	Chopped Fresh Herbs to garnish

Emulsify the Tomatoes and Yoghurt, Garlic, Lemon Juice, Sugar and Seasonings in a blender.

Taste, and if necessary correct seasoning.

Add Worcester Sauce if wished.

Chill for several hours and serve from a chilled Soup Tureen, with a few chopped Herbs (Basil or Oregano) sprinkled over each serving.

SOUPE VERTE

- 1 lb (500 g) fresh spinach, washed
  and spined, or 8 oz (225 g) frozen
  chopped spinach, thawed

- 1 bunch watercress

- 2 oz (50 g) diced cucumber

- 1 oz (25 g) butter

- 1 tbs water

- 8 oz (225 g) smoked haddock, cooked in creamy
  milk and mashed

- 3 tbs cream

- 2½ pints (1.5 litres) vichyssoise soup

- 2 egg yolks

- ½ pint (300 ml) double cream

Sauté the spinach, watercress and cucumber in a saucepan with
the butter and the water until tender, then whirl in a blender.
Add the haddock and the 3 tbs cream and whirl again.   If the
purée is smooth enough use it, but if it is not, push it through
a fine sieve.   Add it to the warm vichyssoise and heat up,
letting it simmer for about 10 minutes.   Remove soup from heat
and cook a little.   Beat up the egg yolks in the ½ pint (300 ml)
cream and carefully add to the soup, off the heat.   Chill until
very cold, and serve with a sprinkling of chopped watercress
and a blob of cream on each helping.

Lady Diana Cooper

TIBETAN MOMOS IN WHITE CABBAGE BROTH

First make the meat stuffing:

1 lb (500 g) beef steak, minced
2 large onions, or the equivalent of spring onions, minced
2 garlic cloves, crushed
2 x ½ inch (1 cm) pieces root ginger (Yeshe measures them by the thumb-nail)
2 pinches 'Vee Tsin Gourmet powder'*
1 tbs thick soy sauce (Tung Chun,* or similar)
1 tomato, skinned and chopped
salt and a very little black pepper
a little water if mixture is too dry

Mix all these ingredients together in a bowl.

Then make the paste or pastry:

8 oz (225 g) self-raising flour
a pinch of salt
a little water
1 egg

Sift the flour and salt together. Make a well in the centre of the flour
heap. Break in the egg and add enough water to make a dough. Mix with
stiff tips of the fingers (like making pasta) until it is a cohesive mass,
then knead well with heel of hand on a board or marble slab, until it is
smooth. Roll out as thin as paper, cut into rounds with a 2½ inch (6 cm)
pastry cutter. Fill each round with 2 teaspoonfuls of the meat mixture.
Pinch together the edges of the rounds so that they make a neat packet, or
fold them over into a half-moon shape, using your thumb to 'pleat' the edge
as is shown in Yeshe's picture. This is a skilful business and it takes
practice to make it look as pretty as he does - but with perseverance you
will learn.

When all the meat and pastry have been used up and you have a couple of dozen
momos prepared, rub some oil round the top of a fairly wide steamer or double
boiler. Bring water in the lower pan to the boil, and put the momos into the
upper pan, packing them in very carefully, if possible in one layer, and
steam for 25 minutes or so (keeping the water below boiling steadily). Test

* can be bought at Cheong Leen, Tower Street, London WC2

to see if the momos are ready by taking off the lid and <u>touching</u> them.
If they are not cooked the pastry will stick to your fingers.   If they
are ready, they will feel slippery - so remove them, and keep them warm.

The soup or broth:

1 pint (600 ml) good strong beef or chicken stock
4 oz (100 g) dried Chinese white cabbage
1 tbs thick soy sauce
pinch of Vee Tsin

Make a good strong beef or chicken stock.   Strain and then reheat it.
Take the cabbage and reconstitute it by putting in a flat dish, pouring
boiling water over it and covering it with a lid for 30 minutes.   When
the cabbage has plumped up, chop it very fine and add it to the stock
together with the thick soy sauce, and Vee Tsin.   Boil for 10 minutes, and
it is ready.

Serve the soup in plates or bowls and hand the momos round separately in a
warm serving dish.   They are to be eaten together and these quantities
make about 4 momos each for 6 people.

Yeshe Tsultim
in co-operation with Lady Egremont

EEL SOUP (La Soupe aux Congres)

Fish soups in Britain are not usually successful and seldom taste like the bony but delicious Mediterranean kind. What seems a pity is that our own Eel Soup is a neglected but perfectly indigenous delicacy. There are many versions of it. Here is one from the West Country:-

1½ lb (750 g) Conger Eel
6 oz (175 g) Coarse Sea Salt
4 oz (100 g) Clarified Butter
2 Medium Onions, chopped fine
3 Pints (1.75 litres) boiling Fish Stock
A Bouquet Garni

A Bay Leaf
6 Peppercorns
A Blade of Mace
¼ Pint (150 ml) Unsweetened Evaporated Milk
½ level tbs Cornflour
¼ Pint (150 ml) Cream

Cut the Eel into 3 inch (7.5 cm) lengths and sprinkle them with salt. Let them stand for a few hours, then wash the pieces of Eel and dry them and sauté them gently in half the Clarified Butter for about 10 minutes - but not long enough to brown them. Add the onions and sauté them till they are soft, then turn both into a soup pan and add the hot stock, a little more butter and the herbs and seasoning. Simmer till the Eels are cooked but not beginning to break up, which will take the best part of an hour. Then remove the Eel and thicken the soup with the evaporated milk mixed with a little cornflour. The pieces of Eel can either be left whole and eaten separately, or they can be skinned and boned and rubbed through a sieve, this Purée being mixed back into the Soup. In either case the Seasoning should be corrected and the Cream added to the Soup just before serving.

Another version adds 4 tbs Tomato Purée and 2 Garlic Cloves to the sautéed Eel and Onions, uses water instead of Stock and thickens the Soup with 3 or 4 Potatoes which are cooked in it.

And a Guernsey Conger Soup thickens the Fish Stock with puréed Peas, adds Milk to it and colours it with "The Petals of 8 Blooms of Marigold" 15 minutes before serving.

Strachur

HERB RIVER OYSTER STEW

2 or 3 Celery Sticks, diced
1 small Onion, minced
4 oz (100 g) Butter
1 Pint (600 ml) Oysters
Salt and Pepper

Chopped fresh Parsley
⅛ tsp Mace
1 Pint (600 ml) Single Cream thinned down with a little Milk

Blanch, then sauté the Celery, and the Onion in Butter until they are soft. Add the Oysters including their liquid. Add Salt, Pepper, Parsley, and a little Mace. Simmer until the Oysters curl. Add the Cream. Heat until bubbles form around the edges, but do not boil. Remove from heat and serve.

Tomato soup with pesto

2 oz (50 g) butter
2 lb (1 kg) canned or fresh
  tomatoes
1 large onion, chopped
salt and pepper

1 pint (600 ml) marrow bone
  stock
$\frac{1}{4}$–$\frac{1}{2}$ pint (150–300 ml) cream
pesto sauce (see recipe below)
croutons

Melt half the butter in a large pan. Add the tomatoes. Gently
sauté until a good colour. Fry the onion in the remaining butter
and add this and salt and pepper to the tomatoes. Simmer
together for 5 minutes. Put the mixture through a blender or
rub through a sieve. Heat the stock and add the tomato purée
to this, mixing well. Remove from the heat, add the cream,
stirring well. Return to the heat, but take care that the soup
does not boil. Just before serving add a good spoonful of the
pesto and some fried croutons to each soup bowl, or hand it in a
sauceboat with the croutons in another.

Pesto al Genovese

2 oz (50 g) fresh basil
2 garlic cloves
1 tbs pine nuts
salt

1 tbs grated Parmesan cheese
1 tbs grated Sardo cheese
3–4 tbs olive oil

Weigh the basil leaves after stripping them from their stalks,
chop them roughly, then pound them in a mortar with the garlic,
nuts and salt until they are reduced to a thick paste. Stir in
the cheeses. Add the oil, little by little, stirring all the
time until the sauce has the consistency of a purée. Use as
required or spoon into a jar, cover with a thin layer of oil and
keep in the refrigerator for up to 1 week.

Note Fresh basil and Sardo cheese are essential for a genuine
pesto. Both are available from good Italian food stores, who
also sell frozen or tinned pesto, which is a lazy way out.
Harrods sell fresh ready-made pesto.

Veronica Maclean

First Course Hot

THOMAS JEFFERSON
1743–1826
Third President of the United States of America
Minister to France, 1784–1789

OEUFS BENEDICT

6 shortcrust pastry shells
6 oz (175 g) jar smoked cod's roe (or smoked haddock that you
    have poached in creamy milk, picked over carefully and mashed
    with some of its own liquid)
6 tbs béchamel sauce (use 3 tbs if using haddock)
6 poached eggs
½ pint (300 ml) Sauce Crème
cayenne pepper

Bake 6 shortcrust pastry shells.   Heat the cod's roe (or
haddock) and stir in the béchamel sauce.   Put a spoonful of
this at the bottom of every pastry shell, a well-drained softly-
poached egg on top and cover with Sauce Crème.   Dust the tops
with a little cayenne pepper.

Sauce Crème

3-4 egg yolks
6 tbs cream
3 tbs butter
salt
cayenne pepper
1 tsp lemon juice

Beat up the egg yolks, put them into a saucepan with the cream,
the butter, a little salt, cayenne pepper and the lemon juice.
Stand the saucepan in a bain-marie and stir with a wooden spoon
until it becomes quite thick and creamy, then pass it through a
nylon sieve and use.

This sauce is also excellent for sweetbreads, or fine quality
plain boiled fish.

H.E. Mrs. David Bruce

42, LOWNDES SQUARE,

LONDON, SWIX 9JL,

TEL. 01-235 5812.

HOUSE OF COMMONS EGGS BENEDICT

6 poached eggs

2 slices lean ham

6 shortcrust pastry shells *

¾ pint (450 ml) Hollandaise Sauce

cream

Poach the eggs and keep them warm in a bowl of hot water on
the side of the stove.   Cut the ham into julienne strips.
Fill each pastry shell with a lightly poached egg which has
been well drained, put a few strips of ham on top and cover
with a creamy Hollandaise sauce.

* or English muffins, split in two, scooped out, toasted
  and buttered.

SUE'S PROCESSOR HOLLANDAISE

6-7 oz (175-200 g) butter

2 tbs lemon juice

1 tbs water

3 egg yolks

salt and pepper

Melt the butter in a small saucepan until very hot.   Heat
the lemon juice and water together in another small pan.
Beat the egg yolks for 30 seconds in the food processor.
Pour the hot butter very slowly on to the egg yolks with
the machine still running.   When it is absorbed, carefully
pour on the lemon/water mixture, still with the machine
running, and lastly add a little salt and pepper.

Mrs. Jeremy Phipps

TUNISIAN CHAGEHOUTIA

4 large tomatoes

3 aubergines

salt and pepper

3 green peppers

¼ pint (150 ml) olive oil

3 onions, chopped

4 courgettes, chopped

2 garlic cloves, crushed

pinch of cayenne pepper, or a hot pimento, finely chopped

6 eggs

Skin, seed and chop the tomatoes. Chop the aubergines
into rounds, sprinkle salt over them, leave them between
two plates for 1 hour, then wash and dry them. Singe
the peppers a little by rolling them on the hot-plate
until they blister. Chop.

Put the tomatoes into a heavy casserole and let them
cook in their juice. Add the olive oil and the other
vegetables, the garlic, salt, pepper, cayenne or pimento.
Cover the pan and simmer together for 30-40 minutes.
Then break in eggs on top of vegetables. Serve in the
casserole as soon as whites have just set.

Mrs. Leo D'Erlanger

EGGS SOMERSET

1 lb (500 g) crab meat (or lobster meat)

4 oz (100 g) butter

½ tsp salt

¼ pint (150 ml) double cream

pinch of cayenne

pinch of paprika

pinch of grated nutmeg

9 eggs

3 tbs sherry

8 oz (225 g) Gruyère cheese, thinly sliced

¾ pint (450 ml) white sauce

Cook the crab meat, butter and salt for 3 minutes in a double boiler. Add cream, cayenne, paprika, nutmeg and heat thoroughly. Add 3 beaten eggs and cook until thickened. Just before removing from heat, add the sherry. Spoon the mixture into individual casseroles or pastry shells. Poach 6 eggs and place one on top of each casserole. Dot generously with Gruyère cheese and cover with sauce. Place in oven at 475°F (240°F) gas mark 9, until mixture is brown and bubbly.

This recipe is equally good with fresh young sweetcorn, scraped off the cob, instead of crab meat.

Mrs. John Sherman Cooper

𝔅𝔞𝔡𝔪𝔦𝔫𝔱𝔬𝔫,
𝔊𝔩𝔬𝔲𝔠𝔢𝔰𝔱𝔢𝔯𝔰𝔥𝔦𝔯𝔢.

BADMINTON EGGS

Boil 6 new-laid eggs quite hard, and when cooked, place
them for a minute in cold water.   Remove the shells and
cut the eggs in halves;   take out the yolks and chop
them finely with 12 pickled mushrooms and 2-3 good sized
truffles that have been previously boiled until tender in
good stock.   Put all this in a stewpan with ¼ pint (150 ml)
of the stock that the truffles have been boiled in, 1 tbs
mushroom ketchup, salt, pepper and 1 tbs of port.

Let all simmer for 10 minutes, then thicken with a little
fresh butter that has been rolled in flour.   Lay the
whites of the eggs the hollow part up, fill them with fried
breadcrumbs, dust them over with a little cayenne and pour
over the mixture out of the saucepan.

The Duchess of Beaufort

SCRAMBLED EGGS CAVENDISH or OEUFS BROUILLES À LA CRÈME for 4

6 tbs butter
6 eggs
salt and pepper
3 tbs double cream

Melt half the butter in a heavy saucepan - copper-bottomed if
possible.   Add the eggs, beaten, with the seasoning.   Stir
continuously with a wooden spoon over a very low heat.   Do
not let the eggs boil or lumps form - it must look like thick
custard.   (Remove pan from heat if eggs cook too quickly).
Add the rest of the butter that you have previously chopped
into pieces, slowly, bit by bit, stirring all the time.   The
whole performance will take 10-15 minutes.   When butter is
all absorbed, and not until then, let the eggs 'catch' and
scramble - but only a little - then add the cream all at once
and stir vigorously.

Serve at once on hot deep saucers or in ramekins.   The eggs
should still be very runny and fingers of hot buttered toast
should be served with them, to mop up.

N.B.   The taste of this dish is very delicate, and some may
like it left strictly alone, but as an alternative, a few tips
of asparagus or some baby new peas can be used to give colour
to each helping.

MRS. RICHARD CAVENDISH

REGENT 7-3900

CREOLE EGGS

4 tbs olive oil

3 tbs flour

14 oz (400 g) canned tomatoes

3 oz (75 g) butter

4 medium onions, chopped

1 fresh chilli, chopped

4 celery sticks, chopped

2 garlic cloves, crushed

1 tbs chopped parsley

1 bay leaf

12 hard-boiled eggs

¾ pint (450 ml) béchamel sauce

1 oz (25 g) fresh breadcrumbs

4 tbs grated Gruyère cheese

salt and pepper

Heat the olive oil in a sauté pan. Make a roux with the
flour and season well. Keep stirring until the roux is a
dark colour. Add the tomatoes and when they are simmering
add the rest of the vegetables, which you have sautéed for
10 minutes or so in butter. Throw in the parsley and bay
leaf, cover the pan firmly and cook until you have a thick,
dark, rich purée. Stir frequently to avoid burning.
Meanwhile, shell and chop the eggs into fairly large pieces.
Mix them carefully into the béchamel sauce. Fill an
earthenware entrée dish with alternate layers of creamed eggs
and Creole sauce. Sprinkle the top with breadcrumbs, and
grated Gruyère cheese and dot with butter. Bake in a hot
oven, 400°F (200°C) gas mark 6, for about 15 minutes.

Mrs. Edward Warburg

Oeufs à la Vaudoise

6 eggs

salt and pepper

2-3 tbs finely grated Gruyère

1 oz (25 g) unsalted butter, melted

Break and separate the eggs. Leave the yolks in their half shells or in separate cups. Beat the whites together to a peak. Butter a soufflé dish or a fairly deep earthenware entrée dish and spoon half the beaten whites into it. Level the surface and sprinkle it with salt, pepper and the grated cheese. Then cover with the rest of the egg whites. With the back of a soup spoon make 6 indentations or shallow holes in the egg whites and carefully slip an egg yolk into each of these. Level the surface again and gently sprinkle melted butter over the dish. Put in a hot oven, 475°F (240°C) gas mark 9, for 15 minutes and serve immediately it is ready.

Oeufs à l'Oseille

1 lb (500 g) French or garden sorrel,
  spined and well-washed

½ oz (15 g) butter

¼ pint (150 ml) cream

salt and pepper

6 eggs

Cook the prepared sorrel in a pan without water until it melts into a purée, thumping it down with a wooden spoon. Add the butter and 2 tbs of the cream, salt and a shake of pepper. Put a spoonful of this purée into the bottom of 6 ramekins. Break an egg on top of each and cover the eggs with a spoonful of cream. Salt and pepper each little pot and place them side by side in a large roasting tin. Pour boiling water carefully into the tin, enough to come half way up the sides of the ramekins, then carefully slide the tin into a hot oven, 400°F (200°C) gas mark 6. Bake until the eggs are beginning to set, about 10 minutes, then flash under a hot grill for a minute or two to finish cooking.

Strachur

Oeufs Rachel

6 eggs

3 tbs butter

6 pieces of beef marrow (see page 164)

¼ pint (150 ml) beef stock

6 thin slices black truffle

8 fl oz (225 ml) Madeira Sauce

Gently fry the eggs in butter.   Trim and sit each egg on a round of fried bread in a serving dish.   Poach the pieces of marrow in beef stock for 1 minute but leave in hot stock for 2-3 minutes until soft.   Lay a piece of marrow, then a slice of truffle, on top of each egg.   Coat with a generous spoonful of Madeira sauce.   Serve at once.

Madeira Sauce

2 small onions or shallots chopped fine

1 tbs butter

1 tbs flour

¼ pint (150 ml) port

3 fl oz (75 ml) Madeira

½ pint (300 ml) rich brown stock (jellied gravy from Sunday joint?)

¾ oz (20 g) meat glaze

2 tsp tomato ketchup

salt and pepper

1½ oz (40 g) butter, softened

Fry the onions in butter until brown, dust with flour and let that colour too.   Add the port and Madeira and boil to reduce almost completely.   Add the brown stock and the meat glaze and reduce again.   Stir in the ketchup and seasoning.   Strain through a fine sieve and, gradually, add the softened butter, away from the heat.   Correct seasoning.

H.E. Mrs David Bruce

Goldeneye
Oracabessa
Jamaica

Oefs James Bond

Warm ovenproof dishes, add
butter to melt. Cook two
eggs slowly in each dish.
As Whites set add cream
liberally, and top with
Tomatoe ketchup at last
minute.

Mrs. Ian Fleming

TARTELETTES VENDOME, or PARIS TARTS

1 tbs butter

1 tbs oil

3 shallots, chopped

½ lb (225 g) button mushrooms

5 hard-boiled eggs, chopped

2 oz (50 g) beef marrow

2 tbs chopped parsley

½ tsp beef extract or soy sauce

salt and cayenne pepper

2 tbs browned breadcrumbs

6 shortcrust pastry shells, half baked in advance

Melt the butter and oil in a saucepan and let it get very hot.   Throw in the shallots and brown them lightly, then the roughly chopped mushrooms and cook till they are soft.   Add the chopped eggs, half the marrow and the parsley. Add a few drops of beef extract or soy sauce, salt and pepper and the breadcrumbs to the ragoût.   Mix well together and put a tablespoonful of the mixture into each pastry shell, laying a slice from the second piece of marrow on top.   Bake for 10 minutes in a very hot oven 475°F (240°C) gas mark 9, and serve very hot.

Georgiana, Countess of Dudley
From The Dudley Recipe Book 1910

FONDS D'ARTICHAUTS AU FONDU

This is a delightful dish and much less complicated than it looks.

Boil 8 artichokes, drain and remove the leaves.   Arrange the 'fonds' neatly in a buttered fireproof entrée dish or shallow casserole.   Make a cheese soufflé, using the recipe on page 48, and pour a sufficient quantity of the soufflé mixture over to cover.   Bake for 15 minutes in a hot oven, 400°F (200°C) gas mark 6, and serve in the same dish.   (If the grated cheese and the egg whites are folded in together, and the dish is immediately refrigerated, it can be prepared up to this moment in advance.)

From the Tour d'Argent, Paris, c. 1908

Aubergine Calvas

4 - 8 Aubergines, depending on size
6 tbs. butter
4 rounded tbs. flour
1 pt (2 cups) milk
½ cup cheese
A little cream
Cooking oil
Salt & pepper

Skin the aubergines. Cut them lengthways in thin slices. Lay them on a clean dish towel, prick them all over with a fork and sprinkle them with salt. Put a plate on top of them. This will make them sweat & get rid of their bitter juices. After about an hour rinse them & pat them dry and deep fry them in very hot cooking oil. Drain & keep warm on absorbent kitchen paper.

Make a pint of good bechanel sauce and add 4 oz grated cheese to it - (½ gruyère & ½ parmesan). Take off fire & stir in a little cream. Season well. Put a layer of aubergines at the bottom of a gratin dish, cover with half the cheese sauce, then another layer of aubergines and cover completely with remainder of sauce. Sprinkle a few crumbs of butter and cheese on top and put into a hot oven for about 3/4 hour.

H.E. Comtesse de Crouy-Chanel   -39-

SAN ZENONE SPINACH ROLL

4 lb (1.75 kg) spinach

4 tbs chopped ham

½ oz (15 g) butter

4 oz (100 g) flour, sifted twice

1 egg

salt

grated Parmesan cheese

Spine the spinach carefully. Wash and cook it in the water clinging to its leaves and squeeze it absolutely dry. Then chop it very fine and mix it with the chopped ham and butter. Make a dough or pasta with the flour, egg, salt and enough water to make a loose dough. Knead it well with the heel of your hand.

Roll this dough out <u>paper thin</u> to a suitably sized rectangle and before it can dry, lay the spinach mixture on it in an even layer to cover it all. Roll it up into a thick sausage. Wrap it in a floured cloth and tie this with string at both ends and in the middle. Boil for about 20 minutes in slightly salted water. Unwrap and cut into finger-thick slices. Lay these in a buttered fireproof dish, which you put into the oven for a few minutes, then serve, with lots of grated Parmesan cheese.

Dame Freya Starke, DBE

SPINACH PUDDING WITH SAUCE MORNAY

2 oz (50 g) butter	2 egg yolks, beaten
1½ lb (750 g) cooked, sieved spinach	pinch of nutmeg
¼ pint (150 ml) Béchamel Sauce	salt and pepper
2 tbs double cream	

Melt the butter in a saucepan, add the spinach and stir so that it is well mixed with the butter.   Stir in the Béchamel Sauce and mix well.   Stir in the cream, egg yolks, nutmeg and seasoning to taste.   Turn into a well-greased mould.   Cover with buttered paper.   Steam gently for 30-40 minutes.

Béchamel Sauce

½ pint (300 ml) milk	6 peppercorns
1 onion, chopped	sprig each of thyme and parsley
1 small carrot, chopped	1 bay leaf
1 celery stick, chopped	2 oz (50 g) butter
salt and pepper	4 rounded tbs flour

Put milk into a small pan with the onion, carrot, celery, seasoning and herbs. Bring slowly to the boil.   In another pan, melt the butter, add flour, cook a few minutes without browning, then gradually add the strained milk.   Stir until smooth and creamy. Cook 3-4 minutes.

Sauce Mornay

2 oz (50 g) butter	a pinch of cayenne pepper
3 rounded tbs flour	salt and pepper
1 pint (600 ml) milk	a few drops of lemon juice
2 oz (50 g) finely grated Parmesan cheese	3 tbs cream

Melt butter in a small pan, add flour, mix to a smooth paste, stir over a low heat a few minutes.   Add milk gradually, stirring all the time.   Bring to the boil, simmer a few minutes to cook the flour, add cheese and seasonings. Stir until cheese has melted.   Add lemon juice.   Stir in the cream at the last minute.

Turn the spinach out on to a hot serving dish, pour half the sauce over it and hand the rest in a sauceboat.

H.E. Madame Velebit

ZELJANICA (for 8)

1 lb (500 g) spinach	3-4 tbs sour cream
salt	8 fl oz (225 ml) milk
1 lb (500 g) cream cheese	sunflower oil, warmed
4 eggs, separated	1 lb (500 g) strudel or 'filo' pastry

Wash the spinach well and spine.   Chop roughly, put in a bowl, sprinkle with
salt, and leave for 1 hour.   Then drain thoroughly.

Meanwhile, mash the cheese with a fork, add egg yolks and sour cream, salt,
milk, and finally the egg whites, beaten stiff.   Oil a 4-5 inch (10-12.5 cm)
deep casserole and cover the bottom of it with 2 or 3 leaves of strudel pastry.
Sprinkle these with warm oil and spoon over them a layer of cheese mixture.
Cover this with a layer of chopped spinach, then another of strudel leaves
and so on until all the cheese and spinach is used up.   Cover the last layer
of spinach with a whole strudel leaf.   Press this down with your fingers all
the way round the edge of the pan and sprinkle with oil.   Bake in a hot oven,
425°F (220oC) gas mark 7, for 35-40 minutes until the zeljanica has coloured
well and risen.   Lower temperature to 350°F (180°C) gas mark 4 and bake for
10 minutes more.   Remove, cool a little, cut into squares and serve.

* This can be bought at any good delicatessen

H.E. Madame Vukica Vidic

CROÛTES PRINTANIÈRES

8 small carrots
8 oz (225 g) cooked young peas
4 fonds d'artichauts
bunch of spring onions
2 celery sticks or a little
   white turnip

2 pints (1.2 litres) stock
butter
salt and pepper
6-8 little puff pastry
   vol-au-vent cases

Cook all the vegetables separately in a good stock until tender.
Then drain, dice, combine, and sauté together in a little
butter for a few minutes only. Correct seasoning. Fill
pastry cases with the vegetable macedoine and serve with Sauce
Espagnole, handed separately.

Sauce Espagnole

2 oz (50 g) butter
4 streaky bacon rashers, chopped
1 large onion, chopped
2 oz (50 g) sliced mushrooms
1 small carrot, chopped
4 rounded tbs flour
1 tbs tomato purée

1 pint (600 ml) good brown stock
½ tsp mixed dried herbs
salt and pepper
peppercorns
mace
1 tbs madeira or sherry

Melt butter in saucepan and fry chopped bacon gently. Add
onion, mushrooms and carrot and fry until lightly browned.
Add flour and fry gently to rich golden brown. Stir in tomato
purée, stock and mixed herbs. Season to taste. Simmer for
40 minutes. Skim and sieve. Reheat sauce, check seasoning
and add madeira just before serving - but boil it up for a
minute or two first, to 'burn off' the alcohol.

Lady Lovat and Mrs Joan Birnie

MUSHROOMS WITH GARLIC BUTTER or CHAMPIGNONS DE CHEZ VICTOR

18 mushrooms	6 thin slices bread
2 oz (50 g) butter	salt

Take 18 fine fresh mushrooms.   NOT the button kind, but the open, flat variety.   Like field mushrooms.   Remove the stalks very carefully, without damaging the cap, and wipe the cap with a damp cloth.   Do not peel.

Cook the mushrooms for 3 minutes only in the butter, in a covered pan. Lift out and keep hot.   Sauté the slices of bread in the same pan, adding more butter if necessary.   Drain the croûtons and arrange them on a serving dish.   Put 3 mushroom caps on each croûton and fill the stalk cavity with the green garlic sauce which you have already prepared.

PROVENÇAL or GREEN GARLIC BUTTER

3-5 garlic cloves, according to taste and size	2½ tbs parsley, very finely chopped
2½ tsp olive or nut oil	about 4 oz (100 g) butter
2½ tbs chervil, very finely chopped	salt and pepper

Chop the garlic and pound in a mortar with the oil, chervil and parsley. Cream the butter in a bowl.   Work in the garlic and herb mixture with a fork.   Season with salt and pepper.   Put in the fridge.   When firm, shape into a roll, wrap in foil and keep in the fridge until you want to use it, when you just chop pieces off the end of the roll.

Walnut oil makes a most delicious garlic butter.

S.E. Comte Victor de Lesseps

PAIN DE CHAMPIGNONS (my grandmother's recipe)

3 eggs
2 egg yolks
18 fl oz (500 ml) milk, boiled
4 oz (100 g) mushrooms, cooked in butter and finely chopped
salt and pepper

Mushroom Sauce
1 tbs butter
a rounded tbs flour
$\frac{1}{2}$ pint (300 ml) cream
$\frac{1}{2}$ lb (225 g) mushrooms, cooked in butter and coarsely chopped

Beat the eggs as if for an omelette. Add little by little the boiled
milk from which you have skimmed off any cream which may have risen.
Add the finely chopped mushrooms that you have cooked first in butter.
Season well, and pour into a buttered mould. Place mould in a bain-marie
and simmer for about 30 minutes when the eggs should be set. Test with
a skewer. Let them cool for 15 minutes and turn out on to a serving dish.

Meanwhile make a creamy béchamel sauce and add to it the cooked chopped
mushrooms - rather more coarsely chopped this time.

Serve with the hot sauce poured over the Pain de Champignons.

You can vary the flavours of this dish by adding to the pain, or the sauce,
a little Parmesan cheese, glace de viande, herbs or tomato purée.

S.E. Monsieur Gérard André

Viennese Mushroom and Pancake Timbale

about 15-20 thin pancakes	2 tbs lemon juice
5 lb (2.25 kg) mushrooms	salt and pepper
butter	½ pint (300 ml) double cream
olive oil	¾ pint (450 ml) béchamel sauce
1 garlic clove, crushed (optional)	2 oz (50g) grated Parmesan cheese

First make 15-20 very thin pancakes, using your favourite recipe, but omitting sugar. This can be done sometime previously, providing the pancakes are layered with greaseproof paper and kept covered.

Next wipe the mushrooms, cut off the stalks, and discard (or use later for soup). Chop the mushrooms roughly, keeping half a dozen or so whole for garnish, and put them all into a large saucepan with enough butter and oil, the garlic if you are using it and a good squeeze of lemon juice. Season well, cover the pan and cook gently until they are tender. Drain the mushrooms, put aside the whole ones, put the rest into a blender and blend to a purée. Remove and add the cream, which you may have to beat a little if it is too thin.

Place a pancake on a fireproof dish and spread it with some of the mushroom mixture, then add another pancake and some more mixture, and so on until you have a pile with a final pancake on top. Cover the pile with béchamel sauce, which you have thinned and darkened with some of the mushroom liquor.

Sprinkle the timbale generously with grated Parmesan, and put it into a moderate oven, 350°F (180°C) gas mark 4, for 20-25 minutes.

Garnish it with reserved mushroom caps and serve.

H.E. Lady Caccia

TARTE AUX CHAMPIGNONS

Mushroom purée

1¼ lb (600 g) fresh mushrooms
1 tbs vinegar
½ pint (300 ml) water

juice of 1 lemon
salt and pepper
¾ oz (20 g) butter

Wash the mushrooms in water in which you have put a tablespoon of vinegar.
Peel and put peelings to boil with half the water in a pan of their own. Put
aside about 20 of the smallest mushrooms. Chop remainder finely and simmer
for 5 minutes in a covered pan with the remaining water, the lemon juice, salt
and pepper and the butter. Drain, reserving juices and keep warm.

Sauce Poulette

1½ oz (40 g) butter
2 rounded tbs flour
8 fl oz (225 ml) chicken stock
salt and pepper

the mushroom juices
4 fl oz (125 ml) double cream
2 egg yolks

Make a white roux with the butter and the flour, add the chicken stock, season
well when it boils and add the juices in which you have just cooked the mushrooms,
plus the water in which you have boiled the mushroom peelings. Let this simmer
and reduce for about 20 minutes, until you have a scant ¾ pint (450 ml) of sauce.
Then pour on to the drained mushrooms. Once mushrooms and sauce are combined,
take the pan off the heat, cool it a little and carefully make a rich liaison by
beating together the cream and egg yolks. Stir into the mushrooms and sauce.
Lastly stir in the remaining butter, which gives the purée a glossy shine.

To Finish

1 x 10 inch (25 cm) shortcrust
  pastry flan

¾ oz (20 g) butter
1 tsp lemon juice

Have ready a shortcrust flan that you have baked blind. Fill with the mushroom
purée, then decorate with a criss-cross (or circles) of small reserved mushrooms
that you have part-cooked in the butter and a few drops of lemon juice while the
sauce was simmering. Season and put in a moderately hot oven 375°F (190°C) gas
mark 5, for 10 minutes to just brown the top.

NOTE   A very little crushed garlic or 2 chopped shallots can be added to the
mushroom purée, but it is really nicer without.

Marquise de Maupeou

BLENHEIM CHEESE SOUFFLÉ

2 tbs butter

2 rounded tbs flour

¾ pint (450 ml) cream

salt and pepper

a little grated nutmeg

6 tbs grated good Cheddar cheese

3 egg yolks

4 egg whites

Melt the butter in a fairly large heavy saucepan.   Stir
in the flour and cook the roux for a few minutes.
Gradually whisk in the cream with a wire whisk until the
sauce is thick and all the taste of flour is gone.   (It
will take 12-15 minutes.)   Then add salt, pepper, a
little nutmeg, and the cheese.   Let this melt while
you continue whisking.   Take the pan off the heat and
beat in the egg yolks.   Then at the last minute, fold
in the absolutely stiffly beaten egg whites.   Tip the
mixture at once into a buttered soufflé dish and put it
immediately into a fairly hot oven, 375°F (190°C) gas
mark 5, for 20 minutes.

Lady Lloyd

'SUISSESSE'

½ pint (300 ml) milk

5 oz (150 g) flour

salt and pepper

grated nutmeg

1 oz (25 g) butter

6 oz (175 g) grated Parmesan cheese

4 egg yolks

4 egg whites

1 pint (600 ml) double cream

Pour the milk into a saucepan, bring to the boil, then shake the flour in, stirring and beating very thoroughly with a wooden spoon until the mixture is smooth.   Reduce by simmering until very thick, beating all the time. Add the salt and pepper, nutmeg, butter and half the Parmesan cheese. Then add the egg yolks, one by one, mixing thoroughly and quickly off the heat.   Beat the egg whites to a peak and fold in carefully.   Grease with butter, about 18 little round or oval tins or porcelain ramekins and spoon the soufflé mixture into them.   Place them in a shallow entrée dish with a little hot water in it and poach them in this in a hot oven, 400°F (200°C) gas mark 6, for 15 minutes.

Take them out, let them cool for 5 minutes, then unmould them carefully on to a shallow earthenware ovenproof dish and sprinkle a little Parmesan cheese over them.   Cover with the cream, sprinkle again with Parmesan cheese and return to a cool oven, 300°F (150°C) gas mark 2, for 12 minutes.

When ready, serve immediately.

H.E. The Hon. Lady Soames

Recette de James Viaene
Chef de Cuisine à l'Ambassade

Lady Minto's Cheese Fingers
(a supper dish for 2)

butter, for greasing
7 fl oz (200 ml) double cream
3 rounded tbs freshly grated Parmesan cheese

4 pieces freshly-made toast,
    cut into fingers
salt and pepper

Grease an oblong ovenproof dish with butter. Pour in half the cream.
Sprinkle with Parmesan, put in the fingers of toast lengthways, sprinkle
with more cheese, add salt and pepper and pour over the remaining cream.
Bake for 5 minutes in a very hot oven, 450°F (230°C) gas mark 8. This
dish must be made with freshly grated Parmesan cheese.

Dolly's Spinach Flan

1 x 9 inch (23 cm) rough puff or
    shortcrust pastry case, uncooked
12 oz (350 g) frozen or fresh puréed spinach
3 oz (75 g) butter
8 oz (225 g) cottage cheese

3 eggs, lightly beaten
4 oz (100 g) grated Cheddar cheese
8 tbs double cream
salt and pepper
grated nutmeg

Prick bottom of the pastry case with a fork and bake blind in a hot oven,
400°F (200°C) gas mark 6, for 15 minutes. Do not let it brown. Cook the
spinach purée with a little butter for a few minutes. Drain, squeeze out
all the water, beat in the rest of the butter and then add the cottage
cheese with the beaten eggs, the grated cheese and the cream. Season and
sprinkle over a little nutmeg. Spoon into the pastry shell and bake in a
moderate oven, 350°F (180°C) gas mark 4, for 30 minutes, until the crust
is brown and the spinach custard is set.

Lady Lovat

Sophia Loren's Neapolitan Crostini

Cut the crusts from 6 slices of bread and cut in half lengthways. Put a
thin slice of Mozzarella cheese on each piece, then one or two filleted
anchovies and their oil and some small pieces of fresh tomato. Sprinkle
with oregano and/or a little basil, salt and pepper. Arrange the crostini
side by side in a well greased or oiled baking dish. Put uncovered into a
hot oven, 425°F (220°C) gas mark 7, for about 10 minutes. Serve at once.

Sophia Loren

Sour Cream Pancakes

6 pints (3.3 litres) milk	12 pancakes
3 egg yolks	½ pint (300 ml) double cream
salt and pepper	4 tbs grated Parmesan cheese

Leave the milk in a tightly closed jar on a warm stove for 36 hours, by which time it should curdle.   Pour it into some double muslin and hang the muslin above a bowl so that the whey drips off.   At the end of 2-3 hours squeeze it gently then take the curds out of the muslin bag and put them in a bowl.   They should be fairly dry.   Add the egg yolks, salt and pepper and mix well.   Make 12 ordinary thin pancakes without sugar and stuff the pancakes with the curd mixture.   Not too full as it swells.   Lay the stuffed pancakes in an ovenproof shallow dish.   Cover them with cream and sprinkle over the grated Parmesan cheese.   Brown in a hot oven, 400°F (200°C) gas mark 6, or under a hot grill and serve.

Lady McEwen

Cheese Croquettes

2 heaped tbs cornflour	cayenne pepper
1 heaped tbs flour	2 oz (50 g) grated Parmesan
3 tbs cold milk	2 oz (50 g) grated Gruyère
1 pint (600 ml) boiling milk	1 whole egg, beaten
3 egg yolks	2 oz (50 g) breadcrumbs
salt	cooking oil or lard

Mix the cornflour and ordinary flour in a bowl with a little cold milk and beat till smooth then pour on the boiling milk a little at a time. When this has been worked to a creamy mixture return it to the heat and boil again for a few minutes.   Then remove and work in the 3 egg yolks, a little salt, the cayenne pepper and the two cheeses.   Pour this mixture into ice cube trays and put these into the freezer for at least 2 hours.   Then turn out as little cheese balls, egg and breadcrumb these carefully and deep fry them in good cooking oil or lard.   They should be golden and crisp outside and hot and creamy inside.   Serve with deep fried parsley and a light tomato sauce.

Strachur

'JULIENNE'

Cut 8 oz (225g) of any kind of game, or dark chicken meat into 'julienne' strips (or tear them into small pieces with your fingers). Mix them with a few chopped gherkins or pickled mushrooms, ¾ pint (450 ml) thick sour cream, some cayenne pepper, a squeeze of onion juice and some salt. Put the mixture into small individual little copper saucepans with handles (two per person) and heat them up until the cream begins to bubble, then sprinkle the top with a little grated Parmesan cheese and brown for a minute under a grill or salamander.

If you can't find 'julienne' pots - and they are difficult to come by even in Moscow where this nineteenth century dish has somehow survived - cook them in those brown earthen-ware cream pots with 'ears' that some good cookery shops import from France.

A salamander was a grid iron with a handle which was heated under the coals of the stove until white hot, then quickly placed over dishes to brown them. It is still the name that professional chefs give to an electric or gas grill under which dishes are 'flashed' to brown them before serving.

Restaurant Praga, Moscow

Rutilio's Risotto

2 tbs olive oil
1 large onion, chopped
½ lb (225 g) Italian rice
bacon rind or salt pork
chopped celery leaves

basil
3 fl oz (75 ml) vermouth or dry
  white wine
chicken or veal stock, boiling
2 oz (50 g) grated Parmesan cheese

Heat the oil in a shallow wide pan or casserole. Sauté the
onion until transparent but not coloured. Wash and drain the
rice. Throw it into the pan and sauté for 5 minutes or so,
until rice looks transparent. You can add a little bacon rind
or salt pork now and some chopped celery leaves and basil.
When rice is clear and beginning to colour, add the vermouth or
dry white wine. Cook a few minutes longer, then pour on boiling
stock, 2½ times the volume of the rice or enough to cover the rice
by 2 fingers. Reduce the heat, cover pan and boil for about
15 minutes or until the liquid is absorbed. The stock must be
a good chicken or veal stock to make a good risotto. You can
always add more stock if the rice gets too dry before it is
cooked. An Italian risotto should be creamy, with each grain
cooked, but also a little hard, i.e. 'al dente'. When nearly
cooked, stir in the Parmesan cheese, and hand some more round,
to sprinkle over each helping.

Risotto alla Romana

Saffron threads or 1 tsp saffron powder can also be stirred in
if yellow rice is wanted. Infuse saffron threads or dissolve
saffron powder in 8 fl oz (225 ml) hot salted water, bring to
the boil, strain if using threads, and pour it on to the rice
just before you add the boiling stock. Reduce the stock,
naturally, by the equivalent amount.

Mrs. Charles Maclean and Rutilio Ferrini

IÇ PILAV

Iç pilav means pilav with things inside it ('icincle' means 'inside' in Turkish) and it is an excellent and versatile dish.

Put the rice for the pilav on a large flat dish and pour boiling water on to it.   When this is cold strain it and wash it under a cold tap.   Drain well.

Melt some butter in a large pan and gently cook a chopped onion, to which you add 1 tbs pine kernels, frying them together until golden.   Now add the drained rice and cook for about 5 minutes.   Then add 1½ tbs currants, 1½ tbs skinned and chopped tomatoes and 1½ tbs finely chopped spring onions or chives.

Season with salt, pepper, a little sugar, dill and a little rosemary.   Finally add ¾ pint (450 ml) chicken or white stock.   Stir together briefly and bring quickly to the boil. Cook uncovered for 5 minutes.   Now cover the pan and cook very slowly for 6-8 minutes until the stock is all absorbed and the rice is cooked to your liking.   Chopped fried liver can be added if it is to go with lamb, or chicken livers with chicken.   Chopped parsley too should be stirred in. Possibly the chives (or spring onions) are better added now if they are very tender - it depends on their size.   Cover with a napkin and the lid and a weight and leave on the side of the Aga or cooker for 30 minutes or so.   Stir before serving and dust with cinnamon or allspice.   It very much depends on what it is to accompany.

The important part with all pilavs is the 'rest' at the end, which is very helpful to a hostess who wants to go and change.

Mrs. G.M. Warr

JOAN'S RISOTTO OR BEAUFORT BROWN RICE

4 tbs good dripping or oil	salt and pepper
6 bacon rashers	9 oz (250 g) rice
1 medium onion, grated	1½ tbs dry vermouth
1 garlic clove, crushed	2 tbs Worcester sauce
8 oz (225 g) button mushrooms, sliced	1 tsp gravy browning
4-8 oz (100-225 g) chicken livers, halved	¾-1¼ pints (450-750 ml) boiling
flour	chicken stock or consommé
1 oz (25 g) butter	2 oz (50 g) grated Parmesan cheese

Melt dripping or oil in a heavy pan or casserole. Put in
the chopped bacon rashers, the onion and garlic and the
sliced mushrooms. Cook gently until onions and mushrooms
are soft, but do not burn. Cut the chicken livers in
half, dust them with flour and sauté them in butter in
a separate pan for 3-4 minutes only. Add them to the onion
and mushroom mixture, scraping in the juices. Season and
add the rice and cook together for a few minutes. Stir in
the vermouth, the Worcester sauce and gravy browning,
simmer and then pour in the hot stock or consommé. (The
liquid should cover the rice by the width of two fingers.)
Stir all together and put in a hot oven, 400°F (200°C)
gas mark 6, for at least 20 minutes.* Look at it
occasionally and stir a few times with a fork, tasting to
see when it is ready. Add a little more stock if necessary,
but this quantity should absorb all the liquid, and cook
to an 'al dente' point without going mushy or sticking.
Remove from the oven, correct seasoning and turn on to a
hot serving dish. Have a bowl of grated Parmesan cheese
ready and hand separately.

*The time depends on the kind of rice used.

Lady Lovat and Mrs. Joan Birnie

22, MONTPELIER STREET,

S. W. 7.

KNIGHTSBRIDGE 3562.

GIORGIANA'S RISOTTO AL GORGONZOLA

3 tbs butter
1 onion, finely chopped
12 oz (350 g) long-grain rice
¼ pint (150 ml) dry white wine
1½ pints (900 ml) boiling stock, or enough
  to cover rice by 2 fingers
6 oz (175 g) Gorgonzola cheese
a little cream
grated Parmesan cheese

Melt a little butter in a heavy saucepan and sauté
the onion in it.   Do not let butter or onion burn.
Pour in the dry rice (about 1 handful per person)
and stir carefully for a few minutes.   Do not let
rice colour.   Then add the dry white wine and simmer
until evaporated, 3-4 minutes.   Then pour on enough
good strong boiling stock (chicken or veal is best)
to cover rice by 2 fingers.   Do not stir, but when
it boils again cover pan.   Reduce heat and simmer
gently for 20-25 minutes.   You can look and stir
occasionally and add more hot stock if necessary.
When the rice is nearly cooked, and still 'al dente',
add the Gorgonzola cheese that you have broken up
with a fork and mixed with a little hot stock and
cream.   Mix into rice and heat up together.   The
risotto should be creamy but the rice should not be
soft.   Serve at once with grated Parmesan cheese
handed separately.

Fiona Fraser and Principessa Giorgiana Corsini

Spaghetti Soufflé with Beurre Noisette

6 oz (175 g) spaghetti, chopped into
   1 inch (2.5 cm) pieces
2 tbs minced onion
2 tomatoes, skinned and seeded
2 oz (50 g) butter
1 tbs oil
4 fl oz (100 ml) milk
4 fl oz (100 ml) double cream

4 egg yolks
2 tbs dry white wine
2 oz (50 g) grated Parmesan cheese
1 oz (25 g) breadcrumbs
salt and pepper
4 egg whites
beurre noisette made with
   6 oz (175 g) butter

Cook spaghetti until "al dente". Drain well. While cooking, stew the onion and tomatoes in a little of the butter and the oil until a purée. Melt the remaining butter in the milk and cream over gentle heat in a large saucepan. Beat up the egg yolks and slowly stir them in before it gets too hot (or they will scramble). Add wine to the tomato purée, and then add the purée, spaghetti, the cheese and the breadcrumbs to the buttery custard in the saucepan. Season and blend well, then take off the heat. Beat the egg whites very stiff and fold them into the slightly cooled mixture. Spoon into a buttered soufflé dish with a greased paper collar and set this in a shallow pan of very hot water which you slide carefully into a moderate oven, 375°F (190°C), gas mark 5. Bake for 30 minutes. Serve the soufflé with a sauceboat of beurre noisette. The soufflé can be made without tomatoes: just add 2 tbs more cream.

Green or Spinach Tagliatelle with Chanterelles

This great dish, like Poulet Marengo, was inspired by necessity - we had run out of spaghetti.

1 lb (500 g) green tagliatelle
2 oz (50 g) butter
1 slice ham, cut in strips (julienne)
1 lb (500 g) chanterelles (or as
   many as you have picked)

butter/olive oil
1 crushed garlic clove
1 tbs chopped parsley
lemon juice
¼ pint (150 ml) double cream

Cook the tagliatelle in the usual way in plenty of fast boiling water for about 12 minutes till 'al dente'. Drain and rinse first under cold, then hot water. Return to pasta pan in which you have melted the butter and heated up the ham. Keep hot.

Clean the chanterelles by wiping with a damp cloth, sauté them in butter and oil with a crushed clove of garlic or 2 minced shallots for 3-5 minutes. Add to them chopped parsley and a squeeze of lemon juice. Combine the chanterelles with the tagliatelle in the pasta pan, being careful not to break them up, correct seasoning and pour over the cream. Dish immediately on to individual hot plates and eat at once. It is wonderfully good.

Crespolini San Ruffillo

Crespolini

8-10 pancakes (crêpes)
½ lb (225 g) frozen spinach purée
2 oz (50 g) butter
salt and pepper
1 tbs flour
½ pint (300 ml) milk
2 tbs tinned (or fresh) tomato purée

2 tbs cream
1 tbs stock
½ lb (225 g) ricotta cheese
freshly grated nutmeg
1 egg
Parmesan cheese, freshly grated

Make the pancakes as thin as possible.   Pancakes will keep for at least a week
in a tin, layered with grease-proof paper, and they deep-freeze particularly well,
so this is an easy dish if you have a batch of pancakes already made.
Melt the spinach purée in a pan in its own ice, then squeeze out every drop of
water by draining and sieving.   Return to pan, beat in half the butter, season
and keep hot.
Make a fairly thin béchamel from the remaining butter, flour and milk and simmer
for 10 minutes.
Thin the tomato purée with the cream and a little stock and keep warm (correct
seasoning and add a pinch of sugar if necessary).
Combine the ricotta with the spinach, season well with salt, pepper and grated
nutmeg and bind with a beaten egg.
Lay a large tablespoonful of this mixture on each pancake and roll up neatly.
Put a little sauce in an oblong overproof entrée dish and place the stuffed pancakes
side by side on it.   Cover with the rest of the béchamel sauce.   Dribble the
tomato sauce over the top and dust with grated Parmesan cheese and a few flakes
of butter.   Bake for 15 minutes in a moderate oven 375°F (190°C) gas mark 5 and
brown under a hot grill if necessary.   Serve with a bowl of freshly grated Parmesan.

Potato gnocchi

4 oz (100 g) butter
½ pint (300 ml) milk
4½ oz (115 g) flour
2 eggs
2 egg yolks

3-4 medium potatoes, cooked and
    sieved
1 oz (25 g) grated Parmesan or
    Gruyère
salt and pepper

Melt half the butter in the milk in a heavy pan.   Bring to the boil and while
boiling shake in the flour while you whisk and stir briskly for 4-5 minutes.
Take off the stove and beat in the eggs and egg yolks one by one, then stir in
the sieved potatoes, the grated cheese and salt and pepper.
Make the gnocchi from this stiff paste using either two teaspoons or a forcing
bag with a 1 inch (2.5 cm) nozzle.   Force out and cut off pieces, the size of
marshmallows, with a sharp knife into a pan of fast-boiling, salted water.
Poach only a few at a time.   When they rise to the top, cook for 3 minutes more.
Drain on kitchen paper and keep hot.
Serve simply, with melted butter and a little grated Parmesan; with a very meaty
Bolognese sugo; or with Pesto (see page 26) poured over the hot gnocchi, which
you serve at once with a bowl of grated Parmesan.

GNOCCHI DI SPINACI

2 lb (1 kg) spinach

just over 1 lb (500 g) ricotta cheese

1½ rounded tbs flour

salt and pepper

grated nutmeg

1 egg

seasoned flour

melted butter

grated Parmesan cheese

Spine, wash, cook and drain the spinach.   Squeeze <u>all</u> the water
out by pressing over a fine sieve with the back of a wooden
spoon, or by wringing in a muslin cloth.   Then chop it
finely on a board.   Put it in a bowl and chop into it the
ricotta cheese, then add the flour, the seasonings and egg.
Mix together thoroughly.   Put this mixture into the fridge
and let it rest there for 20 minutes.

Then shape the gnocchi into little oval cylinders by taking a
spoonful at a time and rolling it between the well-floured palms
of your hands; or (not so efficient) by rolling it into a
thick flat piece on a floured board and cutting this into strips
and then cutting pieces off each strip.   As you finish each
little cylinder dip it lightly into some seasoned and sieved
flour that you have ready and to hand, and lay the finished
gnocchi out side by side on a clean floured teacloth.   Boil up
a large saucepan of salted water - lower about 4-6 gnocchi at
a time into it on a perforated spoon and when they float to the
top, cook for 2-3 minutes.   Fish them out, drain on a clean
kitchen cloth and pile them on to a hot serving dish.   Sprinkle
them with generous spoonfuls of melted butter and Parmesan cheese
and continuing thus until they are all cooked.   Then serve at
once with an extra bowl of grated Parmesan.

Lady Thorneycroft

CRAB ROULADE

1) ### The Cheese Sauce

¼ lb (100 g) butter	pinch of thyme
3 tbs finely chopped onion	pinch of nutmeg
1½ oz (40 g) flour	pinch of white pepper
1 pint (600 ml) warm milk	¼ lb (100 g) grated Parmesan cheese
1 bay leaf	¼ lb (100 g) Gruyère cheese, grated

Melt the butter in a heavy based saucepan. Add the onion and cook until transparent, then add the flour and make a roux which you cook for 3 minutes. Add the warm milk, a little at a time, and beat until smooth. Add the bay leaf, nutmeg and pepper and simmer, stirring occasionally, for 15 minutes. Beat in the 2 cheeses and cook for another 5 minutes until these are melted. Take off the heat and keep warm.

2) ### The Filling

2 oz (50 g) butter	2 oz (50 g) chopped basil
1 tbs each julienne strips of celery, leek and fennel	3 garlic cloves, crushed
	salt and pepper
1 lb (500 g) crabmeat	nutmeg
4 fl oz (100 ml) Cheese Sauce	

Melt the butter in a frying pan and cook the vegetables until tender – about 5 minutes. Add the crabmeat, and sauté for a few minutes, then the cheese sauce and mix together. Lastly add the basil, garlic and seasonings. Keep warm.

3) ### The Roulade

2 oz (50 g) butter	nutmeg
1½ oz (40 g) flour	salt and pepper
16 fl oz (450 ml) warm milk	4 egg yolks
1½ oz (40 g) mixed Parmesan cheese and Gruyère cheese, grated	5-6 egg whites
	a pinch of cream of tartar

Line the base and sides of a 9 x 13 x 1 inch (23 x 32 x 2.5 cm) Swiss roll tin with greaseproof paper. Butter and flour it and shake off excess flour. Make a roux of the butter and flour, add the milk gradually, bring to the boil, beat until smooth and cook gently for 15 minutes, stirring constantly. Remove from heat and cool a little, then add the egg yolks, one by one, mixing each one in carefully, then the grated cheese and seasonings. Beat 5-6 egg whites stiff and fold them into the panada. Mix well and spoon into the tin. Cook in a hot oven, 400°F (200°C) gas mark 6, for 15 minutes.

When the roulade is cooked, dip a clean teatowel in warm water, wring it out and spread it on a flat surface. Immediately invert the roulade on to it. Carefully pull off the paper. Spread over the crabmeat filling. Roll up from one long side, with the aid of the teatowel. Lift on to serving dish. Cover with the rest of the cheese sauce, then sprinkle it with a little Parmesan and just freckle under a hot grill. Slice and serve with a light tomato sauce.

Mrs. Ellsworth Donnell

First Course Cold

THE PALAZZO FARNESE, ROME
Built by Alessandro Farnese, later Pope Paul III
Acquired as the French Embassy in 1871

PORTUGUESE EGGS WITH CRUDITÉS

8 large eggs
2½ tsp grated onion
    or chopped chives
2½ tsp curry powder
2½ tbs mayonnaise

salt and pepper
parsley
lettuce, the heart only
tartar sauce or tarragon
    mayonnaise

raw vegetable to taste - carrots, fennel, cauliflower,
radish, celery, mushrooms, white turnip - all carefully
cleaned and neatly cut up.

Hard-boil the eggs.   When cold, peel and cut in half
lengthways.   Mash yolks with onion (or chives), curry
powder, mayonnaise and seasoning.   Pipe this mixture back
into the egg whites; group them together in the centre of
the serving dish and encircle them with a wreath of parsley
sprigs.
Arrange the raw vegetables in small individual heaps in a
second wreath around the eggs.   Hand a sauceboat of tartar
sauce or tarragon mayonnaise apart, but beware of it, as
this is meant to be a slimmer's first course.

S.E. La Comtesse de Lesseps

Oeufs Mayonnaise Brandolini

Prepare 6 oeufs mollets.

Make ½ pint (300 ml) mayonnaise - not too thick.

Add 2 heaped tbs of aspic jelly, again not too thick.

Add 1 heaped tbs of freshly grated Parmesan cheese.   Mix well.

Place the eggs in a glass bowl and cover with the mayonnaise mixture.   Chill.

Garnish with more chopped up aspic, according to taste and chill on ice until

ready to serve.

<u>Lady Caroline Somerset</u>

Oeufs Brouillés aux Truffes à la gelée de Madère

½ pint (300 ml) aspic	¼ lb (100 g) unsalted butter
2 tbs madeira	8 eggs
1 small truffle	salt and pepper

1. Prepare the aspic; add the madeira; leave to cool to a 'syrupy' and
    just pourable consistency.
2. Slice the truffle into 6 thin little slices, for garnish, and chop
    the rest finely.
3. Melt the butter in a heavy saucepan.
4. Mix 7 eggs in a bowl with a fork, do not beat.
5. Add eggs to the butter, salt and pepper to taste, stir constantly and
    keep the heat low. When half scrambled, add the chopped truffle.
6. Continue cooking and stirring and, just as the eggs are about to set,
    add the 8th whole egg and stir this in to keep the eggs soft and creamy.
    Cook for another minute and then immediately tip the scrambled eggs into
    a bowl to stop them cooking.
7. Spoon the eggs into 6 previously buttered cocotte dishes (size 2) and
    leave to get quite cold.
8. Cover the eggs with a spoonful of the madeira aspic. Allow to set and
    garnish with the reserved truffle slices.

Mrs. John Sheffield

TOMATOES À L'ESPAGNOLE

2 small, or 1 large tomato for each person. Cut some cheese, tongue, apples, celery and raw mushrooms into strips. Mix with mayonnaise and fill the tomatoes which you have previously skinned, seeded, drained and chilled.

Leave for several hours in the fridge before serving.

TOMATO, CAULIFLOWER AND WALNUT SALAD

1 small firm cauliflower
¼ lb (100 g) blanched skinned walnuts
3 tbs finely chopped lean ham

8 fl oz (225 ml) lemon mayonnaise
3 tbs cream
6 large tomatoes

Wash the cauliflower and cut into small pieces. Finely chop the walnuts or put through mincer. Mix cauliflower, nuts and ham with the mayonnaise that you have thinned down with cream. Fill large skinned scooped-out and drained tomatoes with this mixture. Sprinkle with oregano.

Serve very cold.

COLD CHEESE SOUFFLÉ

1 sachet (¼ oz (10 g)) gelatine
hot water
1 chicken stock cube
2 oz (50 g) strong Cheddar cheese,
    grated

1 pint (600 ml) double cream
¼ tsp cayenne pepper
½ tsp ground mace
1 stiffly beaten egg white

Dissolve the gelatine in a little water, make it up to ½ pint (300 ml) with hot water, and dissolve the chicken stock cube in it. Leave to cool and partly set.* Whip the jellied stock and add the grated cheese, cream, cayenne and mace. Mix well and fold in the egg white. Pour into individual ramekins and chill. Sprinkle with cayenne and serve with freshly-made hot cheese straws, a bundle for each person.

*If you have some real jellied veal or chicken stock, use it instead of the gelatine and stock cube mixture.

Marinade of Smoked Haddock

2-3 fillets of smoked Finnan haddock (choose fat ones, which will flake well). Par-boil them in water or milk and water; they should be 'al dente' and not soft. Cool, flake and pick over; remove every piece of bone and skin.

Put into a flat earthenware serving dish and pour over enough good olive oil to soak thoroughly. Add 5-6 peppercorns, 2 small bay leaves and the juice and some thinly peeled rind of a small lemon. Leave in a cold place overnight or for at least 6 hours. Remove rind and bay leaves before serving if you wish.

Mrs. John Noble

Salad Tricolore

This is a simple dish that depends on fresh basil, sun-ripened tomatoes and a really good vinaigrette.

    3-4 beef tomatoes, skinned
    3 ripe avocados, peeled and stoned
    2 mozzarella cheeses
    vinaigrette
    3 or 4 sprays of fresh basil

Slice the tomatoes, avocados and the mozzarella cheeses. Lay 3 or 4 of each in a pattern, alternating the colours, on individual white or green plates, and spoon the vinaigrette, made with 4 tbs oil to one of wine vinegar, (garlic optional), over the salad, scattering a few fresh chopped basil leaves on top. Leave in a cold place for 2 hours or so. Alternatively, use a large round platter and arrange the salad in their separate colours in circles around it.

Mozzarella Salad

6 tomatoes
6 baby leeks
2 Mozzarella cheeses
1 carton of soured cream
1 lemon / corn oil
8 oz bacon.

Peel, seed and slice tomatoes into quarters;
Parboil and drain the leeks (they should be
al dente) – and cut each into three. Slice
the mozzarella and put all these ingredients
into a soufflé dish and into the fridge. Mix
a soured cream dressing (just add soured cream
to a lemon and oil vinaigrette) and grill the
bacon, which must be very crisp. Just before
serving, pour the dressing over the salad
and crumble the bacon on top.
Serve with hot bread.

Jamie Maclean

PARSLEY PÂTÉ

1 lb (500 g) liver sausage, mashed   ½ tsp dried sweet basil, or
1 garlic clove, crushed   1 tbs fresh chopped basil
                                 3 tbs grated onion

Blend these ingredients well together, shape them into a flat
cake, and chill.

8 oz (225 g) cream cheese   1 tsp mayonnaise
1 garlic clove, crushed   a good bunch of parsley
3 drops Tabasco sauce

Mix the cheese, garlic, Tabasco and mayonnaise together and spread
this mixture at least ½ inch (1 cm) thick over the top and sides
of the pâté cake and then sprinkle thickly with parsley. You
will need a lot of parsley, chopped fine, to cover the cake and
make it look completely green. Serve with thin brown toast or
biscuits.

H.E. Lady Burrows

TERRINE DE LIÈVRE

the fillets of a hare   a piece of pork or bacon fat
¾ lb (350 g) minced veal   a bay leaf
salt and pepper   thyme
thin slices of boiled bacon   2 tbs stock
12 slices of raw veal fillet

Bone and mince the fillets of hare and mix them with the minced
veal. Salt and pepper the meat. Line a terrine, first with
thin slices of boiled bacon, then with a layer of the minced meat,
a slice of bacon and a slice of veal fillet, more of the mince
and so on, until the terrine is full. Cover it with a piece of
fat bacon or pork, add the bay leaf and thyme and stock made out
of the hare's bones. Put it in a moderate oven, 350°F (180°C)
gas mark 4, for 1 hour. Take it out of the terrine and serve
it with a green salad.

CAFÉ ROYAL

68 REGENT STREET   LONDON WIR 6EL

FONDS D'ARTICHAUTS CAFÉ ROYAL

6 round fried bread croutons

6 carefully prepared and cooked large fonds d'artichauts

3 Arbroath smokies; milk and water to poach them in

2½ tbs butter

1 small packet Philadelphia cheese

1 lemon

1 egg white

1 cup mayonnaise

1 cup cream

6 black olives

pepper

Cook fish in milk and water and pick free of all bones and skin. Mash carefully with a fork and add the butter, cheese, pepper, lemon juice and a spoonful of cream. Lastly fold in the beaten egg white. Spread this mixture on top of each "fond", place "fonds" on top of cold fried bread croutons (which you have previously fried in olive oil) and coat with mayonnaise which you have thinned down by beating in the rest of the cream. Garnish with a black olive.

CAPONATA OF AUBERGINES

A Sicilian Dish

2 lb (1 kg) aubergines
salt
1 onion, chopped
1 carrot, chopped
1 celery stick, including
  leaf
olive oil

1 tbs sugar
3 tbs wine vinegar
1 lb (500 g) canned, peeled
  tomatoes
8 tbs sliced green olives
8 tbs capers
6 hard-boiled eggs, chopped
fresh basil, lots of it

1.   Cut aubergines into 1 inch (2.5 cm) cubes, leaving on the skin.   Sweat in a little salt and water for 10 minutes.   Rinse and dry.   Meanwhile, prepare the tomato sauce.

2.   Sauté the onion, carrot and celery in olive oil.   Add the sugar and wine vinegar.   Pour in the tomatoes and cook for 20 minutes.

3.   Sauté the aubergines in oil as you would fry potatoes, until they are coloured deep brown, almost black.

4.   Let them and the tomato sauce get cold.

5.   Turn into a big bowl, being careful not to break up the aubergines too much and mix in the tomato sauce, the olives, capers and half the hard-boiled eggs - and a lot of chopped basil.

6.   Either leave in the bowl or transfer to serving dish and garnish the dish with the remainder of the hard-boiled eggs and basil leaves.   Sprinkle a few capers on top.

A very good start to a summer dinner party.

Duca Francesco, Principe di Aragon

Pâté de Foie Gras en Brioche

1. Crumble ½ oz (15 g) fresh yeast over 2 tbs warm water in a bowl. Beat in about 4 oz (100 g) flour to make a dough and leave for 15-20 minutes.

2. Sift another 14 oz (400 g) flour on to a board, add the yeast mixture, 6 eggs, 2 tsp salt and 1 tsp sugar. Knead for 5 minutes then knead in 8 oz (225 g) softened butter.

3. Cover and stand 2 hours, in a warm place, to rise.

4. Roll out, fold into three, cover and leave until doubled in size.

5. Flatten to thickness of 1 inch (2.5 cm) with rolling-pin on lightly floured board.

6. Line a buttered mould with 1 inch (2.5 cm) of brioche dough, allowing enough to cover the whole pâté, which is now placed in the mould. The mould may be round, fluted or oblong but no larger than required to accommodate approximately half the height of the pâté with its surround of dough. Make a ball of the remaining dough and place on top of the brioche.

7. Tie buttered foil or greaseproof paper round mould to prevent brioche overflowing, then stand in warm place for 40 minutes and allow to rise. Brush with egg yolk diluted with a little milk.

8. Cook in hot oven, 425°F (220°C) gas mark 7 for 15 minutes. Reduce oven temperature to 375°F (190°C) gas mark 5 and bake for a further 40 minutes. Serve hot or cold.

Note This is a recipe calculated to break your mixer, your bank account, or both.

Winston S. Churchill

CHILLED TOMATO EMINCÉE

10 fine ripe tomatoes
1 small onion, grated
salt and pepper
6 tbs mayonnaise

2 tbs cream
1½ tbs chopped parsley
1½-2 tsp curry powder

Scald, skin and finely dice the tomatoes and mix with the onion. Season
well. Chill in fridge for several hours. Put into individual chilled
soup cups and top with generous dollops of creamy mayonnaise into which
you have mixed the parsley and curry powder. Sprinkle a little parsley
or chopped basil on top.

BLOODY MARY ICE

6 tbs cream cheese
4 tbs finely chopped Roquefort or
  Dolcelatte
1 tsp grated onion
1 tbs Worcester sauce
2½ tbs lemon juice

salt and pepper
Tabasco sauce
1¼ pints (750 ml) tomato juice
¼ pint (150 ml) vodka
3 egg whites, stiffly beaten
mint sprigs

Cream together the two cheeses in a bowl, add the onion, Worcester sauce,
lemon juice and seasoning. Then the tomato juice, blending smoothly, and
lastly the vodka.

Pour into freezing trays and set fridge at coldest possible. Freeze until
all but a little in the centre is frozen.

Remove and beat smooth in a chilled bowl with a chilled egg-beater. Fold
in egg whites that have been beaten to a peak. Return to freezing trays
and freeze again until firm, then spoon into long glasses and garnish with
a sprig of mint. Of course this excellent and slightly intoxicating ice-
cream can be made without effort and in 20 minutes if you own one of the
new electric Italian sorbetiers.

Mrs. Ronnie Tree

LA TERRINE AUX SIX LEGUMES

carrots, sliced in rounds
leeks
artichoke bottoms (tinned ones are fine)
or any neat and colourful vegetables you
wish
oz (100 g) haricots verts

2 tomatoes
9 oz (250 g) mushrooms
scant 1 pint (600 ml) cream
salt and pepper
½ tbs gelatine

refully prepare the vegetables.   Cook separately in boiling salted
ter the carrots, white parts of the leeks, the artichoke bottoms
d the beans.
in the tomatoes, removing all pips and flesh.
ok the mushrooms in the cream for 30-40 minutes.   Liquidize and
ason with salt and white pepper.   Add the gelatine which you
ssolve first in a little of the vegetable water.
anch the green parts of the leeks and line your terrine with the
st beautifully coloured leaves, leaving ½ inch (1 cm) at the top to
ld over.
ace a thin layer of mushroom cream in the base of the terrine and
ver this with a layer of carrots.   Cover the carrots with mushroom
xture, followed by the artichokes.   Continue layering in this way
th all the vegetables and the mushroom cream.   Finish with a layer
mushroom and more leaves from the green part of the leeks.
ill for at least 6 hours and turn out.   Serve in slices with a fresh
mato sauce.

e Sauce

oz (250 g) tomato flesh
tbs tomato purée
pint (300 ml) fresh or sour cream, or home-made yoghurt
lt and pepper
w drops Tabasco sauce
pinch of sugar

quidize the tomato flesh or pass through a fine sieve.   Add to it
e tomato purée and the cream, and mix thoroughly.   Correct the
asoning.   It should be a little sharp, but not sour.

alcolm Colquhoun

DÉLICES DE SAUMON FUMÉ

Fill a soufflé dish with a good smoked salmon mousse*, put it on a round flat serving dish and arrange very thinly sliced rolls of smoked salmon round the edge of the dish like the spokes of a wheel, with a bunch of watercress garnish in between.

Fill the rolls with a spoonful of small freshly picked shrimps (crevettes) which you have sprinkled with lemon juice and a pinch of mace.

Hand a plateful of <u>very</u> thin brown bread sandwiches spread with watercress butter, and a sauceboat of creamy horseradish sauce.

*An excellent one is on page 56 of my first cook-book (Lady Maclean's Cook Book) but leave out the layer of caviar.   It takes about 10 oz (300 g) of smoked salmon.

Mrs. Vincent Astor

Shell Fish

LOUIS EUSTACHE UDE
1782–1856
Cook to the Duke of York,
Lord Sefton and Crockford's Club

OYSTERS ROCKEFELLER À L'ANTOINE

4 shallots or 1 small onion
1 oz (25 g) parsley
¼ lb (100 g) spinach leaves
1 tbs aniseed
½ pint (300 ml) water
¼ tsp Tabasco sauce
½ tsp salt
½ tsp dried thyme
1 tbs anchovy paste
¼ lb (100 g) butter
2 oz (50 g) toasted breadcrumbs
24 oysters
rock salt

Put shallots, parsley and spinach through a food mincer.
Simmer aniseed in water for 10 minutes.   Strain out seeds.
Add ground vegetables to anise-flavoured liquid.   Simmer,
covered, for 10 minutes.   Season with Tabasco sauce, salt,
thyme and anchovy paste.   Add butter and breadcrumbs.
If sauce is too thick to spread easily, thin it with a
little oyster liquid.   Open oysters with oyster knife.
Place oysters on a bed of rock salt in two shallow baking
dishes.   Grill them for about 5 minutes, or until edges
curl.   Spread each oyster with a spoon of the prepared
mixture and return to grill for 5 minutes longer.   Makes
four servings.

N.B.   American oysters are larger than British or European
(Portuguese) ones: therefore these quantities for Antoine's
sauce would be enough for about 40 British oysters.

H.E. Mrs. David Bruce

BATTER BREAD, VIRGINIA HAM AND OYSTERS (Makes a very good buffet supper - it is a traditional Christmas one in Virginia)

Here are two versions: the batter bread should be served with both.

BATTER BREAD

4 tbs butter	1 tbs sugar
5 oz (150 g) white water-ground cornmeal	8 fl oz (225 ml) boiling water
1 tsp salt	12 fl oz (350 ml) milk (approximately)
1 tsp baking powder	2 eggs, beaten (3 for company)

Pre-heat oven to 450°C (230°C) gas mark 8. Put butter in an ovenproof baking dish (glass or enamelled iron makes best crust) to melt in the oven. Sift dry ingredients into a bowl, and add boiling water. Add milk to beaten eggs, add this mixture <u>gradually</u> to meal, beating hard until smooth. Consistency of batter should be like double cream. Add more milk if necessary. By this time the oven should be hot, and the butter bubbling and beginning to colour. Roll the hot baking dish round so that the butter coats the inside completely, then pour the excess butter into the cornmeal batter. Stir well, pour batter back quickly into baking dish and bake until set and crusty. Time depends on depth of dish.

1. VIRGINIAN PANNED OYSTERS AND HAM

2 tbs butter
2 pints (1 litre) select oysters, well drained
Virginia ham, sliced very thin

Heat butter in frying pan until very hot; add oysters.
Cook until heated through; put slices of ham in, take
off heat, and serve as soon as ham is hot (all this
takes about 2-3 minutes). Serve with batter bread
and a salad.

2. VIRGINIAN STEWED OYSTERS AND COLD HAM

Open oysters and reserve the liquid. Cut off any tough
or rough bits. Put into a shallow casserole or chafing
dish with a little butter, half the oyster juices and
about ½-1 pint (300-600 ml) just boiling cream. Add a
little cracker dust (ground-up water biscuits), salt and
pepper. Cook slowly for 3-5 minutes, until edges of
oysters start to curl. Quantities depend on how many
oysters you use, but they should be semi-immersed in the
cream sauce.

Serve with Virginian ham sliced very thin, and batter
bread.

Mrs. Fitzgerald Bemiss

MOUCLADE D'AUNIS

4 lb (2 kg) mussels (ideally Bouchat)   1 heaped tbs flour
1 lb (500 g) onions, finely chopped   ½ pint (300 ml) double cream
1 oz (25 g) butter   1 tbs curry powder

Clean the mussels well.   Cover with water.   Cook until their shells open.
Remove the mussels from their shells and keep warm.
    Continue simmering the liquid to reduce it.
    Sweat the onions gently in butter then cover the saucepan, adding
if necessary a little mussel liquid, and simmer until they are melted
into a purée;   sprinkle in flour, stirring briskly until smooth;   add
about ½ pint (300 ml) of boiling mussel liquid and remove from heat.
    Just before serving, add the cream, mussels and curry powder.
    Pour into an earthenware entrée dish and hand Riz à la Créole
(see page 262) in another.

Baronne Cecile de Rothschild

MOULES GRILLÉES À LA PROVENCALE

4 lb (2 kg) good mussels, carefully cleaned and washed
¼ pint (150 ml) dry white wine
about ¼ lb (100 g) garlic butter (see page 44)
2 very dry rusks, crushed

Open the mussels by putting them in a large pan and shaking them over a
high heat for 6-8 minutes.   Remove them from the pan, shell them and
leave them to drain on a board covered with kitchen paper.   Reserve half
the shells, choosing the best ones, and discard the rest.
To Serve:
The mussels look nicest served on special metal or china mussel plates,
with 12 small depressions for the mussels to sit in, but if you don't
possess these, spread a ½ inch (1 cm) layer of mashed potato on to
ordinary plates and set the half mussels up on this.   Then, using a palette
knife, cover each mussel with slightly softened garlic butter and sprinkle
a pinch of rusk crumbs over the top.   Slip each plate under the grill for
a moment before serving until the butter softens and bubbles;   serve hot,
and have a few reinforcements ready!

Peoci au Gratin or Moules Marinière en Surprise - a good dish
for an informal dinner party.

6 pints (3.4 litres) mussels

¼ pint (150 ml) white wine

1 small onion or shallot, finely chopped

½ pint (300 ml) water

2 oz (50 g) breadcrumbs

¼ lb (100 g) grated Parmesan cheese

1 tbs chopped fresh parsley

Wash, scrub and beard the mussels.   Cook them in a large pan
with the white wine, onion or shallot and water.   Cover the
pan, bring to the boil and boil for 1 minute.   Take the pan
off the heat and drain the liquid into a second pan.   Put this
pan back on heat and boil briskly to reduce.   Meanwhile pull
away the upper half shells of the mussels which should all have
partly opened in boiling (throw away any that have not opened).
Place mussels in their remaining half shells side by side in
two large shallow fireproof dishes lined with plenty of foil.
Sprinkle breadcrumbs then grated Parmesan and parsley over
mussels.   Add the liquid in which you have cooked the mussels,
which should have reduced to about ¼ pint (150 ml).   Enclose
the mussels in the foil like huge loose parcels.   Bake in a
hot oven, 450°F (230°C) gas mark 8 for 15 minutes.   Split
open the parcels at table, telling everyone to help themselves.

COQUILLES ST JACQUES À LA MEUNIÈRE

6-8 scallops
seasoned flour
6 oz (175 g) clarified butter
6-8 tbs chopped parsley

juice of 1 lemon
duchesse potato mixture
maître d'hôtel butter

Open scallops by putting them on a hot stove.   Remove the black piece and
clean the scallops under cold running water.   Dry them well and chop them.
Shake in a little seasoned flour, then cook them gently in butter, parsley
and lemon juice as you would a sole meunière.
While scallops are cooking, prepare shells by piping duchesse potato around
the edge of the shell and drying this a little under the grill.   (The
duchesse purée is best made of potatoes baked in their jackets in the oven,
then skinned and pushed through a mouli to make it smooth;   add 2 eggs and
season well before you put it into the forcing bag.)
Spoon the scallops into their prepared shells and put a little knob of
maître d'hôtel butter on top of each.   (A good Béarnaise sauce can be handed
separately if preferred.)

H.E. Mrs. Charles E. Bohlen

SCALLOPS, SCALLOPED, FROM BARBADOS

Butter a scallop shell for each person.   Prepare scallop meat as above.
Count two parts of sautéed scallop meat to one part of soft, finely grated
breadcrumbs.   Mix together and then add the following:

juice of a garlic clove
3 tbs chopped chives
a little melted butter
8 fl oz (225 ml) single cream
a dash of Angostura bitters

salt and cayenne pepper
few drops of Tabasco sauce
juice of 1 lemon
2 rashers bacon, fried crisp and
   crumbled

Fill the shells generously with this mixture and brown under the grill with
a few extra breadcrumbs and butter on top.

Brenner's Park-Hotel in Baden-Baden

AN DER LICHTENTALER ALLEE

FRESH CRAYFISH BADEN-BADEN

12-24 fresh crayfish, depending on size

about 1¾ pints (1 litre) good fish stock (made from fish
   trimmings and the heads and (smaller) arms of the
   crayfish, an onion, herbs etc.

2 tbs butter

2 fl oz (50 ml) brandy

1 tsp dill

basil, to taste

parsley, to taste

salt and pepper

Cook the crayfish in the boiling fish stock for 3 minutes
only.   When cooked, remove, drain, shell and pat dry.

Toss in butter and flambé with a little brandy.   Add the
chopped herbs, season and simmer a few moments.

Put sufficient crayfish for one helping into individual
soup bowls and pour over them their pan juices and a little
of the well-reduced and strained stock.

Serve a hollandaise sauce separately and accompany with a
pilaff of rice.

Mr. Ronnie Tree

HAMPTON PLANTATION SHRIMP PILAU

4 bacon rashers
7 oz (200 g) uncooked rice
3 tbs butter
2 oz (50 g) finely chopped
  celery
2 tbs finely chopped green pepper

1 lb (500 g) peeled shrimps
1 tsp Worcester sauce
1 tbs flour
salt and pepper

Fry bacon until crisp.   Drain on kitchen paper and keep
warm.   Cook the rice, adding bacon grease to cooking
water.   In another saucepan, melt butter, add celery and
green pepper.   Cook a few minutes: add shrimps which
have been sprinkled with Worcester sauce and dredged with
flour.   Stir and simmer until flour is cooked (at least
10 minutes).   Season with salt and pepper.

Now add cooked rice and mix well until rice is buttery
and shrimpy.   You may have to add more butter.

Just before serving stir in the crisp bacon, crumbled.
Serve hot.

This pilau can be made with prawns or scampi but the
shellfish should be fresh, not frozen.

From the Charleston Junior League young Ladies and
their wonderful South Carolinian cookery book

PORTUGUESE RISSOIS

These small envelopes of fried pastry stuffed with shrimps are
served in Estoril with cutlets of fried white fish, but they are
so good they can be elevated to a first course in their own
right.   Serve them with some fried parsley with a tartare,
simple normande or sauce of your own choice, handed separately.

8 oz (225 g) shortcrust pastry

1¼ lb (600 g) fresh shrimps, peeled

½ pint (300 ml) thick béchamel sauce

oil for deep-frying

fine breadcrumbs, browned in the oven

Roll out the pastry as thin as possible and stamp into circles
3½ inches (9 cm) in diameter.   Fold the shrimps into the
béchamel sauce and place blobs of the mixture on one half of
each circle.   Wet the edges with cold water, or milk, flap
over and press firmly together.   Deep-fry in very hot oil
until golden.   Lift out and toss immediately in the breadcrumbs.
Serve on a folded paper napkin with fried parsley garnish.

Mrs. Christopher Bridge

Crab Olda

2 medium sized crabs
½ pint (300 ml) mayonnaise
lemon juice
mustard
garlic (optional)
1 lb (500 g) large prawns (half-shelled)

2 tbs melted unsalted butter
cayenne pepper
freshly ground black pepper
Worcester sauce
brown bread toast

Have the fishmonger separate the white meat and the brown from the crabs. Mix the white meat with enough of a lemon flavoured mayonnaise (sharpened with lemon juice and a little mustard and perhaps a touch of garlic) to bind it but not smother it. Shape into a cake in the centre of a round or oblong serving dish, and decorate with the half-shelled prawns.

In another bowl mix the brown crab meat with some unsalted butter, a shake or two of cayenne pepper, 2 tsp lemon juice, some black pepper and a dash of Worcester sauce. This mixture must be mixed to your own taste, as the amount of brown meat varies from crab to crab. It should be fairly 'hot' in contrast to the blander white meat.

Finally toast several pieces of brown bread, butter it and cut into fingers, then spread the brown meat generously on each finger. Arrange the fingers like spokes of a wheel round the central white meat. Make sure the toast is hot and crisp and only dress it at the last moment – then serve immediately. Hand any mayonnaise you have left over in a sauceboat.

Mrs. John Sheffield

Fitzroy's Shrimp Newburg

2 tbs butter
8 oz (225 g) fresh shrimps or small prawns
a very little salt
a little cayenne
a dash of Tabasco

1 tbs sherry
1 tbs brandy
4 tbs double cream
2 egg yolks
English muffins or crumpets

Melt half the butter and sauté the shrimps. Pour off any liquid and, if necessary, add remaining butter. Add seasonings, sherry and brandy and cook for a few minutes until reduced to 1 tbs, then add the cream into which you have beaten the egg yolks and stir until it has thickened. Pile on to toasted and buttered English muffin halves or crumpets. This makes a very good supper at home dish.

Creole Court Bouillon

The basis of a supper dish for twelve.

4 tbs olive oil
3 tbs flour
salt and pepper
¾ pint (450 ml) tomato juice
5 medium onions, chopped and
sautéed in butter
1 fresh chilli
½ green pepper, finely chopped

3 garlic cloves
8 oz (225 g) chopped celery
1 tbs chopped parsley
2 bay leaves
4 lb (1.75 kg) shellfish,
poultry or meat
3 tbs dry sherry (optional)
boiled or fried rice

Heat the olive oil in a saucepan. Make a roux with the flour
adding a little at a time until it is all used. Season to
taste. Keep stirring until the roux is a dark colour. Add
the tomato juice and bring to a simmer. Add all the rest of
the ingredients, except the shellfish, sherry and rice.
Cook on a low heat for 10 minutes. Now put in the shellfish,
poultry or meat you wish to use. Cover the pan firmly and
cook until done. Stir frequently or it could stick and burn.
Before serving, taste to see if the seasoning is correct and
add more salt and pepper if necessary. Finish with the dry
sherry. Serve with a large pilaf of boiled or fried rice.

Seafood Casserole

about 15 oysters
2 oz (50 g) butter
1 oz (25 g) flour
6 fl oz (175 ml) cream
salt and pepper
cayenne
2 tsp onion juice

2 lb (1 kg) cooked shrimps
12 oz (350 g) mushrooms
6 oz (175 g) diced cooked chicken
2 tbs sherry or dry vermouth
1 tbs finely chopped parsley
a little fresh dill, chopped

Par-boil oysters. Make a sauce with the butter, flour and
cream. Thin down with some of the oyster liquid and some
more cream, if you wish. Add seasonings, then the shrimps,
mushrooms, chicken, oysters, sherry and herbs. Do not re-
boil. Serve in a shallow entrée dish, with a big pilaf of
rice to accompany it. Serve hot.

Serves 8.

BROCHETTES DE FRUITS DE MER, SAUCE INDIENNE

Scampi or prawns, steamed mussels, mushrooms, bacon, green pepper, pineapple chunks, pieces of turbot or sole, etc., bay leaf and onion are all threaded on skewers, brushed with olive oil or melted butter and grilled.   The drippings from the grill pan and the mussel juice are incorporated in a sauce lightly flavoured with curry. Serve with rice pilaf.

H.E. Marquesa de Santa Cruz

CRAB CLAWS, SAUCE TARTARE

Allow about 3-5 fresh crab claws per person, depending on size.   You can obtain them fairly easily from a seaside fishmonger or fish-market where dressed crab is sold.   Crack the shell away from the fat part of the claw leaving only the black point, then dip them, lightly seasoned, first in melted butter then in very fine toasted breadcrumbs.   Fry them in a deep pan of hot oil for 5-6 minutes.   Drain and serve in a folded napkin in a wooden bowl with a little deep-fried dry parsley in the middle.   Lots of good homemade sauce tartare must be served with this dish, which is well worth all the effort necessary to find the claws!

VM

PRAWLE PRAWNS

½ pint (300 ml) whipped cream
salt and pepper
1 tsp anchovy essence
2 tsp tomato purée
2 tbs brandy

1 lb (500 g) very fresh shelled prawns, or langoustines
2 lettuce hearts
2 lemons, sliced
paprika

Put the cream in a bowl and mix in the salt, pepper, anchovy essence, tomato purée and brandy, to taste, then carefully fold in the prawns, or langoustines.   Wash the lettuce hearts and put a few leaves on each plate.   Put 2-3 slices of lemon on the side of each plate and 2 large tablespoons of creamy prawns in the centre. Sprinkle a little paprika over each and serve with home made brown bread and butter.

Mrs. Derek Marlowe

SOUFFLÉ DE CRABE SINGAPOUR
(Serves 10)

3 tbs very finely chopped onion

a little butter

6 small crabs or equivalent kamkatkan crab meat

4 fl oz (100 ml) double cream

4 fl oz (100 ml) fairly thick béchamel sauce

4 tbs boiled rice

3 tbs fresh white breadcrumbs

½ tbs curry powder

paprika and cayenne to taste

salt and pepper

8 tbs tomato purée

3 egg yolks

3 egg whites, stiffly beaten

Cook the onion in a little butter for 1 minute, add the crab
meat, the cream, the béchamel sauce, the rice, the breadcrumbs
and the spices.   Bring the mixture to the boil, then add the
tomato purée and the egg yolks, stirring briskly.   Remove
from heat, let it cool a little and fold in the stiffly
beaten egg whites.   Pour into an ovenproof soufflé dish
that has been well greased with butter.   Put a buttered
band of paper round top of dish.   Put the soufflé dish in
a bain marie in a hot oven, 400°F (200°C) gas mark 6, for
30 minutes.   This delicate soufflé cannot possibly wait for
late gourmets, so have the gourmets sit down, and, if
necessary, wait for it.

H.E. The Hon. Lady Soames

Recette de James Viaene,
Chef de Cuisine at the Embassy

MOUSSE DE CRABE (OU DE HOMARD) LUCULLUS

1 lb (500 g) white fish - haddock, plaice or halibut

fish stock

½ lb (225 g) dried breadcrumbs

3 fl oz (75 ml) white wine

2 egg yolks

2½ tbs butter, softened

a few drops pale green vegetable

colouring, if desired

salt and pepper

2 egg whites, stiffly beaten

diced avocado

diced crab meat, or lobster

8 fl oz (225 ml) mayonnaise

2 fl oz (50 ml) double cream

Simmer fish in a simple fish stock (onion, celery, carrot, peppercorns, bay leaf, fish trimmings, boiled together for 30 minutes and strained) until cooked.   Drain fish, reserving ¼ pint (150 ml) of stock. Pick fish over carefully for bones and skin.   Mash fish up with a fork. Soak the breadcrumbs in the fish stock and white wine mixed.   Add the egg yolks and the fish to this purée, then the butter and vegetable colouring, and mix well.   Season sharply and fold in the egg whites which you have beaten to a peak.   Pour the mixture into a well buttered ring mould.   Cover with a greased paper and a heavy lid.   Put the mould into a bain marie and cook gently for about 30 minutes, adding water to pan if necessary.   Cool it, then chill it in the fridge and only turn out when you are about to use it.   Fill the centre of the ring with diced avocado and diced crab meat, or lobster, in a mayonnaise sauce into which you have beaten a little cream.

H.E. Marquesa de Santa Cruz

Shrimp Marguerite

1½ tbs butter
6 oz (175 g) mushrooms, wiped and sliced
1 onion, minced
2 small tomatoes, skinned, drained and chopped
4 fl oz (100 ml) cream
1½ tbs flour
5 tbs dry sherry
1 tbs Worcester sauce
salt and pepper
paprika
few drops Tabasco sauce
2 lb (1 kg) cooked and peeled shrimps
2-3 tbs buttered breadcrumbs

Melt the butter in a sauté pan. Sweat the sliced
mushrooms in it, then add the minced onion and chopped
tomatoes. Simmer together for 10 minutes or so.
Blend the cream and flour together in a small bowl and
add, stirring carefully. When the mixture is smooth
and the flour has cooked a little, add the sherry,
Worcester sauce, salt, pepper, paprika and Tabasco.
Taste and correct seasonings. Now add the shrimps,
mix well, and pour into a buttered entrée dish. Top
with buttered crumbs, a few more flakes of butter, and
cook in a moderate oven, 350°F (180°C) gas mark 4, until
golden brown - about 20 minutes.

This dish can be made equally well with frozen prawns.

Coquilles aux 3 Poivres

(for 2 people)

4 fresh scallops
butter

Sauce
2 tbs fish fumet
1 tbs sherry

3 tbs double cream
1 tsp green peppercorns in brine,
     drained
6-8 hard green peppercorns, ground
salt
freshly ground black pepper

Shell and wash the scallops under cold running water to remove every grain
of sand.   Remove their outer membrane and the black stomach thread and beard.
Pat them dry on kitchen paper and shape into 'medallions'.   You can remove
the pink coral for tidiness sake, but I personally think it is too good to
waste.   Leave them in a warm place for a few minutes, then heat two plates,
butter them and put two scallops on each plate.   After 2 minutes, turn
scallops over and 'cook' the other side.   Spoon the 'trois poivres' sauce
over them.

Sauce   Reduce the fumet, sherry, cream and green peppercorns in a
        saucepan by fast boiling;   add the ground green peppercorns and
        salt.   Lastly, grind a little black pepper over the plates,
        and they are ready.

Mathilda, Duchess of Argyll

Homard à l'Americaine

1 onion
2 garlic cloves
3 shallots
2 carrots
2 celery sticks
1 sour apple
1 tbs chopped ham
butter and oil
2 small lobsters

$\frac{1}{4}$ pint (150 ml) sherry
$\frac{1}{2}$ pint (300 ml) dry white wine
2 tomatoes, skinned
1 tbs tomato purée
tarragon
bay leaf
salt and pepper
cayenne
2 tbs cream (optional)

Chop the first 7 ingredients.   Cook them to a pulp in butter and oil in a
saucepan large enough to hold the lobsters, which are put in last and must
be cut up alive.   Cut off the heads with one blow of a cleaver.   Cut off
the small claws, which you can discard.   Smash the shells of the big claws
a little and cut the bodies into pieces following the rings of the shell.
Moisten with the sherry, white wine, tomatoes and tomato purée.   Throw
in the herbs and cover the saucepan hermetically.   Cook and shake over a
high heat for 15 minutes.   Season with salt and pepper and a pinch of
cayenne.   Add a piece of butter the size of an egg and the cream if you
wish, before serving in hot bowls.   Finger bowls are an essential
accompaniment.

This is a simple and early form of a famous dish which, though now refined,
has become too complicated for most amateur cooks to attempt.

Fish

THE METTERNICH PALACE, VIENNA
Now the Italian Embassy

SHASHLIK OF SALMON WITH RUSSIAN SAUCE

1¾ lb (850 g) middle cut salmon
salt
lemon juice
2 eggs, beaten
2 oz (50 g) fine breadcrumbs
4 oz (100 g) flat mushrooms
2 tbs melted butter

Skin raw salmon and cut into cubes half the size of an ordinary
matchbox.   Don't marinate these, but sprinkle lightly with salt and
lemon juice.   Dip them in egg and breadcrumbs and thread them on
skewers, alternating the pieces with caps of fairly large, flat
mushrooms, which have been dipped in melted butter and salted.
Grill on a charcoal grill, if possible, over moderate or low heat.

Melted butter, sour cream and caviar mixed, or the following sauce
are all good with this dish, and try some unrisen "flat" bread
(pitta) to eat with it.

Russian Sauce, for Salmon, Sea Trout or Sturgeon

¼ pint (150 ml) white wine
2 anchovies, chopped
½ small onion, chopped
grated lemon rind
¼ pint (150 ml) good stock
beurre manié
2-3 tbs cream

Put the white wine into a stewpan with the anchovies, onion, lemon
rind and the stock.   Thicken it with beurre manié and simmer for a
few minutes.   Stir in the cream and either pour the sauce over the
fish or serve it in a sauceboat.

The Rt. Hon. Julian Amery, M.P.

Saumon Beau Lieu flambé au Pernod

1½ oz (40 g) clarified butter

2 x 1 inch (2.5 cm) thick salmon cutlets
(middle cut is best)

salt and pepper

2½ oz (60 g) mixed pine kernels and
chopped macadamia nuts

Sauce

2½ oz (60 g) butter

1 tbs lemon juice

1 tsp grated lemon rind

1 tbs chopped parsley

½ tbs chopped fennel leaves

3 fl oz (75 ml) Pernod

Melt the butter in a frying pan and sauté the salmon in it for 1½ minutes
each side.   Season well and keep warm.   Melt the butter for the sauce
in a small pan and do not let it brown.   Add the lemon juice and grated
rind, the parsley and the chopped fennel.   Pour the sauce over the
salmon and continue cooking them until they colour a little.   Then pour
in the Pernod, basting and cooking for another 2 minutes or so.   (To
test if they are cooked, slide the point of a knife into the flesh near
the bone.   If it is cooked there and comes away from the bone easily,
it is ready.)   Sprinkle over the nuts, tip the pan and ignite, holding
the pan at arm's length.   Baste until the flames die down and dish up.

Truite à la Crème for two

2 trout, each about 4 oz (100 g)

2 oz (50 g) clarified butter

¼ pint (150 ml) double cream

freshly ground black pepper

Take two small very fresh trout, clean, gut and scale them, but leave them
whole.   Melt the clarified butter in a sauté pan and put in the trout.
Cook for about 5 minutes on each side.   When they are cooked, pour off
any surplus fat from the pan and pour on the cream.   Heat it up gently:
it will soon thicken, then grind a little black pepper over them and serve
immediately on hot plates, with all the cream sauce poured over them.
The only garnish suitable, but not necessary, would be a couple of crescents
of puff pastry.

The Creggans Inn, Strachur

COLIN FLORENTINE

1 hake, weighing about 2½ lb (1.25 kg)

a few spring onions or shallots

¼ pint (150 ml) dry white wine

bouquet garni

2 lb (1 kg) spinach

6 tbs butter

salt and pepper

grated nutmeg

1½ pints (900 ml) sauce Mornay*

1½ oz (40 g) grated Parmesan cheese

Fillet fish and make a little fish stock from the bones, onions, white wine and herbs. Spine the spinach, boil it (without adding water), squeeze out every drop of moisture. Toss in butter and season well with salt and pepper and grated nutmeg. Poach the fillets in the fish stock, pour off extra liquid when fish is cooked, reduce it, and add it to the sauce Mornay. Put the cooked spinach at the bottom of an oval entrée dish. Arrange the well-drained fillets on top and cover completely with sauce Mornay. Sprinkle with grated cheese and dot with bits of butter. Put under a hot grill until golden brown and bubbly, or brown in the oven.

* You will find a recipe for sauce Mornay on page 41.

H.E. Lady Reilly

WHITE FISH WITH FENNEL

This recipe is straight from Marseilles and is for grey mullet or other firm white fish, of similar shape.

4-5 lb (2 kg) whole white fish,
  ie grey mullet etc.
large bulb of fennel, chopped
salt and pepper

3 oz (75 g) butter
$\frac{3}{4}$ pint (450 ml) vermouth
fresh or dried tarragon
$\frac{1}{2}$ pint (300 ml) double cream

Take a large white fish, scale it and clean it out properly. Stuff it with celery or fennel, salt and pepper. Spread two-thirds of the butter over all the sides of the fish and wrap it in kitchen foil. Close the end with the head and keep open the end with the tail into which you pour $\frac{1}{4}$ pint (150 ml) of the vermouth. Close that end. Bake the fish in a moderately hot oven, 375°F (190°C) gas mark 5, for 30-40 minutes.

Separately, boil down the remaining vermouth with the tarragon until it is reduced by a quarter. Unwrap the fish and add to the sauce all the juices you manage to save from the packet. Prior to serving, add the rest of the butter which has been well mixed with salt and pepper, and the cream. Re-heat but do not boil. Pour the sauce over the fish which you have carefully skinned and placed on a hot serving dish.

S.E. Madame Louis Roché

SMOKED HADDOCK SOUFFLÉ

½ lb (225 g) smoked Finnan haddock fillets,
   cooked in milk and water then boned,
   skinned and flaked
2 tbs butter
1 tbs flour
¼ pint (150 ml) of the milk the fish was
   cooked in

2 tbs grated cheese
pepper
pinch of cayenne
3 eggs plus 1 egg
   white

Melt the butter, stir in the flour and gradually add the milk
to make a thick sauce.   Mix in the fish, which you have beaten
with a fork until it is fairly creamy, then the cheese and
seasonings.   Break in the 3 egg yolks one at a time, then cool
the mixture and when cool enough fold in the 4 stiffly beaten
egg whites.   Fill an oven-proof soufflé dish full with this
mixture and bake in the middle part of a moderate oven 375°F
(190°C) gas mark 5 for about 30 minutes.   Serve <u>immediately</u>
it is ready.   A beurre noisette can be handed with this soufflé.

The Marquess of Lansdowne

FINNAN HADDOCK FLAN

3-4 Finnan haddock fillets
2 oz (50 g) butter
½ pint (300 ml) milk
shortcrust pastry

3 eggs
black pepper
nutmeg
¾ pint (450 ml) double cream, scalded
4 rashers streaky bacon, grilled
   (optional)

Poach the haddock in butter and milk.   Drain and flake it,
removing all bones and skin.   Add the buttery milk which has
been reduced to a spoonful.   Preheat the oven to 375°F (190°C)
gas mark 5.   Line a 9 inch (23 cm) flan dish or tin with the
pastry and bake blind until three-quarters done.   Beat the eggs,
add the pepper and nutmeg.   Pour in the scalded cream off the
fire, stirring carefully.   Put the haddock in the flan and pour
the custard over it.   Dot with butter and bake in the middle part
of the oven until set, about 25 minutes.   If you like the
combination of bacon and finnan haddock, crumble a few crisply
grilled rashers over the top of the flan, to garnish.

SOLE À L'INDIENNE

1 large lemon sole, or 3
  Dover soles
1 large onion, finely chopped
4 tbs butter
1¼ tbs curry powder

2 dessert apples, peeled and
  chopped
½ pint (300 ml) single cream
4 tomatoes, skinned and chopped
salt and pepper
chopped parsley

Get the fishmonger to skin and fillet the fish.   Cut each
fillet into three or four long strips.   Then tie each
strip into a single knot.   Sauté the onion in the butter
until transparent.   Add the curry powder and fry for
1 minute.   Then add the apples.   Simmer these gently
together for 5 minutes, then add the cream and when it
bubbles add the fish and tomatoes and cook over a low heat
for approximately 8 minutes.   Put on to a hot serving
dish and sprinkle with fresh chopped parsley.

These quantities will serve four people easily, but if
you want to stretch it to six, accompany it with a pilaf
of rice à l'orientale.

Lady Lloyd

SOLE MARGUÉRY

A recipe for a very light and delicate Sole Normande,
given by the head chef at Marguéry's famous
restaurant in Paris c. 1900.

2 medium-sized Dover soles
  (8 fillets)
¼ pint (150 ml) white wine
  (Chablis is best)
salt and pepper
2 egg yolks
1½ oz (40 g) butter
1 tbs chopped parsley

Garnish
2 tbs fresh prawns or
  shrimps
2 tbs fresh mussels
butter

Fillet the soles and lay them in a flat pan.   Moisten
with wine and season with salt and pepper.   When the
fillets are cooked, about 12 minutes, remove them to
a dish and reduce the contents of the pan to about
2 tbs.   Cool, then add the egg yolks to this reduction.
Let them thicken to a cream on a moderate heat, and
add the butter, little by little, taking care that
the sauce is <u>never more than warm</u>.   Throw in some
chopped parsley.   Garnish the fillets with the
prawns or shrimps and mussels which have been cooked
in a little butter, and pour the sauce over all.   Put
the dish in a hot oven, 400°F (200°C) gas mark 6, for
4-5 minutes and serve.

<u>Note</u> If the sauce refuses to thicken, mix a little of
it with ½ tsp of fécule or cornflour and return the
mixture to the pan - but remember it will thicken quite
a lot in the oven.

FILLETS OF SOLE WHITE'S CLUB

12 sole fillets

seasoned flour

4 oz (100 g) butter

1½ tbs wine vinegar

1½ tbs capers

1½ tbs chopped parsley

4 oz (100 g) fresh peeled shrimps or small prawns

2 lemons

Wash, then dry the fillets well. Coat in a little well-seasoned flour and sauté them in half the butter. Remove when cooked to a hot dish. Add the remaining butter to the pan. Let it darken without burning then add the vinegar, capers and parsley, holding the pan at arm's length, for it will splutter. Pour the beurre noire over the sole, pile the shrimps (which you have dried, then heated in a little more butter) on top and surround the dish with thin rounds of lemon.

FILETS DE SOLE EN GOUJON, SAUCE RITZ

8 Dover sole fillets
1¼ tbs flour
2 eggs
salt and pepper
1¼ tbs oil
2 oz (50 g) fresh white breadcrumbs
oil, for deep-frying
1 bunch parsley
lemon wedges

Marinade
12 fl oz (350 ml) dry white wine
2 carrots, chopped
1 onion, sliced
juice and zest of 1 lemon
bunch of thyme
1 bay leaf
8-10 peppercorns

Cut 8 good firm fillets of Dover sole into roughly 2 x ¾ inch (5 x 2 cm) pieces. Steep them in the marinade for at least 2 hours. Drain, wipe dry and shake in a paper bag with a little flour in it. Then dip in the beaten eggs which have had salt, pepper and a little oil mixed into them and roll in the fresh white breadcrumbs.

Keep goujons separate from each other on a pastry board in a warm place as they should dry out a little before being plunged into very hot oil and deep-fried. As soon as they turn deep gold, drain on kitchen paper, then quickly deep-fry a bunch of dry parsley and drain. Pile this in the centre of a serving dish. Arrange fish around it and hand tartar sauce or sauce Ritz separately.

Sauce Ritz

½ pint (300 ml) whipped cream
¾ tsp Worcester sauce
¾ tsp mushroom ketchup

Combine and serve immediately.

Mrs. Ian Fleming and Mrs. Crickmere

THROOPE MANOR
BISHOPSTONE
SALISBURY, WILTS.
SP5 4BA
TEL. COOMBE BISSETT 318
"   0722 - 77 318

Monsieur Bertellot's Filet de Sole Normande

3 Dover sole
salt and pepper
bouquet of fresh thyme
2 bay leaves
3 leeks, chopped
1 head of celery, chopped
2 tbs chopped shallots
¼ pint (150 ml) dry white wine
8 fl oz (225 ml) double cream
juice of 2 lemons
3 tbs butter
2 egg yolks
4 oz (100 g) mussels
2 oz (50 g) mushrooms, sliced
4 oz (100 g) peeled shrimps
croûtons

Fillet the sole, wash the fillets and dry them. Put them
in a saucepan together with the bones of the fish, tail and
head, salt and pepper, thyme, bay leaves, leeks and celery.
Add enough cold water to cover and cook gently for 30 minutes,
then carefully remove poached fillets and place in serving dish.
Keep warm.

To make the sauce, cook together shallots, a little of the
liquor the fillets were cooked in and the white wine.
Simmer slowly until shallots are cooked, then reduce the
sauce to half its quantity. When reduced, add the cream,
the lemon juice and 1 tbs butter, a little at a time. Remove
from the stove and beat in the egg yolks. Pour the sauce
over the fillets and serve with mussels, mushrooms and
shrimps, previously sautéed in the remaining butter, and
croûtons, also fried in butter, arranged in heaps around the
dish.

Viscountess Head

BAKED TURBOT WITH ANCHOVY SAUCE

2 lb (1 kg) turbot, or other large
  white fish, in one piece
1¼ tbs anchovy sauce
2 tbs olive oil
1 tbs wine vinegar or the juice
  of 2 lemons
salt and pepper

1¼ tsp paprika
4 tbs butter
4 tbs lard
a little flour
1 large lemon
3 tbs chopped parsley

Put the turbot into a dish.   Mix anchovy sauce with oil, vinegar
salt, pepper and paprika.   Marinate for 20 minutes or more.
Heat a flameproof casserole and when very hot put in butter and
lard.   When the fat is brown, sprinkle one side of the fish
liberally with flour and put it floured side down in the pan.
Move it to prevent sticking while sprinkling upperside with
flour.   Allow fish 5 minutes on each side.   Add a little hot
water from the kettle to the marinade and then pour the whole
over the fish in the casserole.   Place in the oven for about
15 minutes at 350°F (180°C) gas mark 4, basting at least twice.
Meanwhile, slice the lemon very finely.   Remove fish from the
oven, cover it closely with the lemon slices edge to edge,
sprinkle freely with chopped parsley and replace in the oven
for a further 15 minutes, basting again twice.

H.E. Lady Burrows

TURBOT IN CREAM

3 lb (1.5 kg) turbot, in one piece
butter
salt

lemon juice
1 pint (600 ml) double cream
4 tbs grated Parmesan cheese

Remove skin from fish and place it in a buttered baking dish.
Season with salt and a good squeeze of lemon juice.   Cover with
the cream, sprinkle with Parmesan cheese and dot with butter.
Bake in a moderate oven, 350°F (180°C) gas mark 4, for about
30 minutes, or until the flesh comes clean away from the bone.

Lady Caroline Somerset

POISSON À L'ESPAGNOLE

Take a nice piece of turbot or halibut or 6 very fresh cod steaks and either
grill or bake them in the oven with enough butter and lemon juice to prevent
burning (if baking, cover them well with greaseproof paper). When the fish
is cooked, pour the following sauce over it and serve at once.

Fish Sauce

4 tbs butter or olive oil
2 tbs finely chopped lean bacon
1 carrot, finely chopped
2 medium sized onions, finely chopped
1 garlic clove, crushed (optional)
4 tbs flour

$\frac{3}{4}$ pint (450 ml) very good stock (one made
   from veal and beef bones is best)
bouquet garni
$1\frac{1}{4}$ tbs tomato purée
$2\frac{1}{2}$ tbs chopped mushrooms
$\frac{1}{4}$ pint (150 ml) sherry

Heat the butter or oil and fry the bacon. Add the carrot, onions and, if you
like, a little garlic. Stir over a low heat for 5 minutes or until the carrots
and onions are soft, then add the flour and cook until brown. Add the last
5 ingredients to the sauce and let it simmer gently for 1 hour, skimming off the
fat as much as possible. Either strain the sauce or leave it as it is, but
don't forget to remove the bouquet garni.

H.E. Lady Mallet

SOFT HERRING ROES NORMANDE

1 tbs flour, seasoned with salt and pepper
$\frac{1}{2}$ lb (225 g) soft herring roes, fresh if possible (you can also use a few hard
  roes if they are fresh)
4 tbs dry cider
1 oz (25 g) butter
1 large apple, peeled and sliced

Put the seasoned flour in a paper bag and shake the herring roes in this until
well dusted with flour. Put the cider in a pan and boil it up quickly until
reduced to 1 tbs. Then melt the butter in the pan and fry the roes in it gently.
When cooked lay them on a serving dish and cook apple slices until golden in the
same pan. Garnish the roes with the apple, and pour the sauce from the pan over
them.

POISSON À L'ORIENTALE - for 4 people

7 oz (200 g) rice
1 tbs butter
2 tbs oil
1½ oz (40 g) very finely chopped parsley
4 fl oz (100 ml) vermouth or white wine
¾ pint (450 ml) chicken stock
salt and pepper
1½ lb (750 g) firm white fish (middle cut)
lemon juice
1 large onion,
4 bay leaves
2 tomatoes, halved

First, cook the rice. Put butter and half the oil in a casserole and when hot add the rice, stirring all the time until all the rice is well-heated and becomes transparent. Add the parsley, and a little vermouth or white wine and simmer a little longer. Bring the chicken stock to the boil in a saucepan and pour over the rice, then add salt and pepper. Cover and boil gently for 15 minutes. Then place the casserole in the oven, 300°F (150°C) gas mark 2, until the rice is quite dry.

In the meantime, cut the fish into 1½ inch (4 cm) chunks and marinate in the remaining oil, lemon juice, salt and pepper for about 20 minutes. Oil 4 skewers and put 5 fish chunks on each skewer with a piece of onion between each and a bay leaf in the middle and half a tomato at either end. Place the skewers under a hot grill, turning and basting with the marinade. When the fish is cooked, make a circle of the rice on a hot dish, remove the fish from the skewers and pile it in the middle of the rice circle. Arrange the grilled onions and tomatoes on top.

H.E. Lady Trevelyan

PAIN DE BROCHET VAL DE LOIRE (for 8 people)

Take a nice young pike of about 2 lb (1 kg) and fillet it.   You
should have just under 1 lb (500 g) of fish.   Pound the fillets
in a mortar with a little salt and few peppercorns until quite
smooth, then mix them into a scant $\frac{1}{2}$ pint (300 ml) of very thick
cold béchamel sauce.   (If you have no mortar then cut the fish
into small pieces and put them through the finest part of a
mincer or mouli.)

To this mixture add 3 fl oz (75 ml) double cream, 2 eggs, well
beaten, plus 2 extra yolks, $1\frac{1}{4}$ tbs of finely chopped parsley, a
little chopped chives, salt and pepper.

Spoon the fish purée into a well-buttered mould.*   Set in a
bain marie of hot water and place in the centre of a moderate oven,
$350^{o}F$ ($180^{o}C$) gas mark 4, for 30-40 minutes.

Meanwhile with the bones and fish debris and $\frac{1}{2}$ pint (300 ml) dry
white wine, prepare about $\frac{3}{4}$ pint (450 ml) of a good 'fumet de
poisson' au vin blanc.

Make a white roux of 4 rounded tbs flour and 4 tbs of butter.
Cook together for a few minutes without colouring and then moisten
with the fish fumet.   Add this by degrees until you have about
$\frac{1}{2}$ pint (300 ml) of sauce.   Make a liaison by beating 3 egg yolks
into 8 fl oz (225 ml) of warm cream and add this off the heat to
the sauce.   Pass it through a fine sieve into a clean saucepan.
Warm up very gently but do not let it get too hot or it will curdle.
Unmould your pain de brochet on to a long serving dish that has
a little depth and cover it with the sauce.

Sprinkle the top with very finely chopped parsley and chives.

* A long-shaped tin mould is best - pan loaf, gingerbread or
  fish-shaped, if deep enough.

S.E. Monsieur Gérard André   Recette de Pierre Naegal
                                           Chef de Cuisine à l'Ambassade

ANCHOVY SOUFFLÉ WITH SMOKED COD'S ROE SAUCE

For the soufflé

2 oz (50 g) canned anchovy fillets
1 tbs butter
1 rounded tbs flour
$\frac{1}{4}$ pint (150 ml) milk
3 egg yolks
pepper
lemon juice
4 egg whites

First of all soak the anchovy fillets in cold water for about 15 minutes to remove some of the salt.   Melt the butter in a saucepan, add flour, then milk, and cook for a few minutes.   Cool a little, then add beaten egg yolks, pepper and a good squeeze of lemon juice.

Pound the anchovy fillets to a paste and add to the mixture.   Beat the egg whites until very stiff and fold with a metal spoon into the anchovy mixture.   Put into a soufflé dish and cook in a moderately hot oven, 375°F (190°C) gas mark 5, for about 25 minutes until well risen and golden brown on top.

For the sauce

2 tbs butter
2 rounded tbs flour
$\frac{1}{2}$ pint (300 ml) milk
5 tbs double cream
pepper
lemon juice
chopped chives
2 tbs canned smoked cod's roe

Make a creamy white sauce with the above ingredients mashing down the cod's roe well.   Check seasoning carefully.

Note No salt is added.   You may need a little in the sauce but do not add it indiscriminately.

Lady Amabel Lindsay

FISH PAELLA

about 2 lb (1 kg) of as many different kinds of fish and shellfish as you want

2-3 oz (50-75 g) chopped onion

6-7 tbs olive oil (Spanish if possible)

1 lb (500 g) tomatoes, skinned and chopped

7 oz (200 g) Spanish or Patna rice

4 oz (100 g) mushrooms

4 oz (100 g) shelled peas

2 oz (50 g) pimentos

salt

$\frac{3}{4}$ pint (450 ml) of the fish stock

a good pinch of saffron powder

Boil the fish, drain and keep the stock. Fry the onion in some of the oil until lightly browned, then add the tomatoes and cook for about 5 minutes. Liquidize - it should have the consistency of tomato sauce. Pour the rest of the oil into a paella pan or a thick frying pan or a round earthenware dish. Fry the rice in it gently until transparent. Then add the tomato and onion sauce, the cooked fish, the mushrooms and peas (previously cooked) and the pimentos cut in strips, and any Dublin Bay prawns or scampi - all nicely arranged on the rice. Add salt lightly. Pour over all this the fish stock, which should be boiling, and in which the saffron has dissolved.

Cook fairly fast on top of the stove until the liquid has almost disappeared.* Then put in a moderately hot oven, 375°F (190°C) gas mark 5, for 10 minutes and leave out of the oven for 10 minutes to 'rest', before serving.

* Can be cooked as far as this and then re-heated in a warm oven for a good 20 minutes when wanted later.

H.E. Lady Balfour

RUŽICA'S BOILED FISH WITH PESTO

Use any sizeable firm white fish (about 4-5 lb (2 kg)), such as grey
mullet, John Dory, monkfish or hake.   Clean and scale the fish.
Put it, or them, into a pan of cold water with $\frac{1}{4}$ pint (150 ml) white
wine, 2 tbs olive oil, some parsley, peppercorns and a bay leaf.
Let the water cover the fish by 2-3 fingers.   Bring it to the boil
over a moderate heat and boil for only a few minutes, testing by
sliding the point of a knife into the flesh at the back of the fish's
head to see whether it comes away from the bone easily.   Drain the
fish and let it cool a little in its own steam, then dish up,
surrounded by lemon quarters or slices.   Pour $\frac{1}{4}$ pint (150 ml) good,
strong olive oil and some of the soup it has cooked in over the fish.
Scatter 2 tbs of finely chopped parsley over the whole dish.   Serve
with pesto sauce, in a separate sauceboat or bowl.   The recipe for
pesto is to be found on page 26.

BRODETTO

This is a fish stew made from 4-5 lb. (2 kg) of any, and if possible
several, of the following: cod, eel, haddock, monkfish, hake, striped
bass, whiting, mullet.

Clean the fish and cut it into chunks and include a head or two of
fish as this gives a lot of flavour to the brodet.   Take a large
saucepan and put into it 2-3 tbs olive oil, 2 medium sized chopped
onions, a little crushed garlic, a handful of parsley or chervil.
When the onions are transparent, add 2-3 tbs of fresh tomato pulp and
1 tbs of tomato purée, a little sugar, a little salt, pepper, 1 tbs
wine vinegar and 3 tbs dry white wine.   Boil together for 10 minutes,
then put in the pieces of fish and cover the pan and cook for 20 minutes.
Cut enough pieces of white bread (if you like rubbed with garlic) for
each serving and deep fry them until they are crisp.   Put 1 piece of
fried bread on the bottom of each plate and pour the brodet over.
Serve polenta or boiled rice apart.

Ružića Napotnik

Lapad
Dubrovnik
Dalmatia

MATO'S FAMOUS BLACK RISOTTO

1 lb (500 g) very small squid	salt and pepper
2 large onions, finely chopped	¼ pint (150 ml) white wine
4 tbs good olive oil	12 oz (350 g) rice
chopped parsley	about 1¾ pints (1 litre) fish stock
1 garlic clove, crushed	grated Parmesan cheese
1½ tsp tomato purée	

Clean the squid under running cold water. If they are large, remove bony 'spines' and only use the arms. If small, use the whole fish. In either case be careful to save the small sac of ink from the inside of the squid, which you remove intact and put to one side. Cut the rest into small pieces. Sweat the onions in the olive oil but do not let them brown. When they are soft and transparent add the ink out of the ink sacs that you have previously emptied into a cup and mixed with a little hot water. Stir, and add the chopped squids, the parsley, garlic, tomato purée, salt and pepper. Mix together thoroughly over low heat until it becomes smooth and sauce-like. Now add the wine. Let it boil up once and then stir in rice and half the boiling fish stock. (If you have no fish stock, water can be substituted but your risotto will be the poorer.) This will be absorbed almost at once by the rice and you must continue adding hot fish stock or water every few minutes or so until the rice is cooked, which will take between 12 and 18 minutes, depending on the size and quality of the rice. When you feel it is cooked 'al dente', remove it from the heat, pour it into a well-buttered mould and leave it to rest for 5-10 minutes by the side of your stove. To serve, reverse it on to a hot round dish, sprinkle half the Parmesan cheese over the top of it and serve with the rest of the cheese handed separately.

H.E. Dr. Mato Jaksić

ICED TUNA SALAD

6 oz (175 g) canned tuna fish
14 fl oz (400 ml) canned consommé
2 tsp lemon juice
salt and pepper
few drops Tabasco sauce

¼ pint (150 ml) double cream
1 fennel root
2 tbs lemon vinaigrette
2 hard-boiled eggs
1 heaped tbs capers

Drain the tuna fish.   Flake the flesh with a fork.   Mix the tuna with the consommé and chill in the ice-making compartment of the fridge until set.   Break up the jelly and tuna fish with a fork.   Mix in the lemon juice.   Season with salt, pepper and a drop of Tabasco sauce.   Whip the cream and fold it lightly into the tuna mixture.   Heap on to a serving dish or set in a lightly oiled mould in the fridge.

Meanwhile, slice the fennel and marinate it in the lemon vinaigrette, made with 2 tbs oil and 1 tbs lemon juice.   Drain the fennel, arrange it around the base of the tuna cream. Chop the hard-boiled eggs very coarsely and spoon them and the capers over the lot, but mostly over the fennel.   You can garnish the tuna with a feather of fennel, or some chopped black olives.

Note   If you can obtain it, a can of clam juice makes a better quick aspic for this dish than consommé.   Soak enough gelatine to set in a little of the clam juice; heat up the rest of the juice with a spoonful of lemon juice and a dash of Worcester sauce.   Stir in the gelatine and let it just boil up once.   Cool and when syrupy, flake in the tuna and proceed with the recipe.

Mrs. Derek Marlowe

SALMON MOUSSE FOR 6

Boil 1½ lb (750 g) of fresh salmon. Remove all skin and bones and mince it. Then mix it with 2 tbs of mayonnaise. Season the mixture sharply with some white and black pepper, salt and lemon juice. Add a dash of Worcester sauce, according to taste.

Beat separately the whites of 2 eggs and add to the salmon together with ¾ pint (450 ml) of cream. Mix everything well and add 1 tbs gelatine dissolved in 4 fl oz (100 ml) water. Put the mixture into a mould which has previously been greased with oil. Let the mousse set and chill in the refrigerator for at least 2 hours, preferably longer.

For serving, the mould has to be emptied on to a platter, which can be garnished with boiled scampi or prawns, olives and chopped aspic.

This dish can be prepared the day before but it should be kept in the refrigerator in the mould until required.

A sauce verte (mayonnaise with puréed watercress and spinach juice beaten into it) can be served separately, and looks very pretty with this dish - in which case put a bunch or even a wreath of watercress round the bottom of the mousse.

Another sauce which is excellent with cold salmon is a horseradish cream made from 2 tbs of fresh grated horseradish, a little white wine vinegar, salt and pepper, a large pinch of mustard, a little pinch of sugar, and 8 fl oz (225 ml) of whipped cream.

HE. Mme. Vera Velebit

COD VALENCIENNE WITH SAFFRON RICE

3 tbs olive oil
1 tbs herb vinegar or lemon juice
salt and pepper
paprika
1 large onion, finely chopped
1 garlic clove

1½ lb (700 g) cod, in steaks
 or fillets
15 oz (425 g) canned tomatoes
a pinch of sugar
2-3 oz (50-75 g) grated cheese
boiled rice
saffron or turmeric

Beat the oil and vinegar well together as if for a salad dressing.
Season rather highly and stir in the chopped onion. Rub a fireproof dish well with a cut clove of garlic and turn this mixture
into it. Lay the piece of cod in it and leave to soak for 1-2
hours, turning over once or twice. When ready to cook, cover
thickly with the drained tomatoes, to which you add a pinch of
sugar. Cover and bake in a very moderate oven, 325°F (160°C)
gas mark 3, for 30 minutes or even a little longer, depending upon
the thickness of the fish. When cooked, sprinkle the dish lavishly
with grated cheese and brown under a hot grill. Serve with boiled
rice. Colour the rice bright yellow with saffron or a little
turmeric. In Valencia they use saffron.

HOW TO POACH SALMON

Immerse a well-cleaned and scaled whole salmon in cold water in a
fish kettle. The water should cover the fish by two or three
fingers. Close the kettle and bring the water gently to the boil;
boil briskly for 2 minutes only; then take the fish kettle off
the heat, lift out the strainer and the fish, balancing them both
sideways over the kettle, so that the fish cools in its steam.
Throw a clean cloth over both and, when the salmon has cooled a
little, you will find that (whatever its size) it will be perfectly
cooked, pink and juicy and firm. Eat it hot with a good
hollandaise sauce, or cold with 3 bowls of different mayonnaises:
yellow (plain) or lemon-flavoured; green (spinach juice and
watercress purée added); red (tomato purée added). In this case
only dress the salmon with lettuce and cucumber and/or lemon
slices and forget about all that messy decoration.

Veronica Maclean

Poultry

SIR WILLIAM HAMILTON
1730–1803
Diplomatist and Archaeologist British Envoy Extraordinary
at the Court of Naples, 1764–1800

COQ AU RIESLING (Chicken in white wine) for 4 people

1 capon or large chicken, about 3½ lb (1.5 kg) parsley
1 lb (500 g) onions, sliced   1 carrot, sliced
1 bay leaf   butter
2 cloves   beurre manié
salt and pepper   ¾ pint (450 ml) cream
1¼ pints (750 ml) or 1 bottle of Riesling   1 lb (500 g) mushrooms, sliced

1. Cut the uncooked chicken into portions; take the bone out of the wings
but not the thighs.   Marinate in a deep flat dish on a bed of half the
sliced onions.   Cover with most of the remaining onions, the bay leaf and
cloves and season.   Pour over a whole bottle of white wine.   Leave to
marinate for several hours (1 hour at least).
2. While the bird is marinating, make a stock from the carcass of the chicken,
remaining onion, a sprig of parsley, and the carrot.   Reduce by boiling until
very concentrated.
3. Strain marinade and keep both wine and onions.   Remove bay leaf and cloves.
4. Sauté chicken pieces in butter in a frying pan.
5. Sauté the onions in a cast iron casserole or braising pan until they are
transparent but not coloured.
6. Put the chicken pieces and juices on top of the onions.   Pour over the
wine from the marinade and then the reduced stock from the carcass.
7. Poach the chicken in this liquid for 20 minutes but only let it simmer,
not boil.
8. Remove chicken and keep warm.
9. Drain the onions from the stock and put them through a mouli (or sieve).
10. Continue simmering stock until well reduced, then blend in the beurre
manié to thicken.
11. Add the cream, and be generous with it.
12. Serve the chicken in a deep earthenware cocotte dish, swimming in the sauce.
13. Serve a plain rice pilau apart -
14. - and a dish of the puréed onions into which you mix the sliced mushrooms,
15. - which you have stewed in a little butter.

S.E. Monsieur Gérard André

49 DRAYTON GARDENS

LONDON SW10 9RX

01-373 2867

Grilled Poussins with Lemon and Herbs (for 4)

2 spring poussins (cut into 2 halves)

The Marinade

2 oz (50 g) butter

12 fl oz (350 ml) sherry

2 oz (50 g) bacon fat

4 tbs olive oil

4 tbs lemon juice

2 tbs grated lemon rind

1 tsp salt

6 peppercorns

sprigs of thyme and rosemary

Put the marinade ingredients into a pan and boil
together for 5 minutes.   Cool and when tepid pour
over the poussins which you have rubbed with salt
and arranged in a dish cut side up.   Leave to
marinate for several hours or overnight, turning
once.

Cook them for 20 minutes in a moderate oven, 350°F
(180°C) gas mark 4, in a pan without a covering,
browning birds slightly and basting them with the
marinade sauce.   Then remove them from the oven
and continue cooking under a grill, basting
frequently with the sauce for another 15 minutes,
or until they are cooked.

Laura Hesketh and Jamie Maclean

-115-

POULE AU POT

1 large roasting chicken or poularde, not less than 6 months old and
weighing about 4 lb (1.75 kg) <u>or</u> one fat middle-aged boiling fowl

6 leeks, chopped	2½ pints (1.5 litres) good chicken stock
6 carrots, chopped	2-3 cloves
2-3 small white turnips, chopped	6 peppercorns
1 head of celery, chopped	1 small white cabbage
salt	

For the "farce" or stuffing

4 oz (100 g) lean bacon	2 oz (50 g) crustless bread, soaked in milk
4 oz (100 g) pork, chopped	
1 garlic clove	1 sprig of tarragon
small bunch of parsley	2 eggs
salt and pepper	

First make the farce.   Put all the farce ingredients except the eggs
twice through the finest part of your mincer.   Add the eggs, mix
together and correct seasoning.

Use three-quarters of the farce to stuff the chicken.   Tie it up well
and place it in a large and deep enough pot to accommodate the stock,
leeks, carrots, turnips and celery.   An oval-shaped iron dish with a
well fitting lid is ideal.

Wrap the cut up vegetables separately in clean butter muslin before
you put them in (simply to be able to recover them in whole pieces
at the end).   Salt the stock, throw in the cloves and peppercorns
and close up tightly (if lid does not fit well use foil).   It should
simmer gently in the oven (but never boil) and be ready in 1½ hours.
Meanwhile blanch 6 little packets of cabbage leaves in boiling water
for 2-3 minutes.

Take them out, drain and stuff each with a spoonful of the leftover stuffing. Fold the leaves round it and tie up with fine string. Put these packages to cook in a separate casserole, having poured a ladleful or two of the chicken stock over them. They should not cook more than 30 minutes.

Serve all together in a large deep entrée dish with the vegetables in small heaps all round (muslin and string, of course, removed).

Pommes vapeur or small steamed new potatoes should accompany this dish but if the season is not right then a purée of potatoes will do very well.

Sauce Velouté, made with part of the chicken stock, should be handed apart. Make this in advance, from 2 tbs flour and 2 tbs butter, cooked to a smooth roux. Pour on $\frac{1}{4}$ pint (150 ml) hot chicken stock and bring to the boil. Continue cooking slowly, adding more hot stock for another 20-30 minutes.

S.E. La Baronne de Courcel

POULARDE À LA MAJORQUINE   A Spanish Dish

1 large chicken or capon
3 Spanish onions, finely sliced
3 fl oz (75 ml) orange juice
3 fl oz (75 ml) white wine
3 fl oz (75 ml) olive oil
3 oz (75 g) black olives

Place the chicken or capon in a flat fireproof dish
on a bed of finely sliced Spanish onions.   Pour the
orange juice, white wine and olive oil over the bird
and roast until golden, basting with the juices from
time to time.   Carve the bird and serve it in the
roasting dish, with all its juices; garnish it with
black olives, and accompany it with a dish of saffron
rice, and a salad of lettuce or endive with skinned
fresh orange slices and a vinaigrette dressing.

H.E. Marquesa de Santa Cruz

CHICKEN MARIE LOUISE

6 shallots, or 2 medium onions,
   chopped
1 garlic clove, chopped
1 oz (25 g) butter
3-4 sprigs of thyme, crushed or
   1 tsp dried thyme
1 bay leaf
1 pint (600 ml) chicken stock

2 spring chickens, or 1 roasting
   chicken
2 fl oz (50 ml) brandy
7 fl oz (200 ml) double cream
1 tsp French mustard
2 oz (50 g) grated cheese

Sauté the shallots and garlic in half the butter until golden
and transparent.   Add the thyme and bay leaf, and the stock.
Bring to the boil and simmer over low heat.

    Meanwhile cut each chicken into 6 pieces, and cook without
browning, in the remaining butter, turning often to cook evenly.
When golden all over, pour on the heated brandy and ignite,
holding the pan at arm's length, and shaking it to keep it
burning.

    Pack the chicken pieces tightly into a deep cast iron
casserole and pour on 1) the juices it has cooked in, and 2) the
simmering stock.

    Cover and cook slowly on gentle top heat or in a low oven,
300°F (150°C) gas mark 2, for 35-40 minutes.   Baste or turn the
chicken pieces, if the stock does not cover them, several times
to keep them moist.   When the chicken is just cooked, transfer
it to a shallow oval entrée dish and keep hot.

    Heat the cream in a clean saucepan and add the strained
stock to it, a little at a time until you have a creamy sauce.
It will be much reduced, but you may not need it all.   Stir in
the mustard and half the cheese.

    Stir until the sauce is smooth and then let it simmer gently
until it thickens a little more.

    Add the strained onions if you wish, to the chicken, and
pour the sauce over it.   Sprinkle with the last of the cheese
and put back in a hot oven for 10 minutes, or so to brown.

    Don't cook too long - lots of chicken casseroles are ruined
by overcooking, which dries out the chicken juices.   Serve with
a green vegetable - petits pois or lima beans, or artichoke
bottoms, in another dish.

WATERZOOI À LA GANTOISE

6 half chickens or 3 middle-sized young whole chickens
1 knuckle of veal, weighing about 2 lb (1 kg)
6 oz (175 g) chopped leeks (the white part only)
10 oz (300 g) chopped celery sticks
3 onions (stick a clove in one of them)
2 oz (50 g) well washed parsley roots
1 bay leaf
6 peppercorns
a little thyme
5 rusks (round Dutch ones)*
salt and pepper
butter
finely chopped parsley

The day before, place the chicken giblets in a large soup pan. Add
the chicken feet (well washed) and the knuckle of veal. Cover with
cold water (2 soup ladles per person).
     Bring to boil and skim continually.
     After boiling, cook gently for 2 hours. Store in a cool place
until the next morning.
     Next morning, about 9am, remove the giblets and strain the stock,
return the stock to the soup pan, add the vegetables and herbs and
return the veal knuckle. Boil gently for 2 hours. Moisten the
rusks and add them to the stock, then put it all, except for the veal
knuckle, through the liquidizer.
     Return purée to pan. Place the chickens in the mixture, season
them well. Cover the pan and simmer gently for 1½ hours, by which
time the stock will be greatly reduced and thickened, and the birds
will be cooked.
     Cut up the chicken neatly, put the pieces in a soup tureen, pour
the stock over the chicken and add a few flakes of butter and finely
chopped parsley.
     Serve in hot soup plates with well buttered home-made brown bread
and hand a sauce. Chivry or Poulette, made with enough herbs to make
it look green, would be suitable.

* or 8 Huntley & Palmer's Rusks, if you can't buy the Dutch ones.

Baron Braun

Poulet Corneille

6 oz (175 g) cream cheese
1 large spring chicken, about
   3½ lb (1.5 kg)
salt and pepper
1 large cooking apple

¼ lb (100 g) canned chestnuts or
   peeled and skinned fresh chestnuts
2 fl oz (50 ml) calvados
½ pint (300 ml) double cream
Tabasco sauce

Rub some of the cream cheese over the breast of the trussed chicken and quite a lot over the thighs. Season well, wrap it loosely in foil and put in a baking dish with the rest of the cream cheese. Alternatively, put in dish and cover this tightly with foil and a lid. Roast the chicken in the usual way. Approximately 15 minutes before roasted, open the foil and insert one large cooking apple, peeled, cored and chopped, and the chestnuts, (the kind one buys, skinned and whole in cans of brine, will do at a pinch, but boil them 20 minutes first). When roasting is complete, take the chicken off the bone and keep it warm. To the apple, chestnut and juices now add the calvados, and double cream. Mash this mixture up with a fork or wooden spoon while heating it gently. Do not let it boil. Season with salt and a little Tabasco and pour over the cut up chicken meat.

Anthony Montague Browne

Pollo Pisto

1 free range spring chicken, about
   3½ lb (1.5 kg)
salt and pepper
2 oz (50 g) butter
1 garlic clove, crushed (optional)
1 tbs olive oil
juice and grated rind of 1 lemon
2 chicken livers, chopped

½ onion, grated
2 bacon rashers, chopped
¼ lb (100 g) mushrooms, chopped
flour
water or stock
¼ pint (150 ml) marsala
1 tbs brown sugar
pinch of nutmeg

Split the chicken in two, cutting through the breast bone. Beat the two halves between greaseproof paper until quite flat; brush them all over with threequarters of the butter, melted, and put them, cut half down, in a frying or sauté pan, for which you have a lid which fits inside the pan and rests on the chicken. Weight this down, and cook very gently over low heat for 30-40 minutes. Turn the chicken over, cover again and cook for another 10 minutes. Remove the lid, put in the garlic, and brush the chicken with oil mixed with lemon juice and rind. Fry until chicken is browned all over. When ready, make the sauce. Melt the remaining butter in a pan and add chicken livers, onion, bacon and mushrooms. Cook for a few minutes, sprinkle with flour and add enough water or stock to make a smooth sauce. Boil up, then add marsala, sugar and nutmeg. Simmer for about 20 minutes.

Poulet Tzigane

This is a good recipe for a chicken brick, or an unglazed clay
pot like the gypsies used. It is a delicious and easy way of
cooking old birds, and comes from Portugal.

1 small boiling or roasting chicken
2 tbs butter
24 small whole peeled onions, the kind you use for pickling
2 small garlic cloves, crushed
1 small bay leaf
strip of thinly pared lemon rind
2 oz (50 g) rice
salt and pepper
½ pint (300 ml) good white wine

Partially sever the wing and leg joints of the chicken. Smear
it all over with butter and place in the lower half of the pot.
Pack the onions round it. Add the garlic with the bay leaf,
lemon rind and rice. Season lightly and pour in the wine.
Put on the lid, sealing it hermetically with a little flour and
water paste.
Cook in a slow oven, 300°F (150°C) gas mark 2, until tender -
about 2 hours later, or more if the bird is an old one.

Romany Chicken

Another version of the above dish.

1 chicken
5 oz (150 g) green smoked bacon, cubed
butter
2 Spanish onions, chopped
4 tomatoes, chopped
¼ pint (150 ml) sherry
1 small green pepper, de-seeded, skinned and chopped

Fry the chicken in a stewpan with bacon and a little butter,
then bake it slowly at 300°F (150°C) gas mark 2, with the
onions, tomatoes and sherry in a chicken brick or unglazed
earthenware pot with a lid. A little green pepper is an
improvement, but blister it first on a hot stove before you
chop it. Serve the chicken in the pot it was cooked in.

SUPRÊMES DE VOLAILLES 'EVANGELINE'

6 chicken breasts, or breasts and wings of chicken
1 tbs brandy
1 tsp dried marjoram
1 tsp dried tarragon
salt and pepper
6 tbs butter
1 large bundle fresh or frozen asparagus, cooked
2 tbs sherry
½ pint (300 ml) single cream
1 large egg, beaten
grated nutmeg
2 tbs grated Swiss cheese

Wipe the chicken breasts with a damp cloth and rub all over
with brandy.   Let them stand for 30 minutes to mellow, then
rub with the dried marjoram and tarragon (3 tsp each if herbs
are fresh), and salt and pepper.   Melt the butter in a large
sauté pan, and when it foams put in and sauté the chicken
breasts;   cook them slowly, over a low heat, turning them
occasionally until they are browned and tender.   Remove to a
heated platter and keep hot.   Heat cooked asparagus in a little
butter.

To the butter remaining in the sauté pan add the sherry, blend
well and cook gently, stirring occasionally until evaporated.
Gradually add the cream beaten with a large egg.   Season with
salt, pepper and a little nutmeg.   Cook over very low heat,
stirring constantly, for about 3 minutes until the sauce thickens.
Arrange the breasts of chicken in the serving dish, with bunches
of asparagus in between or round the edge of the dish, and cover
the chicken with sauce.   Sprinkle with grated Swiss cheese and
glaze under a grill.   Serve bubbling hot.

Mrs. Derek Marlowe

SUPRÊMES DE VOLAILLES WITH HAZELNUTS AND APPLES

6 breasts, or breasts and wings of
   2 chickens
seasoned flour
¼ lb (100 g) butter
2½ tbs madeira

1 pint (600 ml) cream
2 tbs meat glaze
3 oz (75 g) ground hazelnuts
4-5 cooking apples, halved and flesh
   scooped out with a melon baller

Coat the suprêmes in seasoned flour and sauté slowly in butter. When
tender, remove from the pan, deglaze it by whirling the madeira round
it and scraping together all the juices. Add the cream and the meat
glaze and simmer together. Blend the nuts into the sauce and keep it
hot, but do not allow it to boil. Fry the little apple balls in butter,
(if you do not have a melon baller that makes balls, cut your apples
into rings instead). Dish up the suprêmes, mask them with the hazelnut
sauce and garnish with the apples.

M. Pelaprat advises a pilaf of rice to go with this dish, but I think a
fresh green vegetable or just a simple salad would be nicer.

POULET AU GRATIN

¼ pint (150 ml) béchamel sauce
1 oz (25 g) meat glaze (or the
   jelly from under the roast)
a little mustard
salt and pepper

remains of 2 roast chickens
2 egg whites
2 tbs brown breadcrumbs
2 tbs grated Parmesan cheese
a little butter

Put the béchamel sauce into a saucepan with the meat glaze and stir it
until it boils. Add mustard and season fairly highly, then stir in the
finely minced remains of the chickens. Let the mixture heat through,
then pour it into a fireproof china entrée dish. Beat up the egg whites
and cover the mixture with them, strewing the brown breadcrumbs and cheese
over all, and adding a few bits of butter here and there. Place it in
the oven, 400°F (200°C) gas mark 6, for 10 minutes, then brown with a
salamander (or under the grill).

Louisa Rochfort

Chicken Cacciatore

1 young chicken, about 3½ lb (1.5 kg)
olive oil
2 shallots, thinly sliced
1 garlic clove, thinly sliced
¾ lb (350 g) mushrooms, wiped and sliced
1½ lb (750 g) tomatoes, skinned,
    seeded and chopped
1 tsp sugar
about ¼ pint (150 ml) dry white wine
    or dry vermouth

2 tbs tomato purée
salt and pepper
bay leaf
oregano
1 tbs butter
1 tbs chopped parsley
grated rind and juice of ½ lemon

Joint the chicken and brown it in hot oil, enough to cover the bottom of a deep sauté pan. This will take at least 10 minutes, as the chicken pieces should be well coloured. When brown on every side, remove from the pan and sauté the shallots, garlic and mushrooms in the oil, adding more if necessary. Put the chicken back in the pan and add the remaining ingredients, except butter, parsley and lemon. Cook, covered, over gentle simmering heat, until tender, about 35 minutes.
Arrange the chicken in a shallow entrée dish. Add the butter and parsley to the juices in the pan. Scrape all together, squeeze a little lemon juice and rind into the sauce and pour it over the chicken. Serve with a hot green vegetable, like courgettes, or sautéed fonds d'artichauts.

The Charleston Junior League

Bulgarian Chicken Casserole

3½ lb (1.5 kg) chicken or 6 suprêmes
2 tbs butter
2 tbs peanut oil
dash of vermouth or white wine
1 tsp cornflour
½ pint (300 ml) sour cream

salt and pepper
bunch of fresh parsley, finely
    chopped
1 tbs chopped fresh dill
1 tbs grated onion
rind and juice of 1 lemon
a little stock

Sauté the chicken gently in a sauté pan in half butter and half the oil, browning it slightly all over, then transfer it to a large casserole with a close fitting lid. Deglaze the pan with a little vermouth or white wine, then blend the cornflour into the remaining juices and add the sour cream, stirring well with a wooden spoon. Season with salt and pepper. Remove from heat when the sauce has boiled for a few minutes and add plenty of parsley, a little dill and onion and the grated rind of a lemon. Mix well and pour on to the chicken in the casserole. Simmer slowly, adding chicken stock if necessary, for about 35 minutes, or less if only chicken suprêmes are used. Finally, add the juice of the lemon and check to correct seasoning. Serve with fresh buttery noodles and a green salad.

Mrs. M. Arthur

QUICK CHICKEN CASSEROLE

Cover the bottom of a generously buttered earthenware
casserole with 2 oz (50 g) of hot, buttered breadcrumbs;
add the meat of half a roasted chicken, pulled apart
into long fragments rather than chopped, and mixed with
6 oz (175 g) of sliced, sautéed mushrooms.   Season to
taste with salt and pepper and a pinch each of nutmeg,
thyme and marjoram.   Pour over ½ pint (300 ml) of
scalded double cream mixed with ½ pint (300 ml) hot
chicken stock.   Top with another 2 oz (50 g) of hot
buttered breadcrumbs and bake for 20 minutes in a moderate
oven, 350°F (180°C) gas mark 4, until brown.   This can
be prepared ahead and then put in the oven 20 minutes
before you need it.   It should be quite moist, so do not
overcook.   A little extra cream added just before serving
improves it.

Note Hot buttered breadcrumbs are white breadcrumbs toasted
on a tray in a moderately hot oven until mid-brown.   Dot
them with butter and take care they do not burn.

H.E. Mrs Giles Bullard

7 Cleveland Gardens
London W 2

Chicken with Parsley – an old English recipe

1 chicken   Seasoning

Parsley   lemon

Stuff a chicken with heads of parsley. Fill very full and season well. Roast the chicken, basting it well, and serve with parsley sauce. This can be poured over the cut up bird. Garnish with tufts of fresh parsley and thin lemon rounds.

Parsley Sauce.

2 large handfuls of parsley $\frac{3}{4}$ pint cream

Put the parsley in a saucepan, season it, cover it with cream and cook it very slowly by the side of the stove for 2 hours. Strain and serve (There must not be any parsley left in the sauce).

Mrs Stephen Clissold

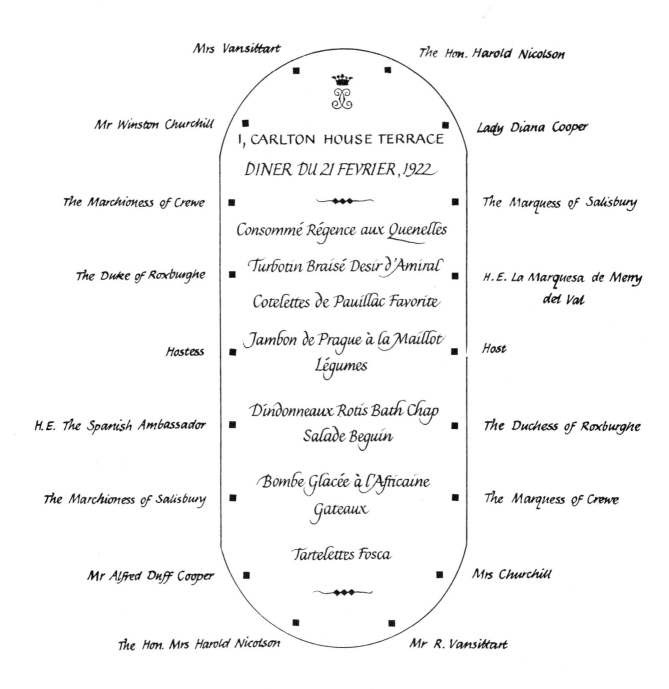

Mrs Vansittart   The Hon. Harold Nicolson

Mr Winston Churchill   Lady Diana Cooper

The Marchioness of Crewe   The Marquess of Salisbury

The Duke of Roxburghe   H.E. La Marquesa de Merry del Val

Hostess   Host

H.E. The Spanish Ambassador   The Duchess of Roxburghe

The Marchioness of Salisbury   The Marquess of Crewe

Mr Alfred Duff Cooper   Mrs Churchill

The Hon. Mrs Harold Nicolson   Mr R. Vansittart

1, CARLTON HOUSE TERRACE

DINER DU 21 FEVRIER, 1922

Consommé Régence aux Quenelles

Turbotin Braisé Desir d'Amiral

Cotelettes de Pauillac Favorite

Jambon de Prague à la Maillot
Légumes

Dindonneaux Rotis Bath Chap
Salade Beguin

Bombe Glacée à l'Africaine
Gateaux

Tartelettes Fosca

Dinner given at 1, Carlton House Terrace
by the Marquess and Marchioness Curzon of Kedleston
Feb 21, 1922

st la même chose

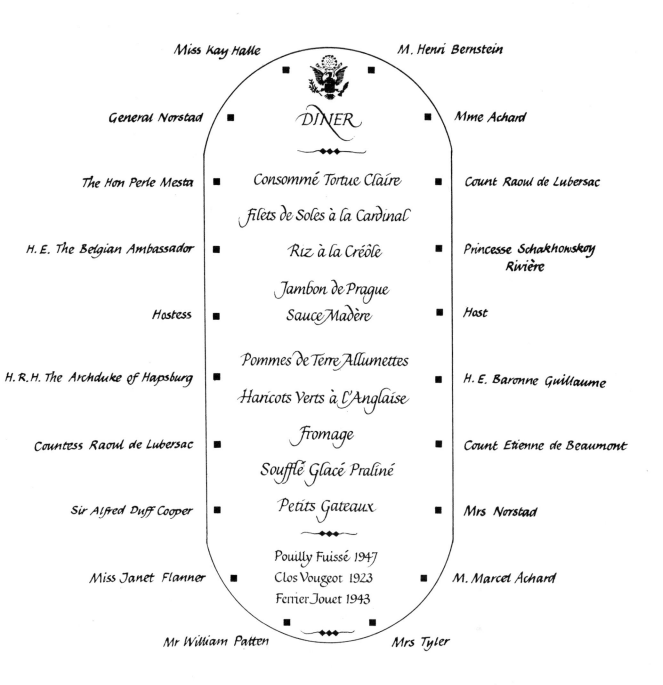

Miss Kay Halle — M. Henri Bernstein

General Norstad — Mme Achard

DINER

◆◆◆

The Hon Perle Mesta — Consommé Tortue Claire — Count Raoul de Lubersac

Filets de Soles à la Cardinal

H. E. The Belgian Ambassador — Riz à la Créôle — Princesse Schakhowskoy Rivière

Jambon de Prague
Hostess — Sauce Madère — Host

Pommes de Terre Allumettes
H.R.H. The Archduke of Hapsburg — — H. E. Baronne Guillaume

Haricots Verts à L'Anglaise

Fromage
Countess Raoul de Lubersac — — Count Etienne de Beaumont

Soufflé Glacé Praliné

Sir Alfred Duff Cooper — Petits Gateaux — Mrs Norstad

◆◆◆

Pouilly Fuissé 1947
Miss Janet Flanner — Clos Vougeot 1923 — M. Marcel Achard
Ferrier Jouet 1943

Mr William Patten — Mrs Tyler

◆◆◆

Dinner given at the American Embassy, Paris, by
H.E. the American Ambassador and Mrs. Bruce
Jan 12, 1950

Poulet au Citron (Chicken with Lemon Sauce)

1 chicken, about 3½ lb (1.5 kg)
1 oz (25 g) salt
3-4 onions, chopped
4 eggs
salt and pepper
2 lemons

Boil the chicken with the salt and onions.   The chicken can be carved after it is cooked, to serve as an entrée, or it can remain whole if the carving is to be done at the table.   In either case, it is served with a lemon sauce.

Strain the chicken stock and measure out ¾ pint (450 ml).   Break the eggs into a bowl, whites and yolks, beat them well with a fork or egg-whisk;   add salt and pepper.   Squeeze the juice from the lemons into another bowl, strain it, and mix it slowly with the eggs, stirring constantly.   Then gradually add the stock.   Pour it into a jug placed in a saucepan full of boiling water, to thicken as for a custard.   When the sauce is the thickness of double cream, it is ready.

Old French Recipe

Poulet Durand

2 fat roasting chickens, about 3½ lb (1.5 kg) each, cooked
butter
salt and pepper
12 fonds d'artichauts, fresh if possible
½ pint (300 ml) béchamel sauce
12 asparagus spears (optional)

This is a very simple and excellent recipe for an entrée of chicken, to serve 8 people.   Take the chickens, carve them, and cook briefly in butter, salt and pepper, turning them on both sides to colour.   They can be browned either in the oven or in a sauté pan on a moderate heat.   In the meanwhile, make a purée of artichokes, using the fonds, add a good béchamel to the purée and place it in the centre of the dish, surrounded by the pieces of chicken.   In the original Edwardian recipe, a small bunch of asparagus spears surmount the purée "like a flag".   And "sometimes the purée is ornamented with carrots and potatoes cut into tiny balls, and cooked in butter;   but the simple purée satisfies the epicure."   It also saves time.

From Durand's Restaurant, Paris c. 1905

ROUTE DE FLORISSANT 86 A

1206 GENÈVE

CHICKEN TETRAZZINI

6-8 large mushrooms
5 tbs butter
1 garlic clove, crushed (optional)
$\frac{1}{4}$ pint (150 ml) pale sherry
2 tbs flour
$\frac{1}{2}$ pint (300 ml) hot milk
$\frac{1}{4}$ pint (150 ml) strong chicken
   stock, strained

salt and pepper
grated nutmeg
$\frac{1}{2}$ lb (225 g) thin spaghetti
$\frac{1}{2}$ pint (300 ml) double cream
2 egg yolks
2 lb (1 kg) diced cold chicken
$1\frac{1}{4}$ tbs chopped ham
$\frac{1}{4}$ lb (100 g) grated Parmesan cheese

This dish is nicer served in individual little casseroles. Chop and sauté the mushrooms in 2 tbs of the butter and garlic, if you like it. Add the sherry and cook for a few moments. Keep hot. Make a white roux of 2 tbs butter and flour. Gradually add the milk. Stir constantly until sauce is smooth and then add the chicken stock slowly. When sauce has a good body (it will take about 15 minutes of cooking), season it well and add nutmeg. Meanwhile, cook the spaghetti in a large pan of boiling water for 10-12 minutes or until al dente. Drain and chop it into pieces. Turn into a buttery bowl and keep hot.

Remove the sauce from the heat, cool it a little, and add the cream into which you have beaten 2 egg yolks. Continue stirring, then add the chicken and ham to the sauce and season again. After 3 minutes add the mushrooms, and it is ready.

Butter a small casserole, soup bowl or large ramekin for each person and put a little cooked spaghetti at the bottom of each. Cover it with the chicken mixture. Sprinkle cheese over the top and put under the grill until brown and bubbling.

Serves 6-8

Mrs. Marjorie Arthur

POULET AUX MORILLES

Cut up a tender young chicken as if for frying.
Put it in a large shallow casserole, together with a lump
of butter; add three large, finely chopped onions, salt
and pepper.
Cover the casserole and simmer gently, or sweat, for 20 minutes.
Three-quarters of the way through the process, add 2 fl oz
(50 ml) brandy, 1 pint (600 ml) double cream, and 1¼ lb
(600 g) morels, which have been chopped into fairly large
pieces, and cooked for a few minutes in butter or peanut oil,
with a garlic clove and 1 tbs chopped parsley.
Finish cooking the chicken and morels, then take the chicken
and large pieces of morel out of the casserole, and keep warm.
Reduce the remaining sauce until it is thick and smooth, add
to it some flakes of butter, then pass it through a sieve
into a clean saucepan (press hard on the onions with the back
of a wooden spoon); reheat but do not let it boil.
Arrange the chicken on a serving dish with the sauce poured
over it, and the larger morels heaped round it.

S.E. Madame de Beaumarchais

N.B. You can buy dried morels in Soho and Pimlico most of
the year round, and these are easily re-constituted by
simmering in a little stock or milk for a few minutes and
then leaving to swell in the liquid.

Fresh morels can be obtained in the late spring only from one
or two gourmet delicatessens; they come from Istria, Central
Europe and Finland, but also grow in Scotland in old birch
woods.

SHIRINI POLO

1 chicken, jointed	a little stock
3 carrots, thinly sliced	saffron
1 onion, chopped	9 oz (250 g) rice
5 oz (150 g) almonds, blanched	¼ lb (100 g) mixed almonds
butter	and raisins
¼ lb (100 g) thinly sliced candied peel	small cinnamon stick, finely chopped

Sauté the carrots, onion and almonds in butter. Add the candied peel to
the mixture. Gently sauté the pieces of chicken in butter until they are
well coloured, about 15 minutes, then put them in a casserole with very
little stock and enough powdered saffron to colour this a rich yellow.
When the chicken is nearly tender add the carrots etc. and continue simmering
for 10 minutes. Boil the rice, adding saffron after 5 minutes to tint it
pale yellow. When just al dente, strain it, rinse it, then toss in butter
with the mixed almonds and raisins and very small pieces of cinnamon.
Serve the chicken on a round platter surrounded by the saffron rice.

ROAST CHICKEN - the way I like it

Cover the breast and thighs of a plump chicken with rashers
of streaky bacon; put a knob of butter rolled in 1 tsp of
chopped dried tarragon inside the bird and roast as usual,
basting it 3 times.   Pour off all but 1 tbs of the fat from
the pan in which the chicken was roasted.   Brown a finely
minced onion in the fat.   Add ½ pint (300 ml) chicken stock
and 2 tbs white wine.   Boil up and de-glaze the pan, scraping
juices together.   Cook rapidly until much reduced and syrupy.
Take off the heat and stir in 2 tbs softened butter.   Serve
in one sauceboat with bread sauce in another.   Good bread
sauce should be made by simmering an onion stuck with 1 clove
in 1½ pints (900 ml) creamy milk while the chicken is
roasting - only add the breadcrumbs to the reduced strained
milk at the last moment.

Chicken Noël

Use poussins weighing about 1 lb (500 g) and cook one for each person.

4 poussins	salt and pepper
$\frac{1}{4}$ lb (100 g) soft home-made or good bought liver pâté	melted butter
	rosemary sprigs
2 garlic cloves, crushed	a little dry white wine
grated rind and juice of $\frac{1}{2}$ a lemon	bay leaves
chopped fresh rosemary	a ladleful of brandy

Make with fresh poussins if possible, but if frozen, defrost slowly. Chop up chicken livers and mix in a bowl with the liver pâté, garlic, lemon rind and juice, rosemary, salt and pepper. Stuff the birds with this mixture and put in a roasting tin. Brush each bird with melted butter, sprinkle with salt and pepper, put a sprig of rosemary on top and pour a little white wine into the tin. Cover the whole tin with foil and cook in a very slow oven, 275°F (140°C) gas mark 1, for $1\frac{1}{4}$ hours.

Remove foil. Baste the chickens with the juices in the tin, move to the top of the oven and turn up the heat to 400°F (200°C) gas mark 6, for 15 minutes to brown the chickens. Baste occasionally to stop them getting dry and when they are done arrange on a serving dish on a <u>bed</u> of bay leaves. Warm the brandy in the ladle and set it alight. Pour it over the chickens and bay leaves and carry flaming to the table. The bay leaves will smoulder slightly, giving a delicious fragrance to the dish. Serve the juices from the roasting tin in a sauceboat, and make bread sauce only if the family insist.

Mrs. Sue Lennan
from 'A Cyprus Cook's Calendar'

Strachur House,
Argyll.
Tel. Strachur 242.

MRS. MACDONALD'S CHICKEN MARYLAND

2 young spring chickens, weighing about 3½ lb (1.5 kg)
    each, carefully skinned and jointed, or 8 chicken breasts,
    boned
2 tbs seasoned flour
2 eggs, well beaten
¼ lb (100 g) fresh white breadcrumbs
½ lb (225 g) clarified butter
¼ pint (150 ml) peanut oil for frying
12 very thin streaky bacon rashers

Discard drumsticks and shake the other 12 pieces of chicken
(or chicken breasts) in a paper bag in which you put the
seasoned flour.   Dip them in the egg and then in the breadcrumbs.   Make sure they are evenly coated in crumbs.   Heat
the butter and oil in one large or two medium-sized sauté
pans.   When it foams, put in the chicken pieces, lower the
heat and cook gently for 5 minutes on each side.   Turn the
chicken pieces very carefully, and if you lose any crumbs
replace them with a shaking of new ones.   Cover the pans
with tin plates or foil for a further 15 minutes, and cook
uncovered for the last 15 minutes.   The thighs may need a
further 5 minutes or so;   leave them in until last.
Continue adding butter and oil when needed and shake the pan
often to prevent sticking or burning.   It is important to
cook the chicken very slowly.   About 5 minutes before dishing
up time, roll up the bacon and fry this in a separate pan
until crisp.   Drain on kitchen paper to eliminate fat.
Surround the fried chicken with bacon rolls, sweetcorn
fritters, small fried bananas, and fonds d'artichaut.   Serve
a large bowl of Sauce Tartare with the chicken.

NIKITA'S RUSSIAN BISTRO

Forshmak Dragomiroff

3 onions, chopped	3 tbs double cream
2 oz (50 g) butter	$\frac{1}{4}$ pint (150 ml) dry white wine
$\frac{1}{4}$ lb (100 g) button mushrooms, sliced	salt and pepper
	pinch of sugar
6 cooked chicken legs	2 small tomatoes, sliced
6 small gherkins, chopped	2 tbs grated Parmesan cheese
3 tbs sour cream	

Fry the onions in butter until they are brown, adding the mushrooms after a few minutes. Then add the meat of the chicken legs, chopped into small pieces and continue cooking gently for another 10 minutes or so. Meanwhile, throw a handful of chopped gherkins plus the sour and the double cream into an ovenproof dish. Add the white wine and bring to a slow simmer. Lastly, add the chicken mixture, season with salt and pepper and add the sugar. Cover with thin rings of fresh tomato and sprinkle with Parmesan cheese. Bake in the oven at 375°F (190°C) gas mark 5, for 5 minutes before serving.

Shura Shiwarg

Rutilio's Chicken Cutlets

remains of a chicken pilaf or 1 small cold roast chicken

cold cooked bacon or ham

2 tbs chopped mozzarella or Bel Paese

2 tbs ricotta or cream cheese

¼ lb (100 g) cooked rice

2 hard-boiled eggs, chopped

¼ pint (150 ml) cold white sauce

salt and pepper

flour

2 egg yolks

2 oz (50 g) white breadcrumbs or frying batter

parsley

Chop up the cold chicken and bacon. Add to it the two cheeses
and mix these in well with the rice, hard-boiled eggs, and enough
white sauce to cohere. The mixture must be stiff and solid.
Refrigerate for 2-3 hours, then turn on to a floured board and
shape quickly with floured hands into pear-shaped cutlets. Dip
each of these into well-seasoned flour, and then either into
beaten egg yolks and white breadcrumbs, or a good coating batter,
according to which you like best. Put two or three at a time
into a frying basket and cook in very hot oil until the cutlets
are golden and crisp on the outside with the cheese just melting
inside. When ready drain on kitchen paper and serve with deep-
fried parsley as a garnish.

A hot tomato sugo sauce can be handed separately, if desired.

Maddalena Ferrini

ROMAN PIE, MARK II

1 chicken or pheasant
6 oz (175 g) mushrooms, sliced
1 oz (25 g) butter
a little lemon juice
salt and pepper
¼ lb (100 g) macaroni
¼ lb (100 g) ham
¼ lb (100 g) tongue
2 oz (50 g) canned anchovy fillets
a large bunch of parsley
10 small black olives
gelatine (sufficient to set stock)
good clear stock

Sauce
1½ tbs butter
1½ tbs flour
8 fl oz (225 ml) milk
2½ oz (60 g) grated Parmesan
   cheese
a little freshly grated nutmeg
¼ pint (150 ml) single cream

Roast the chicken and when cold remove the meat and cut it into slivers. Sauté the mushrooms in the butter. Season with lemon juice, salt and pepper and allow to cool completely before mixing with the chicken meat.

Boil the macaroni. Meanwhile, make a white sauce with the butter, flour and milk. Away from the heat, beat in the Parmesan, nutmeg and cream and season with salt and pepper. Do not over-salt as the ham, anchovies and cheese have a strong salt content. Stir in the drained macaroni and allow to cool.

Cut the ham and tongue into matchstick strips. Mix them with the anchovy fillets, also cut into matchstick strips, and a generous quantity of fairly coarsely chopped parsley.

Arrange half the ham mixture over the base of a dish. Cover it with half the macaroni mixture, then all the chicken and mushroom mixture. Pack it quite, but not too firmly and level the top. Arrange the remaining ham mixture on top, decorating it with a scattering of olives. Pour on enough dissolved gelatine and stock to cover. How much you will need depends on the size of your dish, but I allow 1 tsp gelatine powder for every ½ pint (300 ml) of well-flavoured stock. Cover with cling film or foil and refrigerate until set. Allow the Roman pie to come back to room temperature for at least 2 hours before serving.

A good central dish for a cold buffet; doubled ingredients should feed about 25 people.

This is a modern version of a very old dish: in one of my 18th century cookbooks, it is called 'Norman Pie', and whether it comes from France or Italy is obscure.

Canard aux Olives

1 duck	1 tbs fécule or potato
olive oil	flour, or beurre manié
1¼ pints (750 ml) good, well-seasoned stock or pot au feu	juice of a lemon
	fried croûtons
¼ lb (100 g) green Spanish olives	a little pâté de foie

Truss the duck as for roasting. Put it in a pan with a very little hot olive oil. Brown it on all sides. Pour over the stock. Let it simmer very gently for 2 hours.

Remove the stones from the olives. About 10 minutes before serving up, pour off the juices in the casserole and keep the duck hot. Strain the juices through a sieve, thicken the sauce with the fécule or beurre manié, and add the juice of a lemon. Put in the olives and let it all simmer together for a few seconds. Cut up the duck and serve with the olive sauce poured over. Garnish it with croûtons of bread fried in olive oil that you have spread with a little pâté de foie, and some stoned whole olives.

S.E. Comtesse de Crouy-Chanel

Easton Neston, Northamptonshire

Canard au Raisins

```
2 fat young Aylesbury ducks
about ¼ lb (100 g) butter
4 fl oz (100 ml) brandy
about 1 pint (600 ml) white wine (Pouilly or Muscadet)
2 carrots, chopped
2 small onions, chopped
1 bouquet garni
1 pint (600 ml) good strained stock or pot-au-feu
salt and pepper
3 oz (75 g) sultanas
4 tbs cream
```

Sauté the trussed ducks in butter in a large, deep cocotte or casserole. When they are golden all over, about 15 minutes, drain away the butter. Heat the brandy in a small saucepan, light it and pour it flaming, over the birds, shaking the casserole a little to keep it alight. Now add the wine, vegetables, bouquet garni and the stock. Season well.

Reduce the sauce over high heat, then cover the cocotte and go on cooking gently over low heat for 30-40 minutes or so. A moment before serving, add the sultanas to the sauce (that you have plumped up by soaking in a little wine) and then the cream.

Serve a dish of new potatoes with the duck, and another of small fresh green peas, cooked à la Française.

Lady Hesketh

DUCK IN HONEY - an old English recipe

1 duck
½ pint (300 ml) draught ale, old or mild
3 tbs honey
3 tbs chopped fresh thyme, or 3 tsp dried thyme
2 pounded cloves
a pinch of nutmeg
3 oz (75 g) breadcrumbs
2 egg yolks
2 oz (50 g) butter
3 oranges
olive oil and vinegar dressing

Skin the gizzard of the duck and mince with the heart
and liver. Simmer for 15 minutes in half the ale, half
the honey, thyme, cloves and nutmeg. When the liquid is
quite reduced, cool and mix with breadcrumbs and 2 egg
yolks. Stuff the duck with this.

In a roasting pan melt the butter and stir in the
remaining ale and remaining honey. When the pan is hot,
and the sauce mixed, put the duck in this and roast in a
moderate oven, 350°F (180°C) gas mark 4, basting frequently.
Remove the duck when well cooked, carve it, and pour the
gravy over it. Serve with an orange salad made by
peeling 3 oranges as free as possible from pith. Remove
pips, divide into natural slices and dress with a little
olive oil and vinegar.

TURKEY HASH SUPREME

1½ lb (750 g) white turkey meat
½ pint (300 ml) double cream
1½ tbs butter

1½ rounded tbs flour
salt and pepper
¼ pint (150 ml) milk

Chop up the turkey into pieces the size of a large pea. Combine
with cream and cook over a low heat, stirring frequently, until the
cream is reduced by half. Meanwhile, melt butter in a heavy
saucepan. Then stir in flour and seasoning. When smooth, add
milk GRADUALLY, then cook, stirring constantly, until sauce is as
thick as double cream. Combine with turkey pieces and pour into
shallow baking tin. Keep hot while you make the following cheese
sauce:-

½ pint (300 ml) milk
2 tbs butter
2 rounded tbs flour
1 medium onion, grated

¼ tsp salt
3 egg yolks
1½ tbs butter
3 tbs grated Parmesan cheese

Heat milk until film shows on top, ie scald, but do not boil. Melt
the butter, add flour and stir until smooth. Add grated onion and
salt. Add scalded milk and cook over low heat, stirring frequently.
Then cool. Beat egg yolks slightly. Pour cream sauce into the
yolks VERY SLOWLY so as not to cook yolks. Then stir in butter and
cheese. Spoon this mixture over the hash. Place under the grill
4-5 inches (10-12.5 cm) from the heat. Grill until the sauce is a
pretty golden brown. To make this dish especially festive, border
it with puréed peas.

H.E. Mrs. David Bruce

COLD CHICKEN VASHILSIKOV

1 chicken
fresh grated horseradish, to taste
½ pint (300 ml) whipped cream

½ lb (225 g) cooked spaghetti
  chopped into small pieces
salt and pepper

Roast a chicken and while still warm, shred the meat into small pieces.
Mix the horseradish with the whipped cream and combine with chicken
and spaghetti. Season well and chill. Serve very cold accompanied
by a mixed green salad. This is a good and economical dish for a
supper party. It is easy to increase the quantities.

COLD CHICKEN ROTHSCHILD

2 young roasting chickens, each about 4 lb (1.75 kg)

2 tbs butter

1½ pints (900 ml) dry champagne (you can drink the rest)

salt and pepper

bouquet garni

2 tbs chopped fresh tarragon

1 pint (600 ml) cream

Sauté the chickens in the butter but only let them colour a little, then transfer them to a casserole and fill it half way up with the dry champagne. Season and throw in a bouquet garni and 1 tbs of the fresh chopped tarragon - or a tsp if the tarragon is dried. Poach (simmer gently, but do not boil) the chicken according to size but 35-45 minutes should be approximately right. Do not add any liquid during the cooking and let them cool in their own juices. When cold, skin and joint the chickens as for a chaud-froid. Put them in a shallow entrée dish or bowl.

Warm up the chicken/champagne stock, strain it into a clean saucepan and bring it to the boil. Boil it until it is reduced by one-third. Take it off the heat, and add to its amount twice as much cream. Season well, then return to heat and boil the cream and stock together a few minutes more until the sauce thickens. Continue stirring it all the time it is cooking.

When it is cold add the second spoonful of chopped tarragon. Pour the sauce over the chicken pieces. Put in the fridge and use the next day.

Baronne Cecile de Rothschild

Poulet à la Génoise - a cold chicken dish for summer

1 large fowl for boiling, or capon
1 oz (25 g) salt
For the marinade and sauce
8 fl oz (225 ml) good Italian olive oil
8 fl oz (225 ml) vinegar
salt and pepper
¼ lb (100 g) finely chopped gherkins
¼ lb (100 g) capers
¼ pint (150 ml) white wine
large bunch of parsley, finely chopped

Boil a large fowl or capon with water and the salt, keeping the cover of
the saucepan tightly closed. When the fowl is cooked, remove it into a
colander and let it drain. Then place it in a deep dish, and pour the
following sauce over it while it is still hot. Combine the oil, vinegar,
salt, pepper, gherkins - finely chopped - capers and, if convenient, white
wine. Let the sauce cover the fowl on all sides and remain in this 'marinade'
for at least 24 hours in a cool place. Turn the fowl from one side to the
other. To serve, carve the fowl and arrange on a plain platter; pour some
of the marinade over it and sprinkle liberally with parsley. A green salad
arranged round a small mound of cream cheese with a simple herb dressing
poured over it should accompany this dish.

Coronation Chicken (with Cold Curry Sauce)

One of the best of all chicken dishes: it was invented by Constance Spry
and Rosemary Hume at the Cordon Bleu School of Cookery, to celebrate the
coronation of Queen Elizabeth II.

1 large chicken, cooked as you wish

For the sauce
2 onions, chopped
3 tbs salad oil
1½ tbs curry powder
5 tbs apricot purée
4 tbs red wine

¼ pint (150 ml) water
1 bay leaf
salt and pepper
½ tsp sugar
a squeeze of lemon juice
6 tbs mayonnaise
4 tbs double cream

Either poach the chicken in water with a little wine, an onion, a carrot,
bouquet garni and seasoning, or roast it slowly in the oven, covered with
foil. Allow to cool then joint it and arrange it on a serving dish, or cut
it into small pieces and put in a bowl. Soften the onions in a little hot
oil, curry powder, apricot purée, red wine, water and bay leaf. Bring to
the boil, and add the seasoning, sugar and lemon juice. Cook to thicken and
sieve. By this time there seems to be very little left, but don't despair,
cool that little and mix well with mayonnaise and cream. Serve the curry
sauce spooned over the cooked chicken and accompany it with a bowl of cold
rice salad, in which you have added some chopped green peppers, and mango or
apricot chutney.

Constance Spry and Rosemary Hume

Game

CHARLES ELME FRANCATELLI
1805–1876
Cook to Lord Chesterfield,
Lord Dudley and Queen Victoria

VIRGINIAN BAKED PHEASANT

2 pheasants, cut into serving pieces   2 tbs onion juice
salt and pepper   4 tbs chopped parsley
2 oz (50 g) flour   ¾ pint (450 ml) sour cream
4 oz (100 g) butter   6 bacon rashers

Shake each piece of pheasant in a paper bag in the well seasoned
flour.   Melt the butter in a heavy sauté pan and brown the
pheasant pieces very slowly over a moderate heat for about
15 minutes.   Arrange in a shallow entrée or baking dish.
Add the onion juice and chopped parsley to the sour cream and
pour over the pheasant.   Cover with lid or foil, and bake for
1-1½ hours (depending on the age of birds), at 325°F (160°C)
gas mark 3.   Grill bacon until crisp and crumble over the dish
before serving.

H.E. Lady Caccia

PHEASANT WITH APPLE AND ONION PUREÉ

1 well-hung pheasant
4 streaky bacon rashers
2 tbs good poultry dripping or butter
1 lb (500 g) cooking apples
1 lb (500 g) onions
4 tbs lard
a pinch of cinnamon
salt and pepper
2 tbs white vermouth, or sweet white wine

Lay the rashers of bacon over the breast of the bird,
put it in a baking tin with the dripping or butter and
cover the breast with foil or greaseproof paper.
Roast for 20 minutes per lb (40 minutes per kg), and
10 minutes over, in a moderate oven, 350°F (180°C) gas
mark 4.   Peel, core and slice the apples and the onions,
melt the lard and stew them in it very gently, so that
they soften but do not colour.   When they are good and
soft, drain off any surplus lard, add the cinnamon and
seasonings, and finally the white vermouth.   Simmer on
a very low heat until the final consistency is like a
thick syrup.   Serve hot with the roast pheasant.

The Marchioness of Salisbury

Pheasant with Celery and Cream (for 4)

Another good recipe from 'The Art of British Cooking', by
Theodora Fitzgibbon (Phoenix House).   With her permission
I've altered the amount of celery cooked with the bird,
keeping the second head as a crisp accompanying vegetable,
but this is optional.

1 well-hung pheasant

6 oz (175 g) butter

½ pint (300 ml)   stock made
   from the giblets

2 green bacon rashers, diced

¼ pint (150 ml) port

2 tsp chopped parsley

1 tsp chopped lovage
   (if possible)

salt and pepper

2 heads of celery

1 egg yolk

½ pint (300 ml) whipping cream

lemon juice

Melt ¼ lb (100 g) of the butter in a casserole and brown
the bird all over.   Add the stock, the diced bacon, the
port, 1 tsp parsley and the lovage.   Season to taste.
Cover and simmer slowly in the oven, 300°F (150°C) gas mark
2, for about 30 minutes.   Clean and slice one head of
celery and add it to the pot.   Cook for another 45 minutes,
or until the bird is tender.   Remove from the oven, take
out the bird and put it on a warmed serving dish with the
celery, and keep hot.   Mix the beaten egg yolk with the
cream, and very gradually stir into it the cooled stock of
the bird.   Heat up, but on no account re-boil, or the
sauce will curdle.   Pour a little over the pheasant and
celery, and serve the rest in a sauceboat.
The second head of celery should be washed, sliced at an
angle and blanched for 5-7 minutes in boiling, salted water.
Drain well, and return to a dry clean pan with the remaining
butter.   Cover and simmer until it is cooked 'al dente'.
Drain and serve sprinkled with the remaining chopped parsley
and the lemon juice.

PARTRIDGE AUX CHOUX

An Edwardian Shooting Party Recipe

"Cook a red cabbage with some slices of Lyon sausage, three
pork sausages and three slices of lean bacon; when the cabbage
is partly cooked, remove it into a strainer and drain well;
from the saucepan carefully remove the sausages, etc., leave
a little of the gravy; when the cabbage is thoroughly drained
cut it up and place a layer of it in the saucepan, then a layer
of sausage, slices of carrot and a thin slice of bacon; employ
all your ingredients in this manner; add, of course, salt and
pepper, with the addition of a lump of fresh butter; cover with
a buttered paper; see that you have sufficient gravy, it must
not be dry.   Whilst all this is simmering, put your partridges
in a saucepan with a lump of butter, let them cook slowly,
baste them frequently, add a little of the gravy you have taken
from the other saucepan; when they are cooked and the cabbage
is done, place the cabbage, sausage, etc., carefully on a dish,
place the partridges on the top and the gravy around it.
I do not recommend this as a pretty dish, but it is excellent
if carefully prepared, and all men like it."

The Duchess of Devonshire

Roast Pheasant 'La Fresne'

a brace of pheasants
streaky bacon rashers or pork fat
port or muscatel

For the stuffing
2 Boursin cheeses à l'ail et fines herbes (or any cream cheese with
   crushed garlic cloves and herbs added)
1 heaped tbs chopped walnuts
2 heaped tbs good chutney

Mix the stuffing ingredients together and stuff the pheasants with this
mixture.   Lay them on their sides.   Cover with bacon and roast for
about 50 minutes at 425°F (220°C) gas mark 7.   Make gravy with the
pan juices adding a little port or muscatel to the sauce.

Serve with chanterelles lightly stewed in white wine.

Mrs. Rob MacPherson

Mrs. Chamberlain's Georgian Pheasant

1 pheasant
1 oz (25 g) butter
30 walnuts*
2 lb (1 kg) black grapes
juice of 3-4 oranges

¼ pint (150 ml) port or madeira
¼ pint (150 ml) strong green tea
1½ oz (40 g) butter
salt and pepper
grated nutmeg

Truss the pheasant for cooking; put the butter in an oval casserole
and brown the bird all over in it.   Skin the walnuts by immersing
them in boiling water and then in cold, and add them to the casserole,
along with the juice of the grapes (put the grapes through a liquidizer
and then sieve), and the orange juice.   Add the wine and green tea,
the butter, salt, pepper and nutmeg.   Cook the pheasant in this liquid,
covered, in a medium hot oven, 375°F (190°C) gas mark 5, for 1 hour
until almost done.   Then strain off three-quarters of the cooking
liquid and reduce it by boiling briskly to a good sauce, while the
pheasant browns uncovered in the oven for a further 5 minutes or so.

Carve the pheasant and serve surrounded by the walnuts and a little of
the sauce.   Serve the rest of the sauce separately.

A guinea fowl may be cooked the same way.

* Georgia in the Caucasus, NOT marching through ...

** If you can procure them, fresh walnuts add enormously to this dish.

Faisan Joyeux aux Truffes

3 plump hen pheasants
1¼ pints (750 ml) or 1 bottle red wine
¼ pint (150 ml) port
rosemary
thyme
sage
1 bay leaf
1 garlic clove, crushed

1 lb (500 g) chestnuts
16 shallots, chopped
1 lb (500 g) carrots, sliced
¼ lb (100 g) sultanas
salt and pepper
3 truffles, chopped
½ pint (300 ml) cream

Cut the pheasants up and marinate with the wine, port, herbs and garlic for 24 hours. Prepare the chestnuts in the following way: split the skins at the pointed end of the nut. Put in a saucepan, cover with water, bring to the boil and cook for 5 minutes. Strain the liquid from the nuts and skin them (hard outer and furry inner skin).

Put the birds into a large casserole. Add the marinade, chestnuts, shallots, carrots, sultanas and salt and pepper. Cook gently in the oven at 325°F (160°C) gas mark 3, until tender. Add the truffles and blend in the cream and serve.

Joy Rainbird

About Truffles - the 'black diamonds' of gastronomy

Now, alas, so rare and expensive that they are probably only worth using when fresh, ie during the truffle season, October to January.

The 'perfume' of fresh truffles is much stronger than that of dried ones, consequently you can use fewer; canned truffles do <u>not</u> reproduce the authentic flavour. 'Belle Epoque' recipes are lavish with truffles but the scale of these can usually be cut down, in some instances halved, and they will still produce wonderful results.

Fresh truffles can be ordered from France (mostly from Cahors) or Spain, a week in advance, from the best gastronomic purveyors. They are a marked commodity, and recently cost around £12 for 1 oz (25 g); dried truffles are a little cheaper, and truffle peelings are good, but can only be used to flavour.

To prepare fresh truffles, brush loose earth away, wash them, peel and season with salt and pepper; sprinkle with a little cognac or madeira to 'ripen' before cooking. Poach in stock, or whatever the recipe calls for; they will take a little longer than large mushrooms to cook.

Hot Salmi of Game

The most essential part of a salmi is the sauce, therefore devote your attention to that in the first instance.   Commence by putting into a saucepan ½ oz (15 g) butter, 3 small slices of salt streaky pork or bacon, an onion, chopped, a tomato, 2 fresh mushrooms, a bouquet garni and a little pepper.   Add to this the skinned carcasses and dark meat of some already cooked game birds (pheasant, partridge, grouse, wild duck etc.) from which you have removed the better portions.   Simmer together over low heat for 15 minutes, then mix 1 oz (25 g) flour with ½ pint (300 ml) of stock and ¼ pint (150 ml) of claret and add this to the saucepan, scraping together the juices.   Bring the sauce to the boil and simmer for a further 20 minutes then strain it through a sieve into a clean saucepan.   De-grease the sauce, lay the fillets from the wings and breasts of the birds in it and heat up together.   Serve with braised olives and croutons, the braised olives in the centre and the croutons around the edge of the dish.

Louisa Rochfort

Admiralty House, Sydney, Game Mould

After plucking and cleaning 2 old pheasants, partridge or other game birds roast them very slowly in a 325°F (160°C) gas mark 3 oven.   When cooked, cut all the meat from the carcasses into small neat pieces and reserve, together with the fat and gravy from the roasting tin.   Pound up the carcasses in a braising pan and cover them with just sufficient water, add an onion stuck with cloves, a bay leaf, salt and pepper, and bring to the boil.   Bang down on the bones from time to time with a wooden spoon and let the stock simmer for 40 minutes or so, then strain off the liquid. Lay the pieces of bird very tightly in a suitable earthenware dish or mould, add gelatine (1 oz (25 g) gelatine is enough to set 1 pint (600 ml) stock) to the roast's gravy, (remove the fat first) and the strained stock, then pour over the birds and leave to set.

Turn out the mould, garnish, and serve with a seasonable salad with a sharp French dressing.   This recipe can also be used for chicken.

Viscountess Ruthven

Grouse Stuffed with Bananas

Peel and cut up some bananas, mash them and mix them with 2 tsp black pepper, 1 tsp salt and 10 drops of lemon juice.   Use this to stuff either grouse or partridges.   Tie up and roast as usual.

Boodles Club 1923

ROAST GROUSE IN VINE LEAVES

grouse
streaky bacon rashers
vine leaves
slices of toast

butter
salt and pepper
melted butter

Hang the grouse for some time.   Do not wash them but wipe inside and outside
with a clean cloth.   Truss them like a fowl for roasting, laying over them
thin slices of bacon and then vine leaves, which you tie on with a thin
thread.   Roast them for 30-45 minutes and when done, serve them on a slice
of buttered toasted bread which you have spread with a paste made from
boiling the grouse livers for a few minutes then pounding them with butter,
salt and pepper.   Pour some good melted butter over them as they go to
the table.

Mrs. William Stirling of Keir

COLD GROUSE TERRINE

5-6 grouse (old or young birds)
1 lb (500 g) lean pork
a little pork fat
1 onion, finely chopped
thyme
parsley
1 lb (500 g) streaky bacon, thinly cut
1 oz (25 g) white breadcrumbs

2 egg yolks
4 fl oz (100 ml) brandy
1 black truffle (optional)
very little salt and pepper
3 pints (1.75 litres) stock,
    made with grouse carcasses
    and/or chicken bones

Use only breasts of grouse.   Remove all tough fibres and skin, and cut into
pieces.   Lay each piece of fillet between two layers of greaseproof paper
and beat flat.   Mince the lean and fat pork, and add the onion, the grouse
livers, thyme, parsley, and some of the bacon.   Bind with the breadcrumbs,
egg yolks and brandy.

Take a fireproof pie dish and line it with overlapping rashers of some of the
remaining bacon.   Spread the grouse fillets with mince mixture and lay one
on top of the other until you can't fit any more in.   Bury the truffle,
cut into 3, in the middle (if used).   Season.   Cover with more rashers of
bacon and pour in a good strained grouse stock until the dish is half full.

Cover the terrine with foil and a lid and stand in a roasting tin with water
to come half way up its sides.   Cook in a slow to moderate oven, 325°F (160°C)
gas mark 3, for 2 hours.   Do not let it run dry.   Reduce the remaining
stock by boiling rapidly and when the terrine is ready fill it up with this.

When cool, put a sheet of greaseproof paper on top of the terrine and some
weights.   When quite cold remove these and scrape off the fat which will
have risen to the top.   Garnish with parsley.   Serve with a tossed green
salad and baked potatoes in their jackets.   The terrine will keep for 1 week
and more, in a cold place if you leave the fat on.

PHEASANT PILAU WITH RAISINS AND PINE KERNELS FROM ANATOLIA

Roast 2 pheasants with some rashers of bacon over their breasts.
Cut up and lay the pieces and the bacon on top of a pilau of rice
made according to the recipe for Iç Pilau on page 54, adding more
than usual currants, and pine kernels and a few seedless raisins.

For a good vegetable to go with the Pilau, sprinkle 3-4 aubergines,
sliced lengthways with salt and leave to sweat for 1 hour, between
two plates.   Wipe the bitter juices away with a clean cloth.   Pat
dry, dip in seasoned flour and fry in deep, very hot oil for 3
minutes.   Drain on a paper napkin and serve.   For a good salad,
toss sliced cucumber with a sour cream dressing.

Mrs. G.M. Warre

DEREK HILL'S COLD GROUSE

Stuff the inside of 3 grouse (they need not be young birds)

with good beef dripping to bursting point.   Tie securely

or sew up and put in a roasting tin or covered casserole

with ¼ pint (150 ml) port, or madeira, and water, up to

one-third of the depth of the receptacle.   Cover it tightly

with a lid and foil and roast very slowly, 300°F (150°C)

gas mark 2, for 3½-4 hours.   Leave the birds in a cool

place overnight in their cooking juices.   In the morning

skim off the fat, cut up the jelly and arrange round the

birds.   The flesh when carved will be rosy, juicy and

perfectly tender.   Serve with boiled potatoes over which

you have poured sour cream, and a compôte of cranberry sauce.

Derek Hill

Lièvre à la Royale (Hare)

This recipe for preparing a hare was a favourite with King Edward VII.
The dish comes from Poitou, a part of France that is celebrated for its
cooking. A remarkable fact in connection with this preparation is that,
although there is an abundance of garlic and shallot, the effect of one,
so to speak, counteracts the other, and the guest never suspects that either
of these powerful ingredients has been introduced into the hare.

"Take a hare having passed the baby age. Kill it as cleanly as possible,
in order to lose as little of the blood as possible.

Skin it, and remove the inside. Keep the blood and the liver.

Take about a quarter of a pound of fat bacon, a little parsley, six cloves
of garlic, eight cloves of shallot, a crust of bread soaked in water, and
crumble it over the liver, the bacon, the garlic and the shallot. Break
two eggs over this; salt and pepper and chop it all together as fine, as
fine, as fine ...

This preparation constitutes the 'stuffing'. Fill the hare with it and sew
the opening carefully together.

Line a stew-pan with rashers of bacon and place the hare in it, in a circle.
In the centre put three onions, each onion stuck with a clove; a carrot
cut into slices, salt and pepper. Put the stew-pan into a hot oven.
When the hare is browned, very brown, and the carrot and onions have given
all the moisture they contain, pour in a glass of stock and let it boil
for about five minutes, the necessary time to make the sauce. The stock
can be replaced by a glass of white wine.

The blood, which has been lying in a bowl, is now the chief ingredient of
the sauce. Pour into it three tablespoonfuls of flour, two tablespoonfuls
of vinegar, two of brandy, mix well and work in, little by little,
sufficient white wine to smooth it. Pour this over the hare so that it
partly covers it; add parsley, thyme, bay leaf, fifteen cloves of garlic
and thirty cloves of shallot finely chopped, and let it cook on a slow
fire, simmering like a stew, for at least three hours and a half.

Carve the hare into wafer thin slices and pile on to a dish. Pour the
sauce through a strainer over it. Arrange the stuffing in the centre of
the dish and sprinkle with freshly chopped parsley.

The onions, carrots and bacon must cook with the hare until the end. The
white wine can be replaced by red. The hare is served with a spoon."

Rosa Lewis - A recipe given to my grandfather, Lord Ribblesdale

JUGGED HARE GLOUCESTER-STYLE

1½ lb (700 g) shin of beef

1 large onion, chopped

1 carrot, chopped

1 garlic clove, crushed

salt and pepper

1 hare

flour

cayenne

5 oz (150 g) butter

¼ lb (100 g) mushrooms, chopped

¼ lb (100 g) lean bacon, chopped

2 bay leaves

1 lemon stuck with 5 cloves

12 fl oz (350 ml) port

Put the shin to boil for 4 hours in 2 pints (1.2 litres) of water with the onion, carrot, garlic, salt and pepper. Then cool and when cold remove the fat and strain through a sieve. It should make about 1-1½ pints (600-900 ml) of good beef tea. This is best prepared the day before needed.

Cut the hare into small joints or pieces, dredge with flour, salt and pepper, and cayenne. Melt ¼ lb (100 g) of the butter in a saucepan and fry the hare until brown with the mushrooms and bacon. Put the meat and mushrooms into a very large screw-top jar. Add two bay leaves and the lemon (cut the peel a little to let out the flavour). Add the beef stock, cover the jar and screw the cap tight. Put it into a deep saucepan of cold water and let it boil for 4 hours, or, if you are certain it is a younger hare, 3 hours. Take the jar from the pan, discard the water, pour the contents of the jar into the pan. Shake well over the heat for a few minutes. Add the port and remaining piece of butter, well coated in flour. Stir well until the butter and flour are well blended. Simmer for 10 minutes. Turn out into a serving dish and serve with redcurrant jelly. This sounds rather more complicated than it is, but it is really well worth while.

Joy Rainbird

Lièvre à la Darsy (Hare)

1 plump young hare
5 oz (150 g) butter
12 shallots, chopped
1 tbs flour
8 fl oz (225 ml) double cream

8 fl oz (225 ml) vinegar
juice of 1 lemon
salt and pepper
1 bouquet garni

Cut a hare into small pieces and remove the blood.   Dry it
with kitchen paper.   Melt $\frac{1}{4}$ lb (100 g) of the butter in a
saucepan and add the shallots, and flour, and let them brown for
about 15 minutes.   Then pour in the cream, vinegar and the lemon
juice.   Melt the remaining butter in another saucepan, add the
hare, but do not let it brown.   Season then pour the sauce
through a strainer over it.   Add the bouquet garni, and let it
cook over a low heat for 2 hours.   Remove the bouquet garni
before serving.

A German Way of Roasting Hare

1 saddle of hare
fat bacon for larding
butter for roasting
8 fl oz (225 ml) sour cream
lemon juice
1 tbs meat glaze or jellied gravy
redcurrent jelly

Take the back of the hare (the râble) from the root of the neck
to the tail (the latter being included); remove all tendons
and delicately lard with bacon.   Roast in a hot oven, 400°F
(200°C) gas mark 6, for 20 minutes, so that it is only just
done.

The pan in which the râble has been roasted should be swilled
with sour cream (this cream constitutes the accompaniment), and
a few drops of lemon juice or melted meat glaze may be added,
if liked.

Serve some of the sauce in a sauceboat separately, and some
redcurrant jelly in another.

BEAUFORT RABBIT

Prepare just as you would veal for a Wiener Schnitzel. Cut the
fillets from the backs of 3 young rabbits in one piece (it is
sometimes possible to get 4 schnitzels out of one fat rabbit, but
you had better count on 2). Beat them flat between greaseproof
paper, dip in seasoned flour, then in egg and then in white breadcrumbs. Fry gently and slowly in clarified butter, until the
crumbs are golden and the meat well cooked.

Garnish with a lemon slice on each schnitzel, on which you have
carefully spooned, side by side, a teaspoonful of the white and
a teaspoonful of the yellow parts of a hard-boiled egg, rubbed
through a sieve into 'crumbs'. Surmount this little mound with
a criss-cross of anchovy fillets, split in two, and place a caper
in the centre. (This is the traditional Viennese garnish - and
it really is worth the trouble.) Pour a little of the pan butter
over the schnitzels and serve.

Mrs. Joan Birnie and Lady Lovat

RABBIT IN A SAVOURY SAUCE - A Hungarian Country Recipe

1 rabbit or hare
2 bacon rashers, chopped
2 oz (50 g) lard
4 oz (100 g) chopped onion
4 tbs tomato purée
3 tbs white wine

salt and pepper
3 tbs savory
3 tbs flour
¾ pint (450 ml) sour cream
juice of ½ lemon

Cut the meat from the rabbit carcass, remove membranes, slice in
strips about ¼ inch (5 mm) thick, and wash. Fry the bacon in
the lard and set aside. Fry the chopped onion in the same lard
until golden, then add the tomato purée and wine. Bring to the
boil; add meat, seasonings, and savory. Reduce the heat and
simmer, uncovered, until all the liquid evaporates. Continue
cooking over low heat, letting the meat now fry, until browned,
then add a little water, cover the pan and simmer until tender.
Blend the flour with sour cream and add this, with the reserved
fried bacon, to the rabbit. Add the lemon juice, then stir and
simmer for another 15 minutes or so. Serve with a separate dish
of polenta or rice.

Hungarian Hasenpfeffer

1 plump rabbit

wine, vinegar and water

1 onion, sliced

3 cloves

1 bay leaf

salt and pepper

grated nutmeg

4 tbs butter

½ pint (300 ml) sour cream

croutons

Skin and joint the rabbit. Wipe the pieces carefully with a damp cloth and place them in an earthenware crock with enough white wine, vinegar and water (in equal parts) to cover the meat. Add the onion, a few cloves, a bay leaf, salt, pepper and nutmeg to taste. Marinate the meat for 2 days. Then wipe absolutely dry, and sauté the pieces in hot butter until they are well coloured, turning them frequently. Add, a spoonful at a time, enough of the marinade to come about ¼ inch (5 mm) high in the cocotte pan. Take your time over it, then cover the pan with a tight-fitting lid and continue simmering gently until it is ready. It will take about 30 minutes. Do not let it boil. Just before serving, stir the sour cream into the sauce. Garnish with croutons or little crescents of puff pastry.

This would be very good eaten with baby beetroot cooked à la polonaise, and a purée of potatoes.

From the Charleston Ladies

Rabbit à la Tartare

Place a young rabbit in marinade, that is, in a pickle made with vinegar, salt, pepper, spice, onions, rosemary, sage, fine herbs, cloves, mace etc. (That is, to give an excellent flavour that can only be acquired by this treatment.) Leave it in the marinade for 4 hours, cut it in joints, coat it in egg and breadcrumbs, grill it, and serve with Sauce Tartare.

Louisa Rochfort

LAPIN À L'ANCIENNE

This is a very old recipe for preparing rabbit.

1 rabbit
2 oz (50 g) butter
1½ tbs flour
¼ pint (150 ml) good white wine
stock
6 oz (175 g) mushrooms

3 bacon rashers
thyme
bay leaf
salt and pepper
1 onion, sliced

Cut the rabbit up and put the pieces in a saucepan with the butter, until the pieces of rabbit are brown.   Put the rabbit aside and add the flour to the butter stirring all the time.   Add the white wine (Alsace, Hock, Muscadet, etc.) and replace the rabbit in the pan and put enough stock in the pan to cover it.   Boil. Fry the mushrooms with the bacon and the thyme and bay leaf.   Add this mixture to the rabbit and boil over high heat whilst stirring until the sauce has been reduced by a quarter.   Add a small amount of salt and pepper.   Fry some sliced onions and add them to the mixture.   Finish cooking on a low heat, being careful not to let the food burn at the bottom of the saucepan.   Serve with croûtons, under and around it.

S.E. Madame Louis Roché

SUSIE'S SPECIAL DRESSING FOR ROAST VENISON OR WILD BOAR

3-4 tbs honey
2 tbs lemon juice
1 tbs thick soy sauce
¼-½ tbs minced garlic
salt and black and white pepper

venison
olive oil
1 tsp cornflour
8 fl oz (225 ml) double cream
8 fl oz (225 ml) red wine

Slightly warm honey and mix with lemon juice, soy sauce, garlic and seasonings. Wash the venison (roe or wild boar) under running cold water; dry it and rub into it some olive oil, as much as it will take; roast it without adding any liqui Roast until it is three-quarters cooked, then transfer roasting tin to top of stove and dredge meat with salt and pepper; paste the 'special dressing' generously all over the meat with a pastry brush before returning it to the oven. Repeat this dressing several times (about every 10-15 minutes) until the meat is cooked; it will keep the venison tender and avoid sponginess or 'drying out'. When the meat is done, take it out of the roasting pan.   Add a little water to the juices, then a teaspoonful of cornflour mixed with cream; let these all boil up together for a few minutes and at the last minute add the red wine which you have boiled separately for a minute or two to 'burn off' the alcohol. Pour over the venison and dish up.

Frau Heinrich Krohe, Pirmasens

About Venison

The experts will tell you: "Venison is never cooked in the natural state. After the skin and tendons have been removed it is larded and placed in a deep earthenware dish and marinated with the following ingredients.". This is not strictly true - a freshly killed stag or roe (or fallow deer) produces the most excellent grilling steak if used within a few hours of the beast being shot. But, after that, it has to be 'hung' for 10 days or so and then marinated.

Marinade for Venison

About ¼ pint (150 ml) vinegar, ¼ pint (150 ml) red or white wine, 3 carrots and 1 large onion cut in slices, 3 bay leaves, a sprig of thyme, salt and pepper, all heated in a saucepan until on the point of boiling. The marinade is then put aside to cool, and when tepid is poured over the venison. Once or twice a day the venison is basted and turned in the dish so that all parts are impregnated with the marinade. It is left in the marinade for 3 or 4 days.

Gigot de Chevreuil (Haunch of Roe Deer)

After the joint has been skinned, larded and placed in the marinade for 4 days, it is taken from the dish and cooked in a hot oven, 400°F (200°C) gas mark 6, in a baking pan with several pieces of butter smeared over it, and basted with the marinade. It is served with a sauce poivrade to which some of the marinade is added. (The recipe for this sauce is given on page 162.)

Côtelettes de Chevreuil (Cutlets of Roe)

The cutlets are larded and put into a marinade for a few hours only. They are then placed in a saucepan, with a lump of good fresh butter and a sprinkling of salt and pepper, over high heat and browned on both sides. Serve with a purée of chestnuts into which the gravy from the cutlets has been incorporated. The chestnut purée* is placed in the centre of a round dish, and the cutlets are lapped one over the other around it.

Roast Saddle of Roe or Haunch of Venison

Lard a 5-6 lb (2.25-2.75 kg) saddle of roe or venison haunch with 4 oz (100 g) of fresh pork fat cut into ¼ inch (5 mm) wide strips. Then soak the meat in 1¾ pints (1 litre) buttermilk for 24 hours. Drain it and dry it thoroughly. Put it in a roasting pan or baking dish just large enough to hold it; sear it on all sides in 2 oz (50 g) butter and 2 tbs oil. Rub it with salt and 1 tsp crushed juniper berries and ½ tsp freshly ground pepper. Roast it in a very hot oven, 450°F (230°C) gas mark 8, for 20 minutes.

Continued .....

* see recipe page 162

Roast Saddle of Roe or Haunch of Venison (continued)

Reduce heat to moderate, 350°F (180°C) gas mark 4, and roast for a further 25-30 minutes, or until the top is brown and crisp and the inside slightly pink. Transfer venison to a serving dish. Skim off as much fat as possible from the roasting pan and set over high heat. Add 8 fl oz (225 ml) white wine and scrape in the brown bits. Reduce the wine by half, add a little Tabasco and cook, stirring, until it is well blended. Strain the sauce, add salt and freshly ground black pepper if necessary. Swirl in 2 oz (50 g) butter, cut in pieces. Carve the meat in fairly thick slices and serve the sauce separately, in a sauceboat with redcurrant or rowanberry jelly in another.

Saddle of Roe Nesselrode

Proceed as above, but prepare a creamy purée of Jerusalem artichokes to serve with the saddle and garnish the serving dish with thick apple slices, cored and cooked slowly in butter, then filled with cranberry sauce.

A Simple Sauce Poivrade* for Venison

Chop two onions of ordinary size, put them in a small saucepan with a little butter and let them brown. Add ¼ pint (150 ml) of vinegar and the same quantity of red wine, a good pinch of pepper, 5 or 6 bay leaves, 2 sprigs of thyme, the same of parsley, 2 garlic cloves and a sprinkling of flour. Mix well together with a wooden spoon and let the contents of the saucepan boil for 45 minutes. Then pass it through a fine sieve and add to it the gravy from the venison. If the sauce is not thick enough, let it boil uncovered to 'reduce' it.

When there is no sauce poivrade, 1 tbs flour is mixed with a lump of butter in a saucepan, the marinade and the gravy from the venison are added and boiled for 1 hour. This sauce is then passed through a sieve into another saucepan, and simmered until ready to use: 1 tbs port and 1 tbs redcurrant jelly can be added to it just before serving.

* For the classic sauce, which takes hours to prepare, see my 'Sauces and Surprises' book, pages 48 and 75. Demi glace, which is a refined Sauce Espagnole, is a necessary ingredient for it.

Purée de Marrons (Chestnuts served with Venison)

Make a slight incision in the chestnuts before putting them in cold water and let them boil until the outer skin can be easily removed with the point of a knife. Then put them on the heat in a saucepan with a little butter and shake them until the second skin is loosened. Peel this away and put them again in water with a little salt. When they are quite cooked, pass them through a sieve with some milk; add a little butter and the gravy from the venison with which you are serving the chestnuts.

Beef and Veal

CHARLES MAURICE DE TALLEYRAND-PERIGORD
1754–1838
Statesman
Ambassador at the Court of St. James's, 1830–1834

ENTRECÔTE 'SAUCE BORDELAISE' as cooked at Voisin's in Edward VII'S time

This is a classical dinner party dish for 6-8 people.   It consists of
a whole roast entrecôte or fillet of beef, served with small rounds of
marrow and a red wine sauce.   It should be presented on a large platter
surrounded by little heaps of young vegetables in season.

1 fillet of beef, about 2½-3 lb (1.25-1.5 kg)
2 or more marrow bones, sawn to expose marrow

For the sauce
¼ pint (150 ml) claret
3 fl oz (75 ml) very good stock
a pinch of sugar
1 shallot, chopped
1 bay leaf
1 lemon
salt and pepper
cayenne
1 oz (25 g) butter

The marrow bones should be placed in cold water for 24 hours if possible,
and the water changed several times.   This makes the marrow whiter and
more appetizing;   otherwise it is always more or less grey.   Put the bones
into a saucepan full of cold water without salt.   When the water boils,
remove the saucepan to the side of the heat, to remain hot without boiling.
Cover it and let the marrow poach for 25-30 minutes.   It is shaken from
the bone and cut into slices when the entrecôte is ready to be served.
Alternatively, roast the marrow bones in a low oven, 300ºF (150ºC) gas mark 2,
for 1 hour, then shake the marrow out.

For the sauce, put the claret, stock and a pinch of sugar into a small
saucepan.   Boil without covering it, until it is reduced by half.   Add
the chopped shallot and bay leaf.   Boil for about 5 minutes, then pass the
sauce through a fine sieve.   Add the juice of a lemon, salt, pepper, a
little cayenne and the butter, which you swirl in, in flakes, away from the
heat until the required thickness has been reached.

The entrecôte, which has been roasted for 18-20 minutes in a hot oven,
450ºF (230ºC) gas mark 8, is now carved, seasoned and the pieces placed
one next to the other in the original shape.   The slices of marrow are
cut with a warm knife and arranged down the centre, the length of the steak,
and the sauce is poured over.

QUICK CASSEROLE OF BEEF À LA PROVENÇALE

3 lb (1.5 kg) best braising beef, (rump, chuck or topside)

4 tbs olive oil

4 fl oz (100 ml) armagnac

4 aubergines, sliced

1 lb (500 g) tomatoes, sliced

5 green peppers, deseeded and sliced

3 onions, sliced

1 garlic clove, crushed

3 tbs sugar

salt and pepper

thyme

bay leaf

Sear the meat in the hot oil, and let it colour on all sides.   Then flambé it with the armagnac.   Put into a heavy iron casserole that just fits it.   Add the vegetables, garlic, sugar, seasoning and herbs. Cover, and seal hermetically (flour and water or kitchen foil).   Let it simmer gently and do this by listening, not by looking, on the side of the stove for 2½ hours.   The vegetables should by then have turned into a purée.   Serve the meat sliced, with baby sautéed carrots and courgettes around the dish and the 'coulis' of vegetables you have cooked with the meat in a separate dish.

BEEF ROULADE FROM SAXONY

4 large thin beef steaks, about 2 lb (1 kg) from rump or sirloin

1 tbs mustard

salt and pepper

4 tbs diced bacon

3 onions, finely chopped

4 dill pickles, sliced

2 tbs flour

2 tbs butter or shortening

½-¾ pint (300-450 ml) good stock

cornflour (optional)

5 tbs sour cream

Have your butcher cut extra large thin beef steaks.   Spread mustard thinly and evenly on each steak, sprinkle with salt and pepper.   Cover with diced bacon, chopped onions and some slices of dill pickle.   Roll and tie with string.   Dust with flour, and sauté in the fat until brown on all sides. Cover with boiling stock and braise for 2-2½ hours.   Thicken gravy with a very little cornflour, if necessary, and sour cream, and season to taste.

Filet Diane for Two

thinly cut rump steak
salt and pepper
1 oz (25 g) butter
2 tsp Worcester sauce
1 tbs chopped parsley
1 tbs mixed chopped capers and chopped gherkins
1 tbs vermouth

For this dish you need two thinly cut pieces of rump steak
the size and shape of a saucer, and two frying pans. Beat
the steak flat between greaseproof paper. Season it with
coarse salt and pepper each side. Heat the frying pans
and divide the butter and Worcester sauce between them.
Cook the steaks for 1 minute only each side; dish them on
to two hot plates, then throw the parsley, capers and gherkins
into the first pan with the vermouth and stir briskly to deglaze
it. Pour the contents of the first pan into the second and
deglaze that too. Lastly pour the sauce over the two steaks
and serve at once.

Filet de Boeuf Portugaise

6 anchovy fillets, pounded to a paste
1½ tbs Dijon mustard
scant 1 pint (600 ml) madeira
6 fillet steaks, each about 1½ inches (4 cm) thick
freshly ground pepper
2 oz (50 g) butter
scant 1 tbs cornflour or potato flour
2 tbs cream

Pound the anchovies and blend with the mustard and madeira.
Season the beef with pepper only. Sauté the steaks in a
large skillet in very hot butter, about 2½ minutes on each
side. Remove to a warm dish and keep hot. Scrape together
the pan juices and add a little of the madeira mixture to
them. Then shake in the cornflour and blend well. When
it is smooth and cooked, add the rest of the madeira mixture
and boil briskly until well reduced. Add the cream. Pour
some of the sauce over the steaks, and serve the rest in a
sauceboat.

Tournedos Chasseur from Marguéry's, circa 1905

Cut as many thick slices of fillet of beef as there are guests.
Give them the shape of a five-franc piece.   Put some butter into
a shallow saucepan with the fillets.   Let them colour on both
sides over high heat.   When cooked, take them from the saucepan
and add 1 tbs chopped shallots to the juices.   Moisten with about
5 tbs white wine and the same quantity of sherry, 1 tbs tomato
sauce, 1 tsp sugar and a little concentrated stock or meat jelly.
Simmer down to syrup consistency, then add chopped parsley and
tarragon, and pour the sauce over the tournedos.

Stir-fried Steak à l'Orientale

1½ lb (700 g) fillet steak

2½ tbs soy sauce

1 tbs sherry

1 tbs cornflour

1 tbs sugar

2 tbs water

vegetables in season (tomatoes,
  courgettes, mushrooms or
  sliced peppers)

2 oz (50 g) cooking fat

1 tsp salt

Thinly slice and cut the meat into squares or strips.   Mix 1½ tbs
of the soy sauce, the sherry, cornflour, sugar and water to a thin
paste.   Add the meat to the sauce mixture and stir well, making
sure all the meat is coated.   Cook the vegetables separately in
a little salted water.   Heat the fat in a heavy frying pan
until very hot, add the meat mixture and cook over high heat for
2 minutes, stirring all the time.   Then add the drained vegetables,
the rest of the soy sauce and the salt and cook for 1 minute
longer.   This dish is quickly made and very good.   It can be
served with boiled rice or noodles or, if you prefer it, with
creamed potatoes and a green salad.

SAUERBRATEN

2 lb (1 kg) round or rump beef

For the Marinade

8 fl oz (225 ml) vinegar

8 fl oz (225 ml) water

4 fl oz (100 ml) red wine

1 bay leaf

3 cloves

3 onions, sliced

For Frying

1 marrow-bone

1 tomato, skinned and sliced

2 tbs fat

2 tbs flour

salt and pepper

½ tsp sugar

1 onion, sliced

Mix the ingredients for the marinade and bury the beef in this mixture for 2-3 days. Remove the beef from the marinade, pat dry with kitchen paper, then sauté it, together with the marrow from the marrow bone*, in hot fat until brown on all sides. Sprinkle it with salt and pepper, add the sliced onion and tomato and part of the strained marinade. Simmer for about 2 hours until the meat is tender. Remove to a hot serving platter. For a good gravy, add a little flour and the rest of the marinade to the casserole juices, stirring constantly until the sauce thickens; add a pinch of sugar. Pour the strained gravy over the hot meat and serve the rest separately.

* see page 164.

H.E. Baroness Ungern-Sternberg

SWEDISH MANOR POT ROAST

Beef (topside, sirloin on the bone, or boned top rump, or thick flank.
The French cut of 'aiguillette' is best of all, which is a rump
steak roast.)

$2\frac{3}{4}$ lb (1.25 kg) meat on the bone,
  or $2\frac{1}{4}$ lb (1 kg) boned meat
$2\frac{1}{2}$ tbs butter
salt and white pepper
about $\frac{3}{4}$ pint (450 ml) stock or water
2 onions
1 bay leaf

4 anchovy fillets and some
  anchovy liquor
5 white peppercorns
$1\frac{1}{4}$ tbs treacle
$1\frac{1}{4}$ tbs wine vinegar
$1\frac{1}{2}$ tsp ground allspice

For the sauce
$\frac{3}{4}$ pint (450 ml) gravy from the roast
4 fl oz (100 ml) cream

2 tbs beurre manié

Side sauces
bilberry jam
redcurrant jelly

pickled walnuts
pickled onions

Trim the meat and tie it up if necessary. Heat the fat in a pan and
sear the meat. Season with salt and pepper and moisten with the
warmed stock. Add the onion and other flavourings. Cover with a
lid and cook the meat over gentle heat, or in the oven, 400°F (200°C)
gas mark 6, for $1\frac{1}{2}$-2 hours. Baste during cooking and moisten when
necessary. Lift out the joint. Strain the gravy and if there is
not sufficient, increase it by adding more stock. Add the cream.
Thicken this sauce with the beurre manié and allow it to cook for
3-5 minutes. Taste for seasoning. Serve the roast, with the
sauce in a sauceboat, accompanied by boiled potatoes, boiled
vegetables, a green salad, bilberry jam and redcurrant jelly and
pickled walnuts and onions.

H.E. Madame Belfrage

LOUISA ROCHFORT'S BOEUF À LA MODE

This is not the classical recipe, which takes nearly a day to prepare, and can be found in any French cook book, nor is it one of those over-simplified English versions, which taste like tinned M & V.   It is a French bourgeois version, and a very good one too.   Boeuf 'Mode' should always be made from 'aiguillettes de boeuf' which is a rump steak roast, rolled, or a joint of the rump rolled and sometimes larded.   Get your friendly neighbourhood butcher to do this for you.   Also to bone and blanch the calves' feet.

12 oz (350 g) piece fat bacon
salt and pepper
4 lb (1.75 kg) rump steak roast,
  in one piece
3 tbs rendered pork fat or
  cooking oil
1 scant pint (600 ml) white wine
4 fl oz (100 ml) brandy
1 pint (600 ml) beef stock
1 pint (600 ml) water
2 calves' feet, boned and blanched

1 lb (500 g) carrots
1 large onion, chopped
2 medium tomatoes, skinned,
  seeded and chopped
3 celery sticks, chopped
2 garlic cloves, crushed
3 cloves
bouquet garni (with chervil)
2 bay leaves
24 small glazed onions

Cut the bacon rind off the bacon.   Blanch the rind and set aside.   Cut the bacon into strips for larding and sprinkle them with pepper.   Lard the meat lengthways with this bacon and tie up neatly.   Heat the pork fat or oil in a deep, heavy braising pan (or casserole) until it is smoking hot, and brown the meat in it, searing and sealing it carefully on all sides. This will take a good 10-15 minutes.   Pour off the browning fat.   Now add the white wine, brandy, beef stock, water, calves' feet (already boned and blanched) and the blanched bacon rind.   Put it on the heat again, adding 1½ tbs salt.   Bring to the boil and skim it as you would a pot-au-feu. Having skimmed it add the carrots, the onion, tomatoes, celery, garlic, cloves, bouquet garni, bay leaves and 2 good pinches of pepper.   Cover the pan and allow it to simmer <u>very</u> gently for at least 4½ hours.   Try the meat with a skewer to learn when it is sufficiently cooked.   Strain the gravy through a fine sieve, remove carefully every atom of grease (a bulb baster is a good way of doing this) and reduce it over high heat by about a quarter.   Untie the beef and place it on the dish for serving.   Add the calves' feet cut in pieces and the carrots cut into 1 inch (2.5 cm) pieces. Arrange the calves' feet, carrots and glazed or brown-braised onions round the beef, pour the gravy over the meat, keeping what you do not require for the next day.   Taste first, to ascertain if sufficiently seasoned. The garlic is an improvement, but optional, and red wine can be used instead of white, if preferred.   There should be enough left over from this recipe to eat cold the next day.

Boeuf à la Mode en Gelée

If you have prepared a decent amount of Boeuf à la Mode, you should, after
your hot meal, be left with about 2 lb (1 kg) of beef, bits of calves' feet,
some baby onions and carrots and a good deal of stock that will rapidly
turn into aspic.   So put this into a bowl and the remainder of the meat
into another bowl, and refrigerate overnight.

Next morning, remove the fat from the jellied stock.   Strain and re-melt it
until just sticky, then line the bottom of an ordinary small salad bowl or
a flat round mould with it.   Put it back in the fridge to set.   When it
is half set, arrange the more thinly sliced carrots and onions in it in a
nice pattern, put it back again in the fridge, and allow it to set completely.
Spoon the meat and remaining vegetables into the middle.   Strain the rest
of the stock over the meat until the bowl is full.   If there is not enough
stock, add a little canned jellied consommé.   Put back in the fridge until
completely set then turn out, after holding the dish for a moment in a
basin of hot water, and garnish with salady things.   It is delicious eaten
with a green salad and sauté potatoes.

Note: Only use the calves' feet if cut into very thin strips as they set
         too hard.

Kaldolmar - Cabbage Dolmas

1 good white cabbage
¾ lb (350 g) best minced steak
1 onion, or a few shallots, chopped
   and sautéed
4 oz (100 g) rice, boiled
1 egg, to bind

salt and pepper
butter
1 pint (600 ml) good stock
1 tbs golden syrup
cranberry sauce

Blanch some nice leaves of cabbage for 5 minutes in boiling water.   Drain
them on a clean cloth.   Mix the meat, onion and rice together and add a
beaten egg and seasoning.   Put a spoonful of this mixture on one or two
cabbage leaves and roll up.   Make individual little packages of leaves
filled with stuffing.   Fry them gently in butter until coloured on every
side.   Then lay them side by side in a baking dish or tin and pour a good
stock over to come threequarters of the way up the dish.   Then dribble
over the golden syrup and bake in a moderate oven, 350°F (180°C) gas mark 4,
for 1 hour.   Serve with a bowl of hot cranberry sauce.

H.E. The Hon. Lady O'Neill

Beefsteak, Kidney and Mushroom Pudding - an English classic

1½ lb (700 g) best rump steak

1 garlic clove, halved

½ lb (225 g) kidney

2 oz (50 g) flour

salt and pepper

¼ lb (100 g) mushrooms, chopped

suet crust (see below)

¼ pint (150 ml) well seasoned
beef stock

Rub a very sharp knife with the cut garlic.   Cut the steak into thin slices, each about 3 x 4 inches (7.5 x 10 cm), rubbing the knife with the garlic before cutting each slice.   chop up the kidney.   Mix the flour well with the salt and pepper in a small bowl.   Coat the steak, kidney and mushrooms with seasoned flour.   Roll each slice of beef around a piece of kidney and a piece of mushroom.   Set aside on a floured plate.

Take a large pudding basin and rub it with garlic.   Roll out the suet crust and line the basin with it, leaving a small quantity of dough for the top.   Place the rolls of steak carefully in the basin, packing them as closely together as possible.

Add any remaining pieces of kidney and mushroom and pour in the stock.   Cover the pudding with a lid made from the remaining dough.   Cover the basin with buttered paper and a pudding cloth. Tie this down tightly and steam for 4 hours - do not let the water go off the slow boil.

For the Suet Crust

1 lb (450 g) flour

1 tsp salt

½ lb (225 g) best beef suet, chopped

Sift the flour with the salt and stir in the suet.   Mix lightly with the fingertips.   Slowly add enough water to mix to a soft dough.   Put aside on a floured board until required.   (It should rest a while before being rolled).

Fanny's Moussaka

2 lb (1 kg) aubergines, sliced*
olive or peanut oil, for
  frying
1 lb (500 g) mixed pork and beef
  fillet, minced

½ onion, grate
salt and peppe
1 egg, lightly beaten
2-3 tbs sour cream
butter

For the batter
½ lb (225 g) flour
2 eggs

3 fl oz (75 ml) peanut oil
¾ pint (450 ml) milk or water

For the topping
2 eggs
12 fl oz (350 ml) creamy milk
  or single cream

salt
3-4 tbs grated Parmesan cheese

1. Make the batter and let it stand.

2. Dip the sliced aubergines in the batter and fry in oil.
    Drain on kitchen paper.

3. Sauté the meat and onion in oil for 15-20 minutes, but do
    not let it get too dry. Turn frequently. Season well
    with salt and pepper. Simmer until tender then take off
    the heat. Cool.

4. When it is cool mix in the beaten egg and a little sour
    cream.

5. Take a deep fireproof earthenware dish, grease it with butter
    and put one layer of aubergines at the bottom of it, then a
    layer of mince and then one of aubergines, and so on, until
    you finish with the layer of aubergines.

6. For the topping, break the eggs into a bowl and add the milk
    to them; mix together with a little salt. Pour over the
    moussaka and put immediately into a very hot oven, 450°F
    (230°C) gas mark 8.

7. Bake for 15-20 minutes.

8. Grate a little Parmesan over the top and serve.

*   It is not necessary to 'sweat' aubergines for a moussaka
    if they are fresh and young.

Madame Rafo Ivancevic

RHODA'S BABY BURGERS WITH MUSHROOM AND SOUR CREAM SAUCE

1½ lb (700 g) finely minced steak
  with as little fat as possible
2 onions, very finely chopped
1 tsp English mustard

salt and pepper
a little flour
fat or lard

The sauce

1 garlic clove, crushed
1½ tbs butter
2 tbs sherry or white wine
1 lb (500 g) mushrooms, wiped

clean and sliced T-shaped
squeeze of lemon juice
½ pint (300 ml) sour cream

Combine steak, onions and mustard. Season well. Shape into little balls with floured hands and flatten into little patties no more than 1½ inches (4 cm) in diameter on a lightly floured board. Sear the burgers in a very hot dry pan that you lightly grease with a small piece of fat or lard. When one side is brown, turn and cook the other. Finish under the grill - they should be brown and crusty outside and just pink inside.

For the sauce, fry the garlic in the butter until translucent, add the sherry or wine and boil until the alcohol evaporates. Add the sliced mushrooms and lemon juice and cook, covered, for 3-4 minutes. Pour on the sour cream, heat up, and then pour the sauce round and over the burgers, which you have arranged neatly in a silver entrée dish. Sauté potatoes go well with this dish.

ROAST RIBS OF BEEF STRACHUR

Roast a well-hung rib of beef (allow 5-6 lb (2.25-2.75 kg for 8) as you like it best, but do not overcook it. It should be definitely pink.

Serve on a large ashet (the old Scottish word for platter, derived from the French word 'assiette') with half the meat cut in fairly thick pieces, and surround the dish with small very short pastry tartlets, filled alternatively with a good mushroom duxelles and a creamed spinach purée. Hand Béarnaise Sauce in a sauceboat.

PICADINHO DE PELOTAS

1 lb (500 g) lean beef, chopped	2 hard-boiled eggs, chopped
1 tbs beef dripping	3 oz (75 g) raisins
1 onion, chopped	butter
2 tomatoes, chopped	dry bread slices
salt and pepper	milk
herbs, to taste	2 eggs
¼ pint (150 ml) meat stock	1 tbs sugar
olives	breadcrumbs

The meat, preferably topside, should be finely chopped by hand or machine-ground as coarsely as possible. Melt the dripping and sauté the meat with the onion, tomatoes, salt, pepper and herbs. After the meat is well browned, add enough meat stock to moisten, and then cover the saucepan and reduce heat to moderate. When cooked, and the liquid quite evaporated, add a few olives, hard-boiled eggs, and some raisins.

Butter a baking dish and pile in the chopped beef. Soak slices of dry bread in milk, and place on top of the meat. Beat the eggs with the sugar and pour over all. Sprinkle with breadcrumbs, dot with butter and bake in the oven, $375^\circ F$ ($190^\circ C$) gas mark 5, for 20 minutes to brown the topping.

H.E. Senhora da Costa

Pastičada Korčulanska

A Dalmatian recipe from the island of Korčula.

$3\frac{1}{2}$ lb (1.5 kg) piece of best topside,
  without fat
good wine vinegar
2-4 garlic cloves
4 inch (10 cm) piece of green bacon
flour
2 large onions
2 large carrots
$\frac{1}{4}$ pint (150 ml) olive oil
3-4 cloves

pinch of nutmeg
2 tsp sugar
$\frac{1}{4}$ pint (150 ml) Prosek (a Korčulan
  sweet wine), madeira or sweet
  sherry
6 oz (175 g) prunes, soaked and
  stoned
$\frac{1}{2}$ pint (300 ml) good homemade
  tomato sugo

<u>Sugo</u>   Fresh or tinned tomatoes, onions, celery, carrot, sugar, herbs, olive
        oil and good strong broth, all simmered together for several hours.

Marinate the beef in a bowl for 24 hours, using enough wine vinegar to
cover it.   Turn the meat over once or twice during this period.   Remove
it and pat it dry with a clean cloth.   Cut the garlic into thin slivers.
Cut the bacon into larding strips about 2 inches (5 cm) long and the
thickness of a pencil.
        Make a deep slit in the <u>side</u> of the meat with the tip of a sharp knife.
Insert a piece of bacon and a sliver of garlic into this slit, pushing them
both well into the centre of the meat.   Continue larding all the way round
the sides and then see if you can fit in another row, maybe above or below
the first one, but do not pierce the top or bottom surface of the meat.
        When all the bacon and garlic is used up and the meat is fit to
burst, put some flour on a plate and flour both sides of the fillet well.
Chop the onions and carrots roughly and put them into a heavy iron or enamel
casserole with the olive oil.   Add the cloves, nutmeg and sugar.   When
the onions have softened but not darkened add the meat and sauté it well,
turning it over several times until it is well coloured on every side.
This will take about 10 minutes.   Add the wine and let it cook a little
longer, turning it over once more.
        Pour in the tomato sugo (enough to cover the meat well).   Cook for
a few minutes, then add the prunes, stir and cover the pan.   Continue
cooking gently over low heat until the meat is tender - about 2 hours.   You
can top up the sauce with more sugo or a little stock if necessary.
        Take the fillet out and put it on a flat hot serving dish.   Slice
it vertically about the thickness of a little finger, so that each piece
shows circles of larding.
        Surround it with previously cooked potato gnocchi*, or noodles,
then pour half the rich, dark sauce over the meat.   Serve the remaining
sauce separately.

* see recipe on page 58

Madame Anka Arneric

Strachur House,
Argyll.
Tel. Strachur 242.

RHODA'S POT ROAST

3 lb (1.5 kg) piece of rolled beef (sirloin, silverside or
  brisket, tied tight by the butcher)
dripping
salt and pepper
¼ pint (150 ml) boiling water
¼ pint (150 ml) red wine
6 carrots, chopped
3 onions, halved or quartered (if you have them, baby
  pickling onions are best of all - 15-20 of them)
3 celery sticks, chopped
3 parsnips, peeled and chopped
6 small white turnips, chopped
bouquet garni
stock

    Fry the meat on all sides in good dripping until well
coloured and sealed. This should take about 15-20 minutes.
    Place the meat in a deep ovenproof casserole - cast
iron is excellent as it cooks slowly and evenly. Season
well.
    Deglaze the frying pan with boiling water and red wine.
Let it all boil up then pour it over the meat in the
casserole.
    Put the casserole, covered into the oven, 300°F (150°C)
gas mark 2, and let it just simmer for 2-2½ hours.
    Remove the casserole from the oven and add the carrots,
onions, celery, parsnips, turnips and the bouquet garni.
Now cover the vegetables with good home-made hot stock -
use water and a stock cube, only if necessity demands it.
Re-cover the casserole and put it back in the oven for another
45 minutes or until the vegetables are cooked.
    The meat is then taken from the casserole, carved in
thick slices, re-assembled on a hot entrée dish and surrounded
by the vegetables. The sauce is poured over and a good purée
of potatoes accompanies this delectable and comforting dish.

NOTE If you wish the sauce to be thicker, you can mix 1 tbs
      flour or 1 tsp arrowroot with the same amount of
      butter and let this melt down the sides of the casserole
      once you have taken out the meat, while you stir briskly.
      But I like it the way it is.

RAGOÛT DE VEAU À LA RAMESES

2 oz (50 g) butter
¼ lb (100 g) streaky bacon rashers
2 large onions, sliced into rings
a bay leaf, sprig of thyme and
  parsley tied together

salt and pepper
2 lb (1 kg) veal, cut
  into pieces
½ pint (300 ml) sour cream

Melt the butter in a saucepan with a tight-fitting lid.   Place
the bacon on the top of the butter so as to cover the bottom
of the pan.   Add the onions and the bunch of herbs.   Put the
pan on the heat and leave it uncovered.   Season the veal well
on both sides.   When the contents of the pan begin to smoke,
add the meat.   Cover and cook over a low heat for 1½ hours.
Remove the pieces of veal and bacon with a fork; put them on
a hot dish and throw away the bouquet of herbs.   Put the pan
on the heat again and add the sour cream, stirring constantly.
Pour the sauce, which is now a golden brown, through a strainer
over the meat, and serve at once, with a dish of boiled rice.

Joy Rainbird

VEAL CASSEROLE FOR A PARTY - it serves 20

8 lb (3.5 kg) veal rump
¼ lb (100 g) butter
4 tbs flour
oregano
chervil
salt and pepper
2 large onions, sliced and sautéed
6 oz (175 g) coarsely chopped
  celery
8 fl oz (225 ml) white wine

8 fl oz (225 ml) stock
2 oz (50 g) tomato purée
2 bay leaves
1 lb (500 g) small mushrooms
1½ lb (750 g) frozen baby
  lima beans, thawed
½ pint (300 ml) double cream
½ lb (225 g) bacon, fried
  crisp

Preheat the oven to 300°F (150°C) gas mark 2.   Remove all
gristle and skin from veal, cut it into 1 inch (2.5 cm) cubes
and brown it all over in half the butter.   Sprinkle flour
and seasonings over the meat and mix them in well.   Sauté
the onions and celery in a large casserole in the remaining
butter, then add the wine, stock, tomato purée, bay leaves and
browned meat.   Bake uncovered for 1½-2 hours.   Add more wine
and stock if necessary.   Stir well, add the mushrooms and
lima beans and the cream.   Bake 30-40 minutes longer.   Before
serving, crumble the bacon over the top.

Filet de Veau au Poivre Vert

1 lb (500 g) pickling onions

2-3 tbs butter

1 lb (500 g) mushrooms, wiped and sliced

salt and pepper

6 veal tournedos cut from the fillet, 1½-2 inches (4-5 cm)
   thick, prepared by the butcher with a piece of fat bacon
   tied around the edge

4 fl oz (100 ml) cognac or armagnac

½ lb (225 g) canned green peppers, drained

scant ½ pint (300 ml) good white wine

2 tbs double cream

In a sauté pan fry the little onions gently in butter
until they are golden and nearly soft. Add the sliced
mushrooms and season well. Remove both to a warm dish
and keep hot. Add some more butter to the juices in
the pan and gently sauté the tournedos in it. Let them
colour well on both sides, then remove the string and
bacon and flame them with the brandy that you have heated
in a little saucepan. Now add the green peppers and
the white wine. Let all simmer together for about
5 minutes, then return the mushrooms and the onions to
the pan and finally add the cream. Serve in a very hot
dish with either spinach en branche or Riz à la Créole
(see page 262) to accompany it.

VALDOSTANE DI VITELLO

8 thin veal escalopes

salt and pepper

½ lb (225 g) Philadelphia
   cream cheese

3 tbs freshly grated Parmesan

1½ tbs finely chopped chives

3-5 tbs double cream

4 slices prosciutto (raw Parma ham)

flour

3-5 tbs butter

¼ pint (150 ml) dry white wine

Pound the veal very thinly and season with salt and pepper. Combine the
cream cheese, Parmesan and chives with enough double cream to make a smooth,
spreadable pommade. Place a slice of prosciutto on each of 4 veal
escalopes and spread this generously with cheese mixture. Cover with the
other 4 escalopes and pound the edges of both firmly together. Dip the
now double escalopes in flour and sauté them in butter in a large, shallow
flameproof casserole until well browned on both sides. Add the white
wine, cover and simmer gently for 15-20 minutes, or until the veal is
tender. Serve with a creamy spinach purée and a green salad.

The Hon. Mrs. Robin Allen

VEAL WITH CREAM AND CUCUMBER

1 medium cucumber

¼ lb (100 g) butter

4 veal escalopes

3 fl oz (75 ml) dry white wine

¼ pint (150 ml) cream

a pinch of paprika

salt and pepper

Skin the cucumber and cut it into 1 inch (2.5 cm) long pieces. Steam
these for about 10-15 minutes or until al dente. Drain and keep warm.
Melt half the butter in a frying pan and add the escalopes, which have
been beaten thin and flat. Brown them gently on both sides and then
remove them and keep hot. Deglaze the pan with the wine, scraping it
well to get all the juices together, boil to reduce, then add the cream,
paprika, salt and pepper. Bring to the boil and cook rapidly for a few
minutes to thicken it. Then draw the pan to the edge of the heat, add
the rest of the butter in small pieces and the cooked cucumber. Just
let it heat up and then pour over the escalopes.

Veau aux Noix

3½ tbs butter
2 onions, minced
2 carrots, minced
1 celery stick, minced
2½ lb (1.25 kg) boned and rolled
   loin or rump of veal

salt and pepper
tarragon and parsley
½ pint (300 ml) good white stock
4 tbs chopped walnuts mixed with
   1½ tbs crumbled Roquefort cheese
¼ pint (150 ml) double cream

Melt the butter in the casserole, and brown the onions, carrots, celery and veal in it. When the meat is browned on all sides, season and add the herbs with the stock. Cover and let it cook slowly for 2-2¼ hours. Let the meat cool. Untie and unroll it, spread the stuffing of walnuts and cheese in the middle. Re-roll and tie into a compact bundle. Return it to the casserole and cook for another 1 hour. Place the meat on a fireproof serving dish. Strain the casserole juices over the meat, pour on the cream, and put it under the grill for a minute or two to brown the top. Serve immediately. A Jerusalem artichoke or spinach purée would be good with this.

Mrs. David Sutherland

FRICANDEAU DE VEAU À L'OSEILLE (Veal with a sorrel purée)

2 oz (50 g) fat bacon
½ lb (225 g) button onions
2 carrots
3 lb (1.5 kg) veal (this should be a long piece
   cut from the leg or from the oyster)
¼ pint (150 ml) white wine
1 pint (600 ml) stock
bouquet of herbs
1 garlic clove, crushed
salt and pepper
2 lb (1 kg) sorrel, cleaned and spined
2 oz (50 g) butter
½ oz (15 g) cornflour
1 egg
4 tbs cream
8 fl oz (225 ml) béchamel sauce

Veal Line the bottom of a cocotte with the bacon, scatter in
the onions and sliced carrots. Lard the veal (if possible get
this done for you at the 'French boucherie' counter of a good
butchers), lay it on top, and shake over a brisk heat until the
meat is beginning to brown. Add the wine, stock, herbs and
garlic. Bring to the boil, season then braise in the oven
without the lid, 325°F (160°C) gas mark 3, for about 1¼ hours,
basting well.

Sorrel Purée Put the wet sorrel in a pan without water, and
bash it down with a wooden spoon. Cover the pan, let it
simmer and bash it again. In 3-4 minutes it will be a purée.
Beat in the butter, sprinkle over a very little cornflour, and
cook for a few minutes, season it, then let it 'rest' for
30 minutes in a warm place to lose some of its acidity. Just
before serving, beat in the egg, cream and béchamel sauce,
correct the seasoning and warm up.

To Serve Spoon the sorrel over the bottom of a long dish,
cut the veal into slices, and arrange it on top. Take out
the bacon and herbs, skim the gravy, and reduce it to a syrupy
consistency. Pour this over and round the dish. The gravy
for the fricandeau is not as a rule strained, but of course it
can be so if desired.

Escalopes de Veau
Brunette

4 veal escalopes from fillet
salt and pepper
butter
$\frac{1}{2}$ lb (225 g) mushrooms, cut
  into long strips

1 small garlic clove,
  crushed
1 tbs chopped parsley
$\frac{1}{4}$ pint (150 ml) brandy
$\frac{1}{4}$ pint (150 ml) cream

Beat the veal escalopes to the size of a small saucer.
Remove any fat or skin. Season with salt and pepper.
Melt the butter in a sauté pan, and when sizzling hot, add
the veal. Cook for about 5 minutes, shaking the pan.
Cook the mushrooms in butter and a very little garlic to
bring out their flavour. Stir them in to the meat and
continue cooking. Scatter the parsley over the veal,
which has now been cooking for 8-10 minutes. Heat the
brandy in a little pan, then light it, and pour it over
the meat, holding both pans at arm's length.

Keep off the heat until the first flare up dies down, and
then return it, shaking the pan to keep the now subdued
flame going - when it goes out pour in the cream.

Stir all up together for a few seconds more over the heat
until the cream has thickened and the veal is ready.

It is important to follow the timing of this recipe, which
is easy and delicious.

Marjorie Salter and Adrien Allen Whitney from Delicious Food

Côte de Veau Guizot

2 oz (50 g) butter
8-12 mushrooms, sliced
6 shallots, or equivalent
  onions, finely chopped
salt and pepper
4 veal cutlets

4 tbs breadcrumbs
4 tbs grated cheese, half
  Parmesan and half Cheddar
about ½ pint (300 ml) white wine
finely chopped fresh parsley

Take an earthenware or glass oven dish and butter the bottom.
Sprinkle over the sliced mushrooms and the chopped shallots.
Season well.   Trim and season the veal cutlets and arrange
them on the mushroom bed.   Mix together the breadcrumbs
and grated cheese and cover each cutlet.   Dot with remaining
butter.   Add white wine up to the level of the cutlets.
Do not cover the cutlets as the butter and juice from the
mushrooms form a natural sauce with the wine.   Bake in a
preheated oven, 400°F (200°C) gas mark 6, for about 45
minutes until tender and the breadcrumbs and cheese have
formed a golden crust.   The cutlets should never be dry.
Baste occasionally and add extra wine if evaporation is
too quick.   When cooked, garnish with chopped parsley.

THE CAPTAIN'S PARADISE, or

RISSOLES DE MÉNAGE WITH SAUCE ESPAGNOLE

12 oz (350 g) veal fillet, cooked
½ lb (225 g) mushrooms, finely chopped
butter
2 cooked sheep's brains (cleaned, skinned and poached
   in a little stock), chopped and mixed with 1 tbs bechamel
1 egg white, stiffly beaten
2 egg yolks
salt and pepper
2 oz (50 g) fresh white breadcrumbs
oil or fat for deep-frying
bunch of parsley

Trim the veal of all fat, skin and sinew. Chop finely
or mince. Sauté the chopped mushrooms for a minute or
two in a closed saucepan with a little butter. Combine
veal and mushrooms with the sheep's brains. Fold in a
stiffly beaten egg white and refrigerate for at least
1 hour. Form into rissole shapes on a lightly floured
board.

Dip into beaten egg yolks which you have seasoned with
very little salt and pepper. Roll in breadcrumbs and
plunge in smoking hot oil or fat until golden.

Serve at once with a bunch of deep-fried parsley in the
centre of the dish.

The sauce should be of your own choosing, but a good sauce
must accompany this dish if it is to be lifted into the
'paradise' class: a beurre noisette or a beurre noire
would be good, but rich: a tomato sauce would be good,
but perhaps overpowering. I think a Sauce Espagnole in
which you increase the usual amount of tomato purée
would be best of all.

Mrs. Cockerill

Spinach and Sweetbread Timbale

3 lb (1.5 kg) spinach
1½ lb (700 g) sweetbreads, calves'
  or large, plump lambs'
salt and pepper
veal or chicken stock
about ¼ lb (100 g) cooked ham, cut
  from the bone and then into strips
3 large eggs

grated nutmeg
2 oz (50 g) grated Parmesan cheese
2 oz (50 g) grated Cheddar cheese
butter
1 heaped tbs flour
¼ pint (150 ml) milk
4-6 tbs cream
¼ pint (150 ml) dry white wine

Vegetable 'pains' and 'sformatos' which one often meets with in France and Italy are neglected dishes in Britain. If you have a blender or food processor, Jane Grigson's recipe for this delicious and delicate entrée is easy to make.

Prepare the spinach purée and sweetbreads in advance - the day before if you like - and store them in a refrigerator. Wash and cook the spinach and tip it into a sieve. Drain it thoroughly (very important) and then chop it roughly. Soak the sweetbreads in salted water for an hour, drain and rinse them. Put them into a pan and cover generously with barely seasoned stock. Bring to the boil; lambs' sweetbreads will then need 5 minutes, calves' 15-20 minutes depending on size (be guided by their appearance, the sweetbreads should be opaque, firm yet yielding, not pink and raw looking). Drain the sweetbreads, keeping the stock. Rinse under the cold tap, then remove all bits of gristle and thick skin. Cut into slices or pieces and leave between two plates to become cold and firm, overnight if desired.

To make the spinach timbale: put spinach, ham and eggs into the blender, or processor, and reduce them to a purée. Season with salt and pepper and nutmeg Mix the cheeses, and add about two-thirds to the spinach; turn into a generously buttered ring mould (the mixture may rise a very little, but it does not behave like a soufflé and shoot up). Smooth over the top and cover it with buttered foil. Stand in a pan of very hot water. Put this into the oven, preheated to 475°F (240°C) gas mark 9, and leave for 10 minutes, then switch off the heat and leave in the oven, keeping the door shut, until the sauce and sweetbreads are ready.

To make the sauce: start the moment you put the spinach into the oven, by melting a generous tbs of butter in a pan, and stirring in the flour. After 2 minutes moisten with ½ pint (300 ml) stock from the sweetbreads, the milk and cream. Boil down steadily, stirring occasionally to make sure the sauce is not sticking, or whisking with a balloon whisk.

To make the sweetbread ragoût: start the sweetbreads once the sauce can be left; fry them rapidly to a nice brown in butter. Pour in the wine, and a slightly smaller quantity of the stock. Raise the heat so that these liquids reduce to a small amount of sauce that glazes the meat, with a spoonful of juice or two left in the pan.

Now remove the timbale from its water bath. It should feel firm to the touch, but not hard. Ease round the edges, not forgetting the inner edges and invert a hot serving dish over the mould. Put the sweetbread ragoût into the centre. Stir the remaining cheese into the sauce, pour some over the spinach and serve the rest in a sauceboat.

Jane Grigson

Lamb and Mutton

THE BRITISH EMBASSY, PARIS
Home of the Dukes of Charost and Pauline Borghese
Acquired as the British Embassy in 1814

Gigot d'Agneau Viennoise

a good-sized leg of lamb, not too fat
1¼ pints (750 ml) or 1 bottle red wine
2 garlic cloves, crushed
sprig of rosemary
½ tsp basil
sprig of thyme
pinch of allspice

6 carrots, sliced
3 tomatoes, sliced
3 large onions, chopped
3 apples, cored and chopped
6 oz (175 g) raisins
salt and pepper
½ pint (300 ml) double cream

Marinate the lamb in the wine, garlic, rosemary, basil, thyme and allspice, for 24 hours. Turn once or twice. Prepare the vegetables and apples and arrange these on the bottom of a baking pan, sprinkle the raisins on top and add salt and pepper.

Place the joint on this bed of vegetables and strain the marinade over the top. Cook slowly at 350°F (180°C) gas mark 4, for 2½ hours (or 3 hours if you like it well done). Transfer the joint to a serving dish, and keep hot in the oven while you make a sauce. For the sauce, use half of the cooking liquid. First, sieve or liquidize the now thick mush at the bottom of the pan. Put half the liquid and the sieved mixture into a saucepan and bring it to the boil. Cook until very thick. Add the rest of the cooking liquid a little at a time (you may not need it all). Reduce heat. Blend in the cream and reheat. Serve in a sauceboat. This is a very rich dish, with a delicious sauce, so when planning the menu, choose a light first course, and simple pudding.

Noisettes de Mouton Maison

2 chicken livers, and/or a slice of
  calves' liver
2 garlic cloves
1 shallot
a little chopped fatty bacon
butter

4 tbs port or red wine
bread
oil
6 rashers streaky bacon
salt and pepper
6 noisettes of lamb, 1" thick

Emulsify the livers, garlic, shallot and bacon in a food mill. Sauté in a little butter. Add the port or red wine. Simmer until reduced to a smooth paste. Cool. Fry rounds of bread in hot oil, drain, cool and spread with this paste.

Tie a bacon rasher round each noisette with a fine piece of string. Sauté the noisettes in the usual way in a little butter and oil, and when cooked, put one on each liver croustade.

The Countess of Eldon

Spring Leg of Lamb à l'Armentienne

1 leg of lamb

3½ oz (90 g) butter, melted

thyme

bay leaf

rosemary

dried fennel

salt

4 garlic cloves

2 oz (50 g) chopped parsley

2 oz (50 g) white breadcrumbs

¼ pint (150 ml) milk

pepper

new potatoes

3 tbs cream

Put the leg in a roasting tin. Pour on melted butter and sprinkle with herbs. Put in a hot oven, 400°F (200°C) gas mark 6, for 30-40 minutes. Salt halfway through the roasting. Meanwhile, very finely chop the garlic and parsley, and mix them into the breadcrumbs, which you have soaked in the milk. Add pepper and salt and spread this mixture on to the leg about 10 minutes before you take it out of the oven. Pour some more melted butter over it before serving. New potatoes cut into rounds are served separately. Pour the cream over them before dishing up.

Swedish Cutlets

6 lamb cutlets

1 egg, beaten

2 oz (50 g) white breadcrumbs

2 oz (50 g) butter

3 lb (1.5 kg) tart apples

¼ pint (150 ml) dry white wine

2 oz (50 g) finely grated horseradish

scant ½ pint (300 ml) double cream

Egg and breadcrumb the cutlets in the usual way and sauté them in butter until cooked, but just pink inside. Have ready a purée of apples that you have made by stewing the apples in white wine and a little butter, and then sieving them. Add to this purée finely grated raw horseradish and a little double cream. Turn the purée into a hot entrée dish and lay the cutlets on top of it.

BOLTON HOT-POT - A Lancashire classic

2 lb (1 kg) middle neck of mutton
1 oz (25 g) dripping
1 onion, sliced
1 heaped tbs flour
¾ pint (450 ml) hot stock
salt and pepper

1 tsp caster sugar
2 kidneys, cored
4-5 mushrooms
12 oysters
2 lb (1 kg) potatoes

Cut the meat into chops.   Melt the dripping in a pan and
brown the meat in it.   Lift it out and put it into a brown
Staffordshire pot that·can be sent to table, or if you prefer
it, a deep fireproof baking dish with a lid.   Stew the onion
until soft in the dripping.   Add the flour and cook it until
it is nicely brown.   Add the hot stock to the pan and stir
until it thickens.   Season to taste with salt and pepper and
sugar.

Slice the kidneys thickly over the mutton.   Add the mushrooms,
peeled, and, if large, cut to small size.   Add the oysters
(all these in separate layers).   Peel the potatoes;   cut
them in thick slices and arrange them overlapping round the top
of the meat, etc., with the knobbly ends in the centre to cover
the contents of the pot completely.   Strain the thickened
stock over the potatoes, put on the lid and stew in a moderate
oven, 350°F (180°C) gas mark 4, for 2 hours.   Take off the lid
during the last 15 minutes to brown the potatoes nicely.   This
recipe makes a small hot-pot.   Quantities should be doubled
for 6-8 people except for the oysters and potatoes, which should
be only slightly increased.

And here is an 18th century down-market version, which, from a
literary point of view, is one of my favourite recipes:

Beggar's Dish

"Cut a loin of mutton into chops, take off almost all the fat,
then season it with pepper and salt, shred an onion small, then
put it in, a layer of potatoes and a layer of mutton till all
is in, add a pint of water, cover it close, let it stew ¾ of
an hour, less won't do it, and more won't hurt it".

Elizabeth Raper

Côtelettes de Mouton à la Villeroy

6 mutton or lamb cutlets
1 oz (25 g) butter
1 heaped tbs flour
8 fl oz (225 ml) milk
2 egg yolks
¼ pint (150 ml) cream

For the coating
flour
1 egg
breadcrumbs
1 oz (25 g) butter
1 tbs olive or peanut oil

Take some small mutton or lamb cutlets, half grill them and let them cool.
Melt the butter in a small saucepan.   Stir in the flour to make a roux.
Stir in the milk and cook, stirring with a wooden spoon until it thickens.
Remove from the heat and add the egg yolks and the cream.

Dip the cutlets into this sauce, which should be thick enough to entirely
cover the meat, and let it cool on them.   Then dip them in flour, then in
egg, and then in breadcrumbs.

Melt some butter in a frying pan, and add the oil.   When very hot, fry the
cutlets until golden brown and serve them on a creamy purée of potatoes,
with a green salad to accompany.

Aunt Mary's Lamb Pie

4 lb (1.75 kg) boned loin of lamb
½ tsp ground mace
½ tsp freshly grated nutmeg
1 tsp flour
salt and pepper
shortcrust pastry, made with
   1 lb (500 g) flour etc.

¼ lb (100 g) currants
¼ lb (100 g) raisins
50 g (2 oz) butter, melted
water
½ pint (300 ml) strong sweet white
   wine, hot

Cut the lamb into thin small pieces.   Mix mace, nutmeg, flour, salt and pepper
together and dust on both sides of the lamb with it.   Take a deep buttered
pie dish and line the side and base with pastry.   Put in a layer of meat,
then a layer of currants and raisins.   Continue in this way until all the
ingredients are used, ending with a layer of meat.   Pour the melted butter
over this and add just enough water to keep it moist.   Put the pastry on
top and cook in a hot oven, 400°F (200°C) gas mark 6, for 15 minutes, then
reduce the heat to moderate, 350°F (180°C) gas mark 4 and cook for 1½ hours.
Remove from the oven, carefully take off the pastry top and pour in the hot
wine.   Move the meat about very carefully with a fork so that the wine is
evenly distributed.   Place the crust back on and reheat for 10 minutes,
then serve.

This is a delicious and unusual dish, but make sure the pastry is very 'short'
and light.

Joy Rainbird

Rhoda's Rolled Lamb Maison

1 boned rolled loin of lamb (about 8-10 chops before boning)
½ tsp rosemary

Stuffing

2 bacon rashers, fried and chopped
3-4 shallots, finely chopped
1 heaped tbs finely chopped parsley
2 tsp mixed herbs
salt and pepper
6 oz (175 g) butter

Mix the bacon, shallots, parsley, herbs, a little salt and pepper and the butter together. Spread the lamb out flat and sprinkle the inside of the meat sparingly with rosemary. Spread the stuffing evenly over it and roll up. Tie it firmly with string, or with skewers, and roast it wrapped in foil with a spoonful of fat for about 1 hour, in a moderately hot oven, 375°F (190°C) gas mark 5.

When cooked, cut it into ½ inch (1 cm) slices and serve it with a gravy made from the meat juices that you will find when you unwrap the foil.

Mrs. Cockerill

Hind Quarter of Lamb with Spinach, 1759

1 leg of lamb, including shank
1¾ pints (1 litre) milk
salt and pepper
6 onions
1 oz (25 g) flour
2-3 lemons

1 oz (25 g) suet
bunch of parsley
1 lb (500 g) spinach
1 pint (600 ml) double cream
½ oz (15 g) butter
pinch of grated nutmeg

"Take a hind quarter of lamb, truss in the knuckles neatly, put it in soak for two or three hours in some milk, a little salt, two or three onions and parsley. Then put it in boiling water, skim it well, put in some flour and water well mixed, a lemon or two pared and sliced, a bit of suet and a bunch of onions and parsley, stir it well from the bottom and boil it gently; these ingredients will make it white as curd.

Clean and wash your spinach in several waters, then put it into a pint of cream, a bit of butter mixed with flour, a little pepper, salt and a pinch of nutmeg, stir it on a stove till it is a nice consistency, squeeze in the juice of a lemon, put it on a dish and lay the lamb upon it, but first drain off any fat and water and take off any of the seasonings that may chance to hang to it".

MOUTON À LA SUEDOISE

1¼ tbs mustard

1¼ tbs salt

1¼ tbs sugar

1 leg of mutton, not too fat

enough milk to cover meat

1-2 tbs cream

Mix together the mustard, salt and sugar·, and rub well into
the mutton.   Leave for 24 hours.   Then put the mutton into
a deep saucepan and cover it with milk.   Leave it like this
for 2 or 3 days.   Take it out and roast it, in the ordinary
way, basting it well.   Serve it with the gravy it has cooked
in, to which you should add a little cream.

POACHED LEG OF LAMB

6-7 lb (2.75-3 kg) leg of lamb

1 tbs salt

8 tbs ground black pepper

10 garlic cloves, crushed

12 juniper berries

2 sprigs of rosemary

3 tbs chopped chervil or
   parsley

Have the butcher trim the lamb of all fat and remove the
protruding bone.   Weigh it after this to gauge cooking time.
Wrap the leg in double-thick cheesecloth and sew it up.
Partially fill a large pan with water and bring it to the
boil.   Add salt, pepper, garlic, juniper berries, herbs and
lamb.   Simmer, slightly uncovered, allowing 15 minutes per
lb (30 minutes per kg).   Remove the lamb and cut away the
cloth.   Carve as usual; the meat should be pink in the
centre.   Serve with Béarnaise sauce and boiled new potatoes.
This is also superb eaten cold.

H.E. Madame Belfrage

SHOULDER OF LAMB TABRIZ

(Rice, apricots, raisins, and spice stuffing)

Remove the blade bone (sharp knife and a little patient endurance) from a shoulder of lamb. Or persuade the butcher to do it for you. Boil 8 oz of rice in the usual way. When it is cooked 'al dente', drain it and add:

> 4 oz dried apricots, soaked and roughly chopped
> 2½ tbs. seedless raisins
> 2½ tbs. blanched, split almonds
> ¾ tsp. each cinnamon, coriander and ginger
> salt and black pepper

Use some of this mixture to stuff the shoulder cavity, then sew it up with needle and thread. Roast the lamb in the usual way and serve the remaining rice etc. reheated round the joint. Green vegetables should be kept for a separate course before or after this dish.* Use the juices of the meat to moisten the rice mixture after pouring off the fat.

NB. For this receipt use the little dried apricots from Afghanistan that can be bought at Asian food stores. They have a very aromatic flavour.

* but a side dish of Tunisian carrots and baby onions as on page   would go with it very well.

FOSCOMBE
ASHLEWORTH
GLOUCESTER
GL19 4JN

TELEPHONE 045 270 213

COLD CUTLETS IN ASPIC

1 best end loin of lamb (about 10 cutlets)
1 pint (600 ml) veal or chicken aspic
1 tsp sugar
2 tbs wine vinegar
4 tbs finely chopped fresh mint
1 tsp commercial aspic, if necessary

To garnish
petit pois
mayonnaise

Braise or roast the lamb, and when cold, trim into nice cutlets,
not too thick.   Melt the aspic and flavour it with the sugar,
vinegar and mint.   If you think it is not firm enough, reinforce
it with a little commercial aspic.   When the aspic has cooled
but is still just liquid, stir it well and pour a thin layer into
a flat shallow tin or tray and refrigerate.   When very nearly set
press the cutlets into it and pour more of the just liquid mint
aspic on to them so as to barely cover them.   Refrigerate again.
Then, when the aspic is set and stiff, run a sharp knife round the
outline of each cutlet so as to cut it free from the surrounding jelly.
Hold a cloth wrung out in warm water under the tin, and the cut out
cutlets will separate easily.   Set them carefully on a flat serving
dish, spoon a wreath of peas mixed with mayonnaise, or peas dressed
with oil and tarragon vinegar, round the edge of the dish and
garnish the space between the cutlets and the peas with the
remainder of the aspic chopped up.

Have a large wooden bowl of green salad with sliced cucumber,
avocado and lettuce hearts dressed with vinaigrette and fresh herbs
to accompany the cutlets - and a loaf of homemade brown bread and
farm butter to eat with them.

N.B.   Strawberries and cream to follow?

Mrs. Derek Marlowe

GRILLED CALVES' LIVER SUPREME

This has become a fashionable dish in the best London restaurants simply because it is now cooked in the correct continental way and not stewed into the old boot soles we have all been brought up on.

Only the very best bits of fresh calves' liver should be used with every hard bit of gristle and skin and veins removed. Cut the remaining liver into very thin slivers with a razor sharp knife. Salt and pepper each piece and paint it with 2 tbs melted butter into which you have squeezed the juice of 1 lemon. Grill under a medium hot grill for no more than 2 minutes each side. It is essential that the liver should remain pink and juicy inside. So experiment with a small piece till you get your timing and heat just right. Arrange on a hot plate and sprinkle with a little more of the butter/lemon mixture and some finely chopped parsley. If you do not have an efficient grill the liver can equally well be sautéed in a hot frying pan. In either case serve as soon as it is ready.

Fonds d'artichaut Royale

To dress up and accompany the above recipe, try arranging the thin slivers of liver in a circle round a "Fondation Royale" made from any of the following vegetables: fonds d'artichaut, spinach, salsify or Jerusalem artichokes. It is really a matter of personal preference or convenience which you choose. Make the Royale in a 1 pint (600 ml) dariole mould well in advance and turn it out on to a warm serving dish before you start grilling the liver.

Remember that this vegetable and egg preparation - which is made like a baked custard in a bain marie - must never boil, or your Royale will be as full of holes as a honeycomb. Apart from this incipient danger it is very easy and quick to prepare.

1 lb (500 g) fresh fonds d'artichauts or equivalent vegetables	1 tbs double cream
	3 eggs plus 1 egg yolk
2 tbs béchamel sauce	2 oz (50 g) butter

Make a purée with the fonds d'artichauts and bind them with the béchamel sauce. Rub through a nylon sieve. Add the cream and the beaten up eggs; pour into a buttered mould; place a buttered paper on top, and poach it by standing the mould in a pan containing hot water. Bring this water to the boil on top of the stove and then at once put the pan and its contents into a moderate oven, 350°F (180°C) gas mark 4, for about 30-40 minutes. When a clean skewer or the blade of a knife inserted into the Royale comes out clean it is ready. Allow it to cool a little before turning it out. Crisply grilled bacon can be crumbled over the top to garnish the Royale, according to taste. Use garnishes with discretion as they should not overpower the dish.

Pork, Ham and Tongue

ANTONIN CAREME
1784–1833
Cook to Prince Talleyrand,
the Emperor Alexander and the Baron Rothschild

PORK CHOPS SAVOY

4 tbs butter

6 thick pork chops

1 heaped tsp grated lemon rind

about ½ pint (300 ml) sherry
    or madeira

3 oz (75 g) sultanas

2 apples, peeled and diced

salt and pepper

Melt the butter and brown the chops on both sides quickly.
Add all the other ingredients, cover and simmer gently on
top of the stove for 30 minutes.   It can be cooked in the
oven at 350°F (180°C) gas mark 4, in which case it will take
1 hour.

Serve with new potatoes, spinach or green salad in a bowl.

Theodora Fitzgibbon

BAKED SWEET PORK CHOPS

4 large pork chops

3 oz (75 g) apricot purée*

3 oz (75 g) peach purée*

3 fl oz (75 ml) tomato ketchup

2 fl oz (50 ml) soy sauce

3 oz (75 g) brown sugar

3 fl oz (75 ml) white wine
    vinegar

¼ tsp ground ginger

2 garlic cloves, crushed

salt and pepper

2 bay leaves

Grill the chops to seal in the juices.   Then put them in a
flameproof dish.   Mix all the other ingredients and make sure
that they are well blended.   Pour the mixture over the chops
and cover with a lid.   Bake in a moderate oven, 350°F (180°C)
gas mark 4, for 1½ hours.   Serve with rice, boiled or fried,
mixed with a little coconut and sultanas.

* If you can find tins of puréed apricot and peach baby food,
  these are ideal.

MARINATED PORK

4-6 lb (1.75-2.75 kg) boned loin
   of pork
2 garlic cloves, crushed
pinch of sage
2 bay leaves
good pinch of cumin seeds
salt and pepper

1¼ pints (750 ml) or 1 bottle
   medium-sweet white wine
2 tbs olive oil
1 tbs lemon juice
1 tbs flour
¼ pint (150 ml) vegetable stock

Be sure to ask your butcher to score the crackling and to roll and tie the joint firmly. Put the joint on the bottom of a large casserole, sprinkle the garlic, herbs and salt and pepper over the meat. Pour the wine into the casserole and marinate for 24 hours, turning 2 or 3 times. When ready to cook, remove the joint from the marinade, wipe it dry and rub it all over with the oil and lemon juice. If any oil is left, pour it over the base of the pan, otherwise oil or grease the base of the pan with extra oil. Cook the joint at 450°F (230°C) gas mark 8, for 30 minutes. Reduce the heat to 350°F (180°C) gas mark 4 and continue cooking allowing 30 minutes per lb (1 hour per kg). When the pork is cooked, transfer the joint to its serving dish and make a gravy by putting the flour into the corner of the pan, tipping the pan slightly until enough liquid runs into it to make a roux. Then add the vegetable stock and ¼ pint (150 ml) of the strained marinade.

Blend well together, bring the resultant sauce to the boil and simmer for 10 minutes. If it is too thick, add more wine or stock, and season to taste.

Joy Rainbird

PORK IN MILK

1½ lb (700 g) pork, weighed after boning
1 oz (25 g) butter
2 onions, chopped
4 rashers streaky bacon

salt and pepper
oregano
2 pints (1.2 litres) milk
1 tsp cornflour (optional)

Bone the pork, remove any rind and tie it into a flat, long piece. Melt the butter in a flameproof casserole and cook the chopped onions in it until soft. Add the bacon, cut into strips and cook in the butter. Rub the pork with salt, pepper and a little oregano, and brown it in the butter, turning it to seal it on all sides. In another pan heat enough milk to cover the pork completely. When it boils, pour it over the pork and leave it to simmer until a skin forms on the top. Continue simmering without breaking the skin, for 1 hour and then stir the skin into the sauce. It may be necessary to top up the milk. Simmer for a further 45 minutes, stirring occasionally, and turning the meat to see that it doesn't catch on the bottom. If the meat is cooked, and the sauce is still too thin, remove the meat to a serving dish, keep it warm and boil the sauce to reduce it, adding a very little cornflour if you wish. Pour a little over the sliced meat and serve the rest in a sauceboat. A compote of hot stewed prunes and/or a purée of spinach sharpened with a handful of sorrel leaves make good companions to this dish.

Côte de Porc à la Flamande

4-6 pork chops, about 1 inch (2.5 cm) thick
salt and pepper
oil or butter
2 onions, sliced

½ pint (300 ml) white wine
½ pint (300 ml) stock
1¼ tbs butter
1¼ tbs flour
2½ tsp French mustard

Season the chops, brown them in oil or butter and transfer them to a flameproof casserole fitted with a lid.   Pour off most of the fat in the pan, leaving just enough to cook the onions.   Add the white wine and the stock and cook, stirring, for 1 minute.   Pour this sauce over the chops, bring it again to the boil, then cover the casserole and braise the chops in a moderately slow oven, 325°F (160°C) gas mark 3, for 1-2 hours or until the meat is very tender. Strain the pan juices and skim off the excess fat.   In a clean saucepan melt the butter, stir in the flour and cook the roux for a minute or two.   Stir in the strained pan juices and cook, stirring until thick.   Simmer the sauce gently for 10 minutes.   Add the mustard and adjust the seasoning.   Pour over the chops which you have piled at one end of the serving dish and arrange some buttered broad beans at the other.

H.E. Madame Velebit

Pork and Quince Casserole

1½ lb (700 g) boned pork
2 tbs oil
4 large tomatoes, sliced
salt and pepper

pinch of cinnamon
½ pint (300 ml) water
1½ lb (700 g) quinces
2 oz (50 g) sugar

Cut the pork into cubes and brown it in hot oil in a heavy, flame-proof casserole.   Add the sliced tomatoes, salt, pepper, cinnamon and water.   Cover and simmer, gently, for 1 hour.   After 30 minutes, peel and core the quinces and cut them into slices. Sprinkle with sugar and leave aside to 'draw' for 30 minutes, then add the quinces and their juices, to the casserole, and simmer for a further 45 minutes.   Serve with roast potatoes.

FILLETS OF PORK WITH BAKED APPLES AND GARLIC POTATOES

2-3 pork fillets
¼ lb (100 g) clarified butter
rosemary
sage
salt and pepper

6 cooking apples
12 bacon rashers, grilled and
    crumbled
6 large potatoes
¼ lb (100 g) garlic butter

Wipe and dry the pork fillets then seal them in hot clarified butter, turning often to brown them all over. Sprinkle them with the herbs and seasoning and roast in a hot oven, 400°F (200°C) gas mark 6, for the first 20 minutes, then in a moderate one, 350°F (180°C) gas mark 4, for another 20 minutes (approx.) covering the roasting pan with a lid or foil until the last 10 minutes or so. In the same, or another roasting pan, bake 6 small tart cooking apples, preparing them as you would baked apples. When they are cooked, fill their centres with well-grilled, crumbled bacon.

Scrub 6 large potatoes and slice them vertically, not quite all the way through, about 4-6 slices in each potato. Prepare some garlic butter (2 garlic cloves, ¼ lb (100 g) butter, lemon juice and chopped parsley) and squeeze it between each slice. Then wrap the potatoes in foil and bake them with the meat and apples.

Cut the meat into slices on the serving dish and garnish with the stuffed apples. Hand a sauce made from the pan juices and accompany with the garlic potatoes in another dish and green salad with a sharpish dressing.

DEVILLED HAM

Take as many rather thick ham slices as you want. Trim the fat away and marinate them for 2 hours in sherry or vermouth. Then put them in a buttered entrée dish, pouring the marinade over it. Mix 4 tbs double cream with 2 tbs tomato purée and as much hot chilli sauce and curry powder as you like. Spread this over the ham. Dot with butter and bake in a moderate oven, 350°F (180°C) gas mark 4, for 45 minutes. Serve with a purée of peas.

H.E. The Hon. Lady O'Neill

MOUSSE AU JAMBON

12 fl oz (350 ml) chicken stock
1 sachet (¼ oz (10 g)) gelatine
2 eggs, separated
2 lb (1 kg) cooked minced ham
¼ pint (150 ml) double cream, whipped
¼ pint (150 ml) cognac

Heat the chicken stock in a pan. Dissolve the gelatine in
the normal way and stir it into the stock. Beat the egg
yolks together in a bowl and stir a little hot stock into
them, then return the eggs to the pan and cook until thickened.
Leave to cool. Mix the ham with the cream, cognac and stiffly
beaten egg whites. Combine with the cooled stock mixture
and spoon into a rinsed out mould. Chill for 2-3 hours until
set, then turn out on to a flat dish.

The traditional garnish is watercress and chopped skinned
tomatoes. Serve with a rice salad made by mixing cooked
(al dente) rice with mayonnaise, Dijon mustard, chopped
pimentos, pistachio nuts, a little chutney, and a few black
grapes, seeded but left unpeeled.

H.E. Madame Velebit

JAMBON AU PORTO

1 10 lb (4.5 kg) canned cooked ham
6 oz (175 g) brown sugar
1 tbs Dijon mustard
1 tsp ground cloves
6 oz (175 g) seedless raisins
1¼ pints (750 ml) port

Preheat the oven to 400°F (200°C) gas mark 6. Put the ham
in a covered baking dish, with its juices and gelatine. Blend
the brown sugar, mustard, cloves, raisins and port together
and pour over the ham. Bake for 1 hour, basting once or twice
with the sauce. If you wish to serve the ham hot: carve it
into slices, boil down the juices in the roasting pan, correct
seasoning, and pour it over the meat. If you wish it for a
cold buffet, it can be prepared the day before and refrigerated.

Fillets of Pork (or Veal) in Sour Cream

2 pork fillets (about 1½ lb (700 g))
   or veal escalopes
2 onions, thinly sliced
1 oz (25 g) butter
flour

½ pint (300 ml) sour cream
salt and pepper
1 tbs dry sherry
croûtons

Slice the pork or veal to paper thickness, beat flat and trim to pieces
about 3 x 2 inches (7.5 x 5 cm). Fry the onions in the butter until
tender and golden. Remove the onions from the butter and place them in
a baking dish. Sprinkle the meat very lightly with flour and fry it in
the same butter until a pale golden colour. Add it to the onions in
your baking dish together with the pan juices. Cover the baking dish
tightly and cook in a low oven, 300°F (150°C) gas mark 2, for 1½-2 hours.
When cooked, add the sour cream, salt and pepper and the sherry.

Serve with croûtons, cut into triangles, and arranged round the edge of
the dish.

Ham à l'Hypocras (Old French Recipe)

This is an unusual dish, pleasing to those who like the sharp contrast
of sweet and salt, as achieved with baked ham and Cumberland sauce, but
no doubt anathema to others.

½ lb (225 g) raw ham or gammon steak
1 tbs butter

2 tbs stock
2 tsp soy or Worcester sauce

For the sauce
1 tbs sugar
1 large or 2 small macaroons, crushed
2 tbs red wine

10 bruised white peppercorns
¼ pint (150 ml) orange juice

Cut the ham up into thin strips like for a Boeuf Stroganov. Cook it in
a casserole, sealing it first in butter and then simmering it in the
stock and sauce for 10-15 minutes.

Make a sauce by putting the sugar, the macaroons (use a mouli or cheese
grater to crush them), the red wine and the peppercorns into a little
pan and boiling them together. Strangely enough they soon turn into a
rich sauce, to which you add the juices of the ham and, at the last
minute, the orange juice. Pour this sauce over the meat in the
casserole and serve with a good purée of potatoes and a dish of petits
pois à la française.

SWEET AND SOUR PORK FROM HONG KONG for 2-4 people

½ tsp five-spice powder

2 tsp light soy sauce

2 tsp sherry

½ tsp finely chopped root ginger

½ tsp salt

½ lb (225 g) pork fillet, cut
into ½ inch (1 cm) pieces

Batter

1 tbs cornflour

1 tbs flour

pinch of salt

2 eggs, beaten

oil for
frying

Sauce

4 fl oz (100 ml) water

4 fl oz (100 ml) sugar

2 fl oz (50 ml) red wine vinegar

1 tbs cornflour

1 tbs thick soy sauce

1 tsp shredded sweet gherkins

1 tsp shredded preserved ginger

1 large tomato, skinned and
cut into thin wedges

Mix the first five ingredients together. Dip the pieces of pork
in this mixture and coat them well with it. Put on one side while
you make the second coating batter.

Mix the cornflour, flour and salt together; add the eggs. Beat
to a creamy paste. Dip each piece of pork in the batter and deep
fry them in boiling oil until they are crisp and brown. Put in
shallow fireproof dish and place in the oven to keep hot.

To make the sauce, put the water in a small saucepan, add the sugar,
vinegar and cornflour, mixed with a little water, then the soy sauce,
and stir and mix well together. Add the gherkins and ginger, and
stir continually over low heat until it comes to the boil. Simmer
for 5 minutes, then add the tomato.

Simmer again for a few minutes, and it is ready. Pour the sauce
over the pork and serve at once. Fried rice or Chinese noodles
are the best accompaniment. For 6-8 people, the quantities
should be doubled.

Jambon Persillé en gelée

1 meaty shin or knuckle of veal,
chopped into pieces

2 calf's feet, prepared by butcher
and split into 4 pieces

1 generous bouquet garni (4 sprigs
parsley, 4 sprigs tarragon, 2 bay
leaves and 2 sprigs thyme)

4 shallots

6 black peppercorns

1¾ pints (1 litre) dry white wine,
plus 4 tbs

a large thick slice of ham, weighing
about 2½ lb (1.25 kg) uncooked

1 large bunch of parsley, finely
chopped

1 tbs tarragon vinegar

Put the shin bone or knuckle with plenty of meat on it, and the calf's feet,
into a saucepan with the bouquet garni, shallots, peppercorns and 1¾ pints
(1 litre) white wine; add enough water to cover the bones. Bring slowly to
the boil, removing the scum as it rises; then cover the pan and simmer the
stock over a low heat for about 3 hours.

Soak the ham in cold water for the same amount of time to remove some of the
salt. Then put the ham slice into the stock and bring it slowly back to the
boil, carefully removing the scum as it rises. When the liquid is barely
simmering, cover the pan and continue simmering gently over low heat, until the
ham is tender. Drain and cool it, then dice the ham coarsely, meat and fat
together, and press it gently into an oiled glass bowl which you have dusted
with plenty of finely chopped parsley.

Strain the ham stock through a fine sieve; cool it. Skim all the fat from
its surface, and moisten the diced ham with a little of it. Clarify the rest
of the stock; then strain it through a sieve lined with a wet flannel cloth*.
Cool until syrupy, stir in the tarragon vinegar, the 4 tbs wine and a large
amount of finely chopped parsley. Pour the aspic over the pink ham chunks
and let it jell in the refrigerator. Serve in slices from the bowl, and
accompany with a simple green salad, or a dish of new peas.

* This is such a pretty dish that it is worth the trouble of clarifying and
straining the stock — but can be eliminated if you haven't time for it.

Matilda, Duchess of Argyll

The Reform Club Banquet to Ibrahim Pacha

Puddings Hot

FREDERICK AUGUSTUS HERVEY, EARL OF BRISTOL
1730–1803
Bishop of Derry
Dilettante and traveller extraordinary

BREAD AND BUTTER PUDDING

Bread and Butter Pudding is a controversial Nursery pudding —
you either love it, or you hate it.   But one thing is certain,
it has out-lived many generations of its critics.

An 18th Century Bread and Butter Pudding

"Take a pint and a half of thick cream, boil it with a little
mace, nutmeg, and sugar to your taste, have ready laid in a
china deepish dish some thin slices of French rolls spread thin
with butter, pour the cream over it warm, and set it in a pretty
quick oven, bake it half an hour, you may if you please add
currants to the cream".

Elizabeth Raper

And here is a light and crisp modern version that is good enough
for grown-ups.

Line (bottom and sides) a deep ovenproof pie dish with ordinary,
lightly buttered, sliced bread.   Sprinkle this with 1 tsp sugar
and 1 tbs each of currants and sultanas, and fill up the middle
of the dish with more bread and butter, cut to fit, each layer
being sprinkled with currants, sultanas and a very little sugar.
When the dish is full, press down on it lightly, dust it with a
very little nutmeg and mace, sprinkle it with ½ tbs of mixed peel,
and pour over the bread, by degrees, about 1 pint (600 ml) milk
which has been heated and mixed with 2 well beaten eggs.   Wait
until the bread swells and absorbs all the eggy milk (that is
the secret) then bake in a hot oven until well risen, golden
and very crisp on the top and sides of the pudding.   Serve
with pouring cream.

Nanny Tansy

26 WHITFIELD STREET, LONDON W.1. TEL: 636 2323

MALINA RUSSE   A Russian Raspberry Pudding

1 lb (500 g) raspberries
3-4 tbs caster sugar
½ pint (300 ml) sour cream
2 eggs
1¼ tbs flour
extra sugar, to decorate

Turn the raspberries into a shallow oval gratin
dish and sprinkle them with 2 tbs of the sugar.
Stand the dish in the middle of a slow oven,
300^{0}F (150^{0}C) gas mark 2, until the raspberries
are hot through.

Beat up the sour cream with the eggs, flour and
the rest of the sugar.   Pour the mixture over
the raspberries and replace in the oven at the
same heat but nearer the top.   Cook until the
topping is pale golden brown and firm, about
45 minutes.   Sprinkle with a little more sugar
before serving.

Margaret Costa

MINT AND MINCEMEAT PASTIES WITH ZABAGLIONE SAUCE

12 oz (350 g) shortcrust pastry
4 oz (100 g) currants
4 oz (100 g) stoned raisins
2 oz (50 g) very finely chopped
   candied peel

1½ tbs chopped fresh mint leaves
2 oz (50 g) brown sugar
a little butter
grated nutmeg
allspice

1. Roll out pastry about ¼ inch (5 mm) thick.
2. Cut into large rounds or squares.
3. On one half place a layer of currants, raisins and candied peel.
4. Sprinkle with the mint.
5. Then sprinkle with brown sugar.
6. Add some more of the currants etc.
7. Then some dabs of butter, grated nutmeg and allspice.
8. Wet the edges of the pastry.
9. Turn the plain half over to cover the filling.
10. Pinch the edges together and bake in a moderate oven, 350°F (180°C) gas mark 4, for about 30 minutes. Serve with:

SAUCE SABAYON (ZABAGLIONE)

4 egg yolks
5 tbs marsala or madeira
2 tbs hot water

4 tbs caster sugar
2 egg whites, stiffly beaten

Put a pan of water on to heat. Wedge a bowl into it, so that the water very gently simmers against the sides. Pour the egg yolks, sugar, wine and hot water into it and start whisking briskly. Whisk until the sauce is like thick cream and then cool a little and fold in the stiffly beaten egg whites. Be careful not to overheat. Serve warm in a sauceboat.

The only difference between this sauce and real Zabaglione - a lovely pudding in its own right - is the addition of the egg whites.

The Marchioness of Salisbury

GÂTEAU DE POMMES (can be eaten hot or cold)

2 lb (1 kg) cooking apples
lemon juice
7 oz (200 g) fresh breadcrumbs
7 oz (200 g) molasses sugar
1 tsp cinnamon
2 oz (50 g) melted butter
¼ pint (150 ml) cream
3 tbs apricot jam
juice of 1 lemon

Butter a charlotte tin thoroughly.   Into this drop thin
slices of apples, previously cored, and peeled, of course,
and sprinkled with lemon juice, to form a 1 inch (2.5 cm)
layer.   Cover the apples with a layer of breadcrumbs,
dribble over a little melted butter, then spoon on a layer
of the sugar, mixed with cinnamon.   Go on alternating the
various ingredients until the tin is really full.   Press
down very firmly.   Finish with a layer of apples, over
which you pour the rest of the melted butter.   Set in a
baking tin half-full of hot water in a moderate oven, 350°F
(180°C) gas mark 4, for about 3 hours.   Cool for 30 minutes
at least before turning out.   Serve with either fresh
pouring or whipped cream, or a sauce made from warmed apricot
jam, lightly moistened with hot water, into which you squeeze
the juice of a lemon.

This recipe was given by H.R.H. the Comtesse de Flandres
to my mother the Duchesse d'Ursel in 1910.

Marquise de Maupeou   -211-

Macaroon Soufflé – a hot or cold soufflé

1 oz (25 g) sugar
pared rind of 1 lemon
pinch of cinnamon

½ pint (300 ml) milk, plus extra
8 large macaroons, crushed
4 eggs, separated

Put the sugar, lemon rind and cinnamon into a saucepan with the milk and bring it very gently to the boil.   Then take out the lemon rind, add the macaroons and cook for a few minutes.

Take it off the heat, cool and add the egg yolks, stirring carefully.   Then return to the heat for a moment to thicken, but not boil.

1.   For a cold soufflé: Dissolve ½ sachet (⅛ oz (5 g)) gelatine in the mixture.   Cool it and fold in the stiffly beaten egg whites.   Pour it into a soufflé dish or a deep bowl.   Sprinkle ¼ lb (100 g) finely chopped almonds over the mixture and colour the surface of the soufflé by putting it under a hot grill for a few moments.   Refrigerate for 2-3 hours.

2.   For a hot soufflé: Stiffly beat the egg whites and add to the mixture. Turn it into a greased soufflé dish and bake for 20 minutes in a moderately hot oven, 375°F (190°C) gas mark 5.

In either case, serve it with Sauce Cardinale, made with fresh or frozen raspberries and hand whipped cream in a second sauceboat.

Lady Amabel Lindsay

Soufflé Rothschild

8 eggs
3 tbs icing sugar
1 pinch of salt

2 fl oz (50 ml) white rum
about ½ lb (225 g) crystallized
    fruit, finely chopped

This is a sweet dish, said to have been a favourite with King Edward VII, and, according to my informant "always served by the amphitryons who had the honour of receiving His Majesty.   It is so simple that even the ordinary cook can make it, given the necessary care in the quantity and quality of the ingredients".

Break the egg yolks into one bowl, the whites into another.   Beat the yolks, adding the sugar, salt and rum.   Beat the whites until stiff, then fold into the egg yolk mixture.   Add the fruit and pour into a soufflé dish. Bake in a moderate oven, 350°F (180°C) gas mark 4, for 10 minutes, and serve at once.

ORANGE PUDDING - an Edwardian Recipe

½ pint (300 ml) orange juice, strained
4 fl oz (100 ml) brandy
2 tbs white rum
2 egg yolks

2 oz (50 g) sifted icing sugar,
  plus extra for dusting
3 slices sponge cake, crumbled
3-4 macaroons, crushed

Mix the orange juice with the brandy, rum, egg yolks and sugar. Stir
in the cake crumbs and crushed macaroons. Pour into a buttered soufflé
dish and bake in a moderately hot oven, 375°F (190°C) gas mark 5, for
30 minutes. Dust with icing sugar before serving.

This is a delicious pudding served just as it is, with a golden top
dusted with icing sugar, but if you should wish to rise to further
heights like a soufflé, tie a band of greased greaseproof paper round
the soufflé dish, add 3 stiffly beaten egg whites to the mixture.

Sit the soufflé dish in a roasting pan of very hot water, which should
come one third of the way up its side. I used 3 inch (7.5 cm)
macaroons and 3 large slices of (bought) almond Victoria sponge cake
which I dried in the oven before putting through a mouli. It should
be served with whipped cream.

SPICED SAUCER PANCAKES

2 oz (50 g) butter
2 oz (50 g) brown sugar
grated rind of 1 lemon
½ tsp ground mixed spice
2 eggs

2 oz (50 g) flour
½ pint (300 ml) warm milk
caster sugar
3 tbs lemon curd

Cream the butter with the sugar until nearly white and beat in the lemon
rind and spice. Beat the eggs, add little by little, with half the
flour, to the creamed butter, still beating vigorously. Stir in the
rest of the flour with the warm milk - it may look curdled but this doesn't
matter. Let the mixture 'rest' for at least 1 hour, then stir it up and
spoon it into 8 well-greased 4 inch (10 cm) ovenproof saucers. Bake at
375°F (190°C) gas mark 5 for about 20 minutes, or until golden brown
and just set. Loosen round the edges of the saucers with a knife and
turn out on to sugared paper. Spread at once with warm lemon curd, then
fold over into half-moons and serve.

Another version: Leave out the spice and lemon, use white sugar and
fill with slightly warm apricot jam instead of lemon curd.

Veronica Maclean

127, avenue
des champs-élysées
225 26.72
359 50 21
association déclarée
sous le n° 16.049
(loi du 1ᵉʳ juillet 1901)

TARTE À L'ORANGE

10 oz (300 g) flour, sifted
1 tsp salt
½ lb (225 g) unsalted butter
2 tbs ground almonds
2 egg yolks
4 thin-skinned ripe oranges
sugar

Make the sablé pastry: sift the flour and salt into
a bowl, rub in the butter and stir in the ground
almonds. Mix to a dough with the egg yolks, and add
cold water if necessary. Use to line a buttered and
floured loose-bottomed flan tin. Bake blind in a
hot oven, 400°F (200°C) gas mark 6 for 12-15 minutes.

Put the oranges into enough water to cover them. Add
their weight in sugar and boil until their skins are
quite soft. Then liquidize and sieve.

When the pastry has cooled, fill the flan with the
orange purée and bake again, just enough for the
pastry to colour and for the oranges to glaze.

Anne de Marcuil

TARTE AUX POIRES

3½ oz (90 g) unsalted butter, softened
6 sugar lumps, dissolved in 3 tbs water
¼ lb (100 g) flour, sifted
3 pears, peeled, halved and cored
1 pint (600 ml) double cream
1 tbs caster sugar
3 eggs, separated
icing sugar

Cream the butter and dissolved sugar together with a wooden spoon.
Tip all the flour in at once and work it very rapidly into a dough
with the tips of your fingers. As soon as it is smooth and pliable,
roll it into a ball and put in a cool place to rest (not a fridge) for
at least 4 hours. Lay the pears (choose prime pears - Cressane,
Grande Duchesse or Williams) on a plastic sieve (they will blacken if
they come into contact with metal) and let them drain. Beat the cream
in a bowl, add the sugar to it, and then the egg yolks. Beat the
egg whites until stiff then beat into the mixture. Beat together for
at least 10 minutes.

Roll out the pastry on a floured surface to ¼ inch (5 mm) thick.
Flour a loose bottomed flan tin and press pastry into it. Don't worry
if it breaks, just pinch together again with your fingers. Dust the
bottom of the flan lightly with icing sugar. Bake blind in a hot
oven, 400°F (200°C) gas mark 6, for 6-10 minutes, then take it out
and cool in the tin.

The pears by now are well drained, so when the pastry is quite cold,
arrange them carefully in the flan in a circle. (You may have to cut
one to fill up the middle.) Then cover them with the cream and egg
mixture.

Put the flan back in the oven for long enough for the egg cream to
cook. It should take from 8-12 minutes, depending on your oven, but
watch it carefully, for as soon as it colours it will be ready and if
you leave it longer it will burn.

Take it out immediately, and when it is quite cold, brush the top of
the pears with a little apricot or gooseberry jam glaze.

H.E. Comtesse de Crouy-Chanel

SUSSEX POND PUDDING, a Victorian nurserymaid's recipe for a family lunch

"1. Make a good suet crust, put in some currants, and a little
     sugar.

 2. Divide in two and roll each piece into a rather thick round.

 3. Put into the middle of one round a ball of butter mixed with
     sugar using the proportions of 1 lb (500 g) butter to
     $\frac{1}{4}$ lb (100 g) Demerara or molasses sugar.

 4. Gather up the edges of the crust, and enclose the butter ball
     securely by covering the join with the second round of crust
     and pinching that up.

 5. Put into a well floured cloth, tie up tightly and boil 3 hours
     or more, according to size".

Mr. Glover, from whom this recipe originates, says: "If you don't
know this and think it uninteresting, try it - the melted butter
and sugar make a delectable sauce just right for a cold winter's
day".

The Scottish version of this dish is called 'Cloutie Dumpling' and
is made with currants but no butter/sugar ball.

Mrs. Sue Lennan has a 'Cyprus' version. She leaves out the
currants but buries a whole ripe lemon, thin-skinned but unpeeled
in the butter/sugar ball. This makes a rich, and much sharper sauce.

Deep South Fried Peaches

Peel and halve, or slice, fresh ripe peaches (but not overripe).
Melt some unsalted clarified butter in a frying pan to cover the
bottom by about $\frac{1}{8}$ inch (3 mm). Put in the peaches, which you have
drained of excess juice on a silk or nylon sieve and fry them until
they are very lightly browned. Then add soft brown sugar and
finish cooking in a hot oven till the sugar melts. Transfer to
serving dish and eat at once.

Southern Spicy Gingerbread

A hot gingerbread cake served with a lemon and honey sauce.

2 eggs
4 oz (100 g) brown sugar
9 fl oz (250 ml) dark molasses
6 oz (175 g) butter
½ tsp cloves
½ tsp grated nutmeg
½ tsp baking powder

2 tsp bicarbonate of soda
2 tsp ginger
1½ tsp cinnamon
1¼ lb (600 g) flour
grated zest of 1 lemon
8 fl oz (225 ml) boiling water
chopped nuts

Beat the eggs, and add to the creamed sugar, molasses and butter; beat well together. Add the dry ingredients which have been mixed and sifted, then the boiling water. Bake in a greased shallow pan, in a moderate oven, 350°F (180°C) gas mark 4, for 30-40 minutes. Turn out on to a hot plate and slice - but reshape and leave whole. Heat a handful of chopped nuts in 1 tbs melted butter and pour these over the top of the gingerbread. Then serve at once with one sauceboat of whipped cream and one of honey and lemon sauce.

NB Gingerbread improves with keeping, and it is possible to make this cake in advance, if you keep it in an airtight tin and reheat it in a very slow oven (useful if you want a quick pudding).

Miss Adkins Crisp Buttermilk Waffles

3 oz (75 g) flour
¼ tsp bicarbonate of soda
¼ tsp salt
2 tsp baking powder

2 eggs
¼ pint (150 ml) (approx.)
  buttermilk
5 tbs cooking oil

Sift together the flour, soda, salt and baking powder. Beat the eggs in a bowl. Add to them a portion of the flour mixture, then a small amount of buttermilk, mixing well. Continue to alternate the dry and liquid ingredients three times, using all the flour mixture and enough buttermilk to make a thin batter. Lastly add the cooking oil and stir carefully, just blending. Then use immediately. Cook in a hot, lightly greased waffle iron and serve with hot strawberry jam and whipped cream handed separately.

Makes 4 waffles. Double the ingredients for 8.

LEMON PUDDING

3 tbs flour	8 fl oz (225 ml) milk
¼ tsp salt	2 eggs, separated
½ lb (225 g) sugar	juice and grated rind of 1 lemon

Sift the flour and salt into a bowl and stir
in the sugar.   Add milk, the well-beaten egg
yolks, the lemon juice and grated rind.
Carefully fold in the stiffly beaten egg
whites.   Pour into a buttered baking dish.
Set this in a pan of warm water.   Bake in a
moderately hot oven, 350°F (180°C) gas mark 4,
about 35 minutes, or until a knife blade
inserted comes out clean.   When cooked, this
pudding forms a light fluffy cake on top and a
rich lemony sauce at the bottom.   Serve warm,
with a bowl of whipped cream.

TURKISH SNOWBALLS OR LEMON PUFFS BIGE

A quick and easy light pudding.

Take 4 eggs and the juice of 2 large lemons.   Add the
eggs to the lemon juice and let them curdle.   Stir in
enough flour to make a creamy batter.   Meanwhile make
a light syrup by boiling 1¾ lb (800 g) caster sugar with
1¾ pints (1 litre) water.   Put the squeezed half of one
of the lemons into the syrup while it is boiling.   When
ready pour into a wide bowl and cool.   Thoroughly heat
a pan of lard or corn oil (as if for chips), and drop
spoonfuls of the batter into it when smoking hot.   Remove
with a wire spoon when golden and crisp;   drain well on
kitchen paper and then float in cooled-off syrup, with the
lemon removed.   Serve with fresh cream.

BLACK MOLASSES SOUFFLÉ

4 tbs butter	1 tsp cinnamon
4 tbs flour	½ tsp grated nutmeg
8 fl oz (225 ml) milk	pinch of salt
6 fl oz (175 ml) black	4 eggs
molasses treacle	2 tbs sugar
1 tsp ginger	

Melt the butter in a double boiler, add the flour and blend well. Stir in the milk gradually and cook until it thickens taking care not to let it get too stiff. Remove from the heat, stir in the treacle, spices and salt. Cool slightly. Beat the egg yolks until creamy, beat in the sugar; add to the treacle mixture. Fold in the stiffly beaten egg whites. Pour into a buttered 8 inch (20 cm) soufflé dish. Bake in a moderate oven, 350°F (180°C) gas mark 4, in a pan of hot water for 40-45 minutes. This soufflé should be custard-like at the bottom and spongy on top.

Serve with the following sauce:

Brandy Sauce

2 egg yolks	½ pint (300 ml) double cream
2 oz (50 g) sugar	4 tbs brandy

Beat the egg yolks until light. Beat in the sugar, fold in the cream, whipped until it is thick but not stiff. Fold in the brandy. Chill thoroughly before serving.

Madame Pol-Roger

OMELETTE SOUFFLÉ AUX FRAMBOISES (for 2 omelettes for 4-6 people)

1 pint (600 ml) milk

1 vanilla pod

6 tbs sugar

4 tbs butter

5 tbs sifted flour

a pinch of salt

5 eggs

clarified butter

raspberry jam

icing sugar

Put the milk with the vanilla pod and sugar in a saucepan.
Bring them slowly to boiling point, take off the heat and
leave to infuse.   In another saucepan, make a roux with
the butter and flour.   Cook for a few minutes but do not
let it change colour.   Remove vanilla pod and pour the
hot milk over it and cook for a few minutes longer.   Turn
this sweet white sauce into a bowl, add the pinch of salt,
and then the egg yolks, beating them in one by one.   In
another bowl beat up the whites until stiff, and gently and
carefully fold them into the white sauce.

Put a little clarified butter into 2 omelette pans.   When
the butter is hot, half fill each pan with the mixture and
cook it as you would an ordinary omelette, stirring it with
a fork and letting the base solidify, then transfer the pans
to a hot oven, 400°F (200°C) gas mark 6 and finish cooking.
After about 20 minutes remove from the oven and put a large
tablespoon of raspberry jam (homemade if possible) in the
middle of the omelettes.   You may have to thin it down with
a little hot water.   Flip half the omelettes over as you
turn them on to the serving dish.   Dredge them with icing
sugar and glaze them under the grill.

S.E. La Baronne de Courcel

Tangerine Soufflés in Tangerines

(Soufflés aux Mandarines)

20 fine tangerines, mandarines or netsukas
the grated rind of 4 of these
½ pint (300 ml) milk
2 eggs, separated
2 tbs sugar
2½ tbs flour, sifted
icing sugar

First, grate the rinds from 4 tangerines, then cut the tops off
all the tangerines and scoop out their insides, being careful
not to pierce or rupture the skins.   Empty the flesh and juices
into a bowl.   Keep the ungrated tangerine shells and put aside.
Meanwhile emulsify their flesh in an electric blender, then push
the pulp through a sieve.   Pour the resultant purée into a
saucepan, and add to it the grated tangerine rind which you have
already prepared.   Reduce by boiling until it looks like jam.

In another saucepan bring the milk to the boil.   Beat the egg
yolks and sugar in a bowl until they are pale and very frothy.   Add
the flour, a spoonful at a time, then the boiling milk, beating
and mixing all the time so that there are no lumps.   Lastly mix
in the reduced tangerine syrup, pour back into the tangerine
saucepan, and bring to the boil.   Simmer for a few minutes until
you lose the taste of the flour, then take off the heat and cool.
When cool enough beat the egg whites until stiff and fold them
into the mixture.

Fill the tangerine shells with the mixture but leave a little room
for them to rise.   Put them on a baking sheet in a hot oven,
400°F (200°C) gas mark 6, for 5 minutes only.   When they come out,
dust them with icing sugar and glaze with a salamander or by flashing
under the grill.   A few drops of Grand Marnier go well with this
soufflé, but be careful not to drown the very delicate and delicious
tangerine flavour.

H.E. The Hon. Lady Soames

Recette de James Viaene
Chef de Cuisine à l'Ambassade

49 DRAYTON GARDENS
LONDON SW10 9RX

01-373 2867

POOR MAN'S SUPPER

A recipe that has evolved from several countries.

2 lb (1 kg) dried apricots (the small
   wild ones from the Middle East
   are best)
3 tbs Hungarian apricot brandy
½ pint (300 ml) water
8 thin slices white bread
1½ pints (900 ml) milk

2 eggs, beaten
2 tbs caster sugar
butter for frying
a little cinnamon and allspice
1 pint (600 ml) sour cream

Spread the unsoaked apricots out on a baking dish, sprinkle with the
apricot brandy and water.   Set the oven at low 275°F (140°C) gas mark 1,
and leave the apricots to bake for 3-4 hours.
Cooked like this they will plump up and make a little of their own juice
and taste exotic and fragrant and delicious.   Do not overcook: they
should be just a little bit chewy.
Meanwhile, reduce the milk to half by gently simmering.   Stir in the
beaten eggs and sugar and pour into a large flat dish.   Cut the crusts
off the bread slices and halve them.   Soak them thoroughly in the
fortified milk, then drain and fry in foaming butter, over gentle heat.
When the 'French bread' or 'pauvre homme' is hicely coloured on both
sides, and crisp, take from the pan, sprinkle sparingly with the spice
and arrange in a hot serving dish.   You can now either heap the hot
apricots over each piece, and pour some sour cream on top, or you can
leave your guests to assemble their own: serving the apricots and the
'pauvre homme' in separate dishes and sending round a large bowl of sour
cream and a small one of brown sugar.

Sarah Maclean

EASY APRICOT SOUFFLÉ

2 eggs
2 tbs caster sugar

2 fl oz (50 ml) Hungarian
   apricot brandy
3 tbs whole fruit apricot jam

Separate the eggs.   Put the yolks in a basin (or an electric mixer) and
beat with the sugar for 20 minutes.   Whip the whites very stiff and fold
into the yolks.
Cover the bottom of a soufflé dish with apricot jam (the rough tinned
kind that has bits of whole apricot in it).   Sprinkle with apricot brandy.
Spoon on the egg mixture and bake for 5-8 minutes in a very hot oven,
425°F (220°C) gas mark 7.   Serve with pouring cream.

HOT CHOCOLATE CAKE

5 oz (150 g) best quality plain chocolate
3 oz (75 g) butter
1 tsp cold black coffee
5 oz (150 g) caster sugar
1½ tbs flour
3 eggs, separated

Melt the chocolate and butter together with the cold coffee in a bowl
over hot water.   Then stir in the sugar, sift in the flour and beat
in the egg yolks.   Lastly fold in the beaten egg whites.   Spoon the
mixture into a greased and floured deep sandwich tin with a loose
bottom, and bake quickly, at 400°F (200°C) gas mark 6, for approximately
15 minutes.   Turn out very carefully, allow to cool.   Don't worry if
the inside of the cake is still slightly runny, it is meant to be.
Pour over a thick chocolate icing sauce.   Serve immediately, eat with
whipped cream and don't count the calories.   It is also delicious cold.

Mrs. Alexander McEwen

SOUFFLÉ AU CHOCOLAT

3 oz (75 g) best quality chocolate
½ pint (300 ml) scalded milk
   plus extra for melting chocolate
2 oz (50 g) caster sugar
3 egg yolks

½ tsp vanilla essence, or 2 tbs
   strong black coffee
1 oz (25 g) flour or potato flour
pinch of salt
6 egg whites

Melt the chocolate in a double boiler, with a little milk, without letting
it boil.   Mix 1½ oz (40 g) of the sugar in another saucepan, with the
egg yolks and vanilla essence or coffee.   When this mixture becomes
smooth like a cream, add the flour, followed by the milk, the chocolate,
and salt.   Put the pan over the heat and remove it when boiling.   Pour
it into a bowl to cool it.   Meanwhile beat the egg whites until stiff
with the remaining sugar.   Mix the whites carefully with the chocolate
mixture when the latter is cold.   Lightly butter a soufflé dish and fill
half-full with the mixture, to leave space for the soufflé to rise.✱
Bake in a hot oven, 400°F (200°C) gas mark 6, for about 20 minutes.
Serve the soufflé as soon as it has risen and is firm.

✱ You may like to know that this soufflé can be prepared several hours in
advance: put it in the coldest part of the fridge and shut the door on
it gently.   Take it out carefully 30 minutes before dish-up time and quickly
bake it in a hot oven, as usual.   The cold of the fridge will have
stopped it collapsing.

NORMANDY APPLE FRITTERS WITH CALVADOS BUTTER

2 lb (1 kg) good firm cooking apples	corn oil for frying
7 oz (200 g) caster sugar	4 tbs icing sugar
Vieux Calvados liqueur	6 tbs butter
frying batter	

Peel, core and slice the apples into rings at least ½ inch
(1 cm) thick.   Dust them with ¼ lb (100 g) caster sugar
and sprinkle with a little Calvados.   Leave them on a plate
for 30 minutes.   Just before you serve them, dip each ring
in a good frying batter and throw them into a pan of fast
boiling cooking oil.   As soon as the batter is golden
coloured, fish out with a perforated spoon and drain on a
wire rack.   Dust with icing sugar.   Put into a very hot oven,
450°F (230°C) gas mark 8, on the wire rack so that the sugar
caramelizes a little.   Then serve immediately on a large
plate on which you have folded a white napkin.
Serve with 'brandy' butter that you have made without brandy
but by creaming the butter, remaining caster sugar and a little
Vieux Calvados (apple liqueur) together.

S.E. La Comtesse de Lesseps

LEMON AND RUM OMELETTE SOUFFLÉ SURPRISE

6 tbs rum	3 tbs caster sugar
juice of ½ lemon	butter
6 eggs, separated	

Heat up the rum and lemon juice almost to boiling in a small
saucepan, and have a very hot, unbreakable serving dish ready.
Whisk the egg yolks with 2 tbs of the sugar until a pale cream,
then fold in the stiffly whisked egg whites, and quickly make
an ordinary fluffy omelette.   Fold it, slip it on to the
serving dish and dust it with the remaining sugar, then pour
the hot rum around and light it.   That's the surprise.

C. Hackett-Smith

REGENCY PUDDING

1.   First line a 2½ pint (1.5 litre) metal mould with caramel:

boil 3 oz (75 g) sugar and 2 tbs water in the mould itself over
a moderate heat, swirling the syrup round (do not stir it) until
it finally goes toffee brown and begins to caramelise (wear
oven gloves for this operation).   When it is the right colour
dip the outside of the mould immediately into a pan of cold
water for 2-3 seconds, to cool it slightly, and then holding it
firmly in gloved hands, tilt it in all directions to film the
bottom and sides all over with a thin coating of caramel.
When the caramel has ceased to run turn the mould over a plate
and put aside.

2.   Make a lemon soufflé cream:

cream 6 tbs butter and 6 tbs sugar, add 5 egg yolks and the grated
zest and juice of 1 lemon and beat lightly over moderate heat
until they become like thick cream.   It is best done in a basin
over a bain-marie.   Take off the heat and cool.   Beat the 5
egg whites until stiff and add to the yolks when these are cool.

3.   Steam the lemon soufflé in the caramel mould:

spoon the lemon cream into the caramelised mould, cover it with
a tin plate and put it into a large saucepan of very gently
shuddering water, enough for it to come two-thirds of the way
up the side of the mould.   The water round the mould must not
boil nor should it go higher than 210ºF (100ºC).   It should be
ready in 40-50 minutes.

4.   Turn out on to a hot dish, and serve with caramel sauce
poured round it, and whipped cream in a separate sauceboat.
This is easily made by pouring 1 beaten egg and 2-3 tbs cream
into the now empty mould, putting it back over gentle heat and
whisking hard so that the egg cream absorbs the last traces of
caramel.   Do not overheat or the egg will scramble.   It should
only take a minute or two, and can be done over the hot water
of the bain-marie.

Lady Lovat and Joan Birnie

Languedoc Almond Tart

Shortcrust Pastry
6 oz (175 g) flour
pinch of salt
4 oz (100 g) butter
1 egg yolk, beaten

4 egg yolks
4 oz (100 g) ground almonds
2 oz (50 g) caster sugar
1 tsp grated orange rind
blanched almonds

Sift the flour and salt into a bowl and rub in the butter.
Mix in the egg yolk and add enough cold water to make a dough;
knead and roll as usual.

Line a baking tin or flan case with the pastry, beat the 4 egg
yolks and mix them with the ground almonds, sugar and orange
rind.   Fill the flan case with this mixture and decorate the
top with the blanched almonds split in two.   Bake in a
moderate oven, 350°C (180°C) gas mark 4, for about 40 minutes
until golden brown,   A compôte of oranges goes well with
this dish.

Algerian Cream

4 eggs
1 tbs icing sugar
2 tbs orange flower water
grated zest and juice of 1 lemon

1 oz (25 g) flour, sifted,
   or potato flour
¾ pint (450 ml) cream heated
   with 3 tbs milk

Separate the eggs, then beat the egg yolks and the sugar in a
bowl until pale cream.   Add the orange flower water and lemon
zest.   When the mixture is smooth, add the sifted flour and
the hot cream which you have diluted with a little milk.   Add
them alternately and beat and mix briskly to avoid lumps.
Transfer the mixture to a thick saucepan and bring it slowly
to the boil over low heat, stirring carefully all the time.
When it boils take off the heat and beat until smooth.   Return
and cook very slowly until there is no taste of flour and the
mixture thickens to a thick custard.   Then remove and cool a
little.   Add the lemon juice and fold in carefully the stiffly
beaten egg whites.   Pour into a lightly greased soufflé dish
and dust with more icing sugar.   Put it into a hot oven for
10 minutes to make it rise, then serve at once with a lemon
sauce and pouring cream.   The remainder, if there is any,
is very good put into ramekins and served chilled.

Puddings Cold

THE BRITISH EMBASSY, ISTANBUL
The old summer residence on the Bosphorus.
Now destroyed by fire

TWO-STRAWBERRY COMPÔTE FROM MELLS

2-3 lb (1-1.5 kg) strawberries   ½ lb (225 g) caster sugar

This is a good dish if you have a lot of wet or damaged fruit
and only a few good strawberries.
Select about ½ lb (225 g) of the best strawberries and keep in
a cool place.   Hull the rest and sprinkle with the sugar.
Leave for a few hours or overnight and then turn them, sugar,
juice and all into a large enamel saucepan with about 1¾ pints
(1 litre) of cold water and a squeeze of lemon juice.   Bring
to the boil and simmer, skimming frequently until the syrup
below is clear with some strawberries floating around on top.
Pour into a glass bowl and cool.   If the compôte is not pink
enough add a drop of cochineal.   Then add the carefully hulled
selected fresh strawberries and chill.   Serve very cold with
a dish of Yoghurt Cream, or junket.

Mrs. Raymond Asquith and Mrs. Gould

YOGHURT CREAM TO ACCOMPANY A COMPÔTE

Drain about 1¾ pints (1 litre) of yoghurt (homemade is much the
best) overnight in a muslin bag.   Squeeze out the last drop of
the casein.   Mix about ¼ pint (150 ml) double cream with the
remaining yoghurt curd and turn it out into a glass dish, or
earthenware bowl.   You can flavour it with a little vanilla or
cointreau if you wish, but I like it plain.   Garnish with a
few candied violets (or strawberries).   This is a Turkish
sweet-meat.

H.E. Lady Kelly   -228-

ICED APRICOTS BRÛLÉES

1 lb (500 g) canned apricots or peaches   ½ pint (300 ml) cream
¼ pint (150 ml) brandy   soft brown sugar

Put the apricots in a soufflé dish, discarding most of the juice.
Add the brandy.   Whisk the cream until thick and completely cover
the apricots with this and then completely cover the cream with
soft brown sugar: it should be a very generous covering.   Pat
down, making quite sure it touches the edge of the dish all round
and that no cream is showing.   Cover and leave in the fridge
for at least 2 hours.   Remove, caramelize the surface under a
hot grill and serve immediately.

NB   It is important that the sugar layer comes to the very top
of the soufflé dish, so that it caramelizes quickly and evenly.

Mrs. Bertie Procter

FOOD FOR THE GODS

8 oz (225 g) good quality macaroons   4 tbs icing sugar, sifted
2 egg yolks   ¾ pint (450 ml) double cream
5 tbs kirsch   a little almond oil

Rough-crumble either macaroons or ratafia biscuits from a good
patisserie, to yield 8 oz (225 g).   Mix the egg yolks with the
kirsch and icing sugar.   Blend this into the chosen crumbs.

Whip the cream very stiff.   Fold it into the blended mixture,
then press this down into a lightly-oiled round cake tin or
mould, and cover the top, first with greaseproof paper, then with
foil, and either freeze or refrigerate it until needed.

Serve with a compôte of peaches or pears, and a fresh raspberry
purée made by emulsifying fresh raspberries in a blender with
1 tbs of raspberry jam and 1 tbs redcurrant jelly.   Sieve the
purée and dribble it over the top of the turned out macaroon
gâteau.   Rum can be used instead of the Kirsch, if preferred.

Beaufort Pears Cardinale

4 pears
6 oz (175 g) sugar
½ pint (300 ml) water
½ vanilla pod

6 oz (175 g) raspberry jam
6 oz (175 g) redcurrant jelly
angelica
whipped cream

Make a creamy vanilla flavoured bavarois in a flat bottomed mould and
when it is set turn it out into a rather larger round glass dish (see
below).   Cut 3-4 pears in half; peel them and remove the pips.   Cook
them in a thin syrup made with the sugar and water and the vanilla pod.
When they are quite tender take them off the heat, cool and add the
sieved raspberry jam and redcurrant jelly to the syrup.   If necessary,
colour it with a drop of cochineal.   Arrange the pears standing up round
the sides of the bavarois - give them angelica stalks and dribble the
sauce over the pears.   Garnish with a few puffs of whipped cream.

For the Bavarois:

4 egg yolks
½ lb (225 g) sugar
½ pint (300 ml) milk
½ vanilla pod

½ oz (15 g) gelatine
½ pint (300 ml) cream, stiffly
   whipped
sugar, if desired

Put the egg yolks in a saucepan and beat to a cream with the sugar, then
gradually add the scalded milk in which you have infused the vanilla pod.
Add the gelatine, dissolved in a little water.   Stir over a low heat
until the mixture begins to thicken and coats the spoon.   Do not allow
it to boil, or the custard will curdle.   Strain through a sieve into a
bowl and let it cool.   When nearly cold and set fold in the cream, which
you have sweetened to taste.   Spoon into a flat-bottomed mould and set
on ice or in the fridge for at least 2 hours.

Lady Lovat and Mrs. Grady

BOODLES FOOL

4 oranges	1 pint (600 ml) double cream
2 lemons	8 sponge fingers
icing sugar	

Grate the zest of 2 oranges and 1 lemon into a bowl. Add the strained juice of both the oranges and lemons. Sweeten to taste and add to the juice the lightly beaten cream. Fill a soufflé dish with sponge fingers that you have cut into two or three pieces and pour the orange cream over. Chill in a fridge for several hours.

FRAISES SABLEUSES A strawberry gâteau

Bake 4 layers of sablé biscuit, cooked about ¼ inch (5 mm) thick and not too golden, about the size of a breakfast plate. When cold cover each layer with crême chantilly, then with firm red strawberries that have been sliced in two, sweetened, and marinated in a mixture of grand marnier and orange juice. End with a layer of sablé biscuit, and then cover the gâteau entirely with plain whipped cream that you smooth over and then flick up with a palette knife. Sprinkle the top with toasted chopped almonds and a few halved strawberries.

NB Be careful how you handle the sablé biscuits as they are very fragile. You will find the recipe for making good sablé pastry in Constance Spry or Pelleprat, or on page 214.

LEMON MINCEMEAT FLAN WITH ROYAL ICING

Make a 'sablé' pastry flan, as for Tarte à l'Orange on page 214. Bake blind, and, when cool, fill it with mincemeat, which you have mixed with the grated rind and the juice of ½ a lemon. Put it back in the oven to finish cooking for about 15 minutes. When the flan is quite cold, ice the top with royal icing (icing sugar mixed with egg white and thinned with lemon juice). Chill, and serve when the icing is not quite set. Decorate dish with white and green flowers, like lemon blossom.

S.E. La Comtesse de Lesseps

Brandy Cream — A Victorian Recipe

20 sweet almonds, and 3-4
  bitter ones
1-2 tbs milk
3 egg yolks

1 pint (600 ml) double cream
3 tbs caster sugar
¼ pint (150 ml) brandy

Blanch and pound the almonds, or emulsify them in a blender — a spoonful
of iced water will prevent them oiling, then boil them in the milk.
Cool and sieve. When cold stir in the egg yolks that you have beaten
up until thick with a spoonful of the cream. Add the sugar and the
brandy. When thoroughly mixed pour in the cream. Set it over the
heat, but do not let it boil. Stir one way until it thickens, then
pour into custard cups. Serve with a ratafia on the top of each.

Lady Alexandra Metcalfe

Crème de Marrons

½ lb (225 g) canned sweetened
  chestnut purée (or ½ lb (225 g)
  unsweetened purée and 2 oz (50 g)
  caster sugar)

2 tbs marsala
2 tbs rum
¾ pint (450 ml) whipped cream

Empty the purée into a saucepan. Gently warm to soften the consistency,
add the marsala and rum, stir well — it should be like a very thick
custard. Have ready the whipped cream, spoon into it the cooled purée
and gently blend. Be careful not to whip too much or it will curdle.
Turn it out into individual glass dishes, and put them into the
refrigerator. Decorate with a marron glacé sitting on a puff of
whipped cream — or a spoonful of marrons debris, which you can buy at
good grocers, and a crystallized violet.

GINGER CREAM

Heat 6 oz (175 g) ginger marmalade and 1 tbs of
chopped preserved ginger in the top of a double boiler.

Add 1 sachet of gelatine soaked in ¼ pint (150 ml)
water and stir until dissolved. Whip ¾ pint (450 ml)
double cream stiff. When the ginger mixture is cool,
add gelatine, fold it into the whipped cream and pour
into a chilled 1¾ pint (1 litre) mould. Set in the
refrigerator and turn out of the mould on to a plate
just before serving. Pipe a double ruff of thick
whipped cream round the base of the ginger cream and
decorate with a top-knot of cream and a few pieces of
preserved ginger.

For 6-8 people

IMPERIAL CREAM

1 pint (600 ml) double cream
thinly pared rind of 1 lemon
8 tbs icing sugar
juice of 2 lemons

Boil the cream with the thinly pared (no pith) lemon
rind for exactly 5 minutes, then stir the cream off
the heat with a wooden spoon or flat whisk until nearly
cold, adding the sugar as you stir. (It can be put
into a mixer set to lowest speed). Strain the lemon
juice into a glass dish, and pour the cream over it from
a jug with a narrow spout, holding it as high as possible
above the dish to form bubbles, and moving it about to
mix with the lemon juice. The drainer of the jug will
hold back the peel, or you can remove it before you pour.
Chill for several hours before serving, or overnight.

Lady McKean

MARRONS DE MONSIEUR L'AMBASSADEUR (for 10-12 people)

8 egg whites
a few grains of salt
½ tsp cream of tartar
1 lb (500 g) sugar (vanilla
    sugar is best)
1 pint (600 ml) whipping cream

14 oz (400 g) canned marrons
    glacés
½ lb (225 g) canned sweet
    chestnut purée (crème de marron)
1-2 tbs rum

Beat the egg whites with salt until they are stiff. Add cream
of tartar and continue beating until well blended. Gradually
beat in half the sugar, then fold in the remainder all at once.
Place very small mounds of this meringue mixture - 1 inch (2.5 cm)
diameter - on slightly oiled greaseproof or parchment paper laid
in a shallow pan or baking tray. Bake in a slow oven, 300°F
(150°C) gas mark 2, for 1 hour. When cooked, remove the paper
and crush the little meringues slightly, so that they look rough.
Whip the cream stiff. Fill the meringues with a spoonful of
cream, then pile them one on top of each other into a small
craggy mountain, inserting chopped pieces of marrons glacés
here and there to look like rocks. Surround the base of the
meringue pile with sweetened chestnut purée which you have
thinned with a tablespoon or two of rum. Chill and serve.

S.E. Monsieur Jacques de Beaumarchais

PORT WINE JELLY FROM FROME

1½ oz (40 g) gelatine, dissolved
½ inch (1 cm) cinnamon stick
grated nutmeg
¼ lb (100 g) lump sugar

¾ pint (450 ml) water
grated rind of ½ lemon
1 pint (600 ml) port

Put all the ingredients except ½ pint (300 ml) of the port into a
saucepan. Heat up until well blended. Strain. Add the remaining
port and put into well-wetted moulds or coffee cups. When cold, turn
out when required on to pretty coffee saucers and eat with a silver
teaspoon.

NB   In this way the jelly has both the flavour of the cooked and
uncooked port.

SUE'S SUMMER PUDDING

My daughter-in-law is an artist and she says she makes this by blending
the colours of the fruits, but as her summer puddings, though never
identical, are the best I know, I have watched her carefully, and this
is approximately what she does:

She puts enough fruit of 2 or 3 different kinds to fill a pudding basin,
into a large bowl, and covers it generously with sugar. She leaves it
in the larder overnight. The next morning it will have made a lot of
juice.

She lines a pudding basin carefully, bottom and sides, with pieces of
white sliced bread, from which the crusts have been removed, then spoons
half the fruit into it, followed by a single layer of bread, then the
rest of the fruit, and finishes with a bread layer, making sure there
is enough sugary juice to completely soak the bread. She squashes and
presses it all well down with her fist until it is a solid mass, then
puts the basin back in the fridge for a further 8 hours (minimum) but
if she can, she leaves it overnight as it then tastes even better.

Fresh fruit, of course, is best. Blackcurrants, redcurrants and
raspberries are the classic mix but frozen fruits prolong the season
and are almost as good. Defrost them overnight with the sugar, be
sure you have at least a third of blackcurrants, or brambles, or black
cherries to give a rich dark colour. Frozen strawberries make a lot
of juice and give a delicate scented flavour.

Finally, she turns the pudding on to a pretty plate and pours fresh
cream over the top.

Mrs. Jeremy Phipps

MERINGUES DE MADAME LA DUCHESSE

Tiny meringues stuck together with Crème Chantilly - piled into
a mountain on a plate and with a raspberry purée poured over.

Crème Chantilly: whipped cream sweetened by icing sugar.
Raspberry purée: use fresh raspberries or frozen ones. Simmer
with sugar for 5 minutes, mix in 1 tbs raspberry jam, and 1 tbs
redcurrant jelly. Sieve and cool.

3, WEST EATON PLACE,

S.W.1.

01-235 3852.

NÈGRE EN CHEMISES

½ lb (225 g) bitter chocolate (any good black chocolate)
2½ tbs very strong black coffee
4 tbs butter

a little rum or brandy
6 tbs praliné (see below), ground
about ½ pint (300 ml) double cream

Melt the chocolate, broken into pieces, in the coffee,
stirring over a low heat until it is smooth and creamy.
Remove from heat and beat in the butter, cut into small
pieces.   (If the chocolate 'oils', add more coffee).
Flavour with rum or brandy.   When cool stir in the ground
praliné and whipped cream and turn into an oiled basin (use
almond or corn oil).   Chill in the fridge.
To serve, turn out and pipe a double ruff of thick whipped
cream round the base.

To make Praliné

3 oz (75 g) caster sugar
2½ tbs water

3 oz (75 g) whole unblanched almonds

Put these together into a thick old cast iron saucepan and
set on low heat to melt.   Do not stir until sugar is melted.
Then stir briskly with a metal spoon until it assumes a
rich brown colour and the almonds are well toasted.   Pour
immediately on to an oiled tin or enamel plate, smoothing it
out with the spoon to keep it as thin as possible, and leave
it to cool.   When cool break into pieces between 2 sheets
of greaseproof paper and then put through a mincer or
grinder.   It can be coarse or fine whichever is preferred.

H.E. Lady Bowker

THE CREGGANS INN
STRACHUR
ARGYLL PA27 8BX

A.A. ★ ★ ★ R.A.C.
CHAÎNE DES RÔTISSEURS
EGON RONAY

TELEPHONES:
STRACHUR 036.986.279 and 777
TELEX: 727396 ATT. CREGGANS

MEG'S CHOCOLATE ROULADE

5 eggs
5 oz (150 g) caster sugar
½ lb (225 g) good quality dark
  chocolate

3 fl oz (75 ml) water
1 tsp strong instant coffee
½ pint (300 ml) double cream
icing sugar

Line an oblong baking tin about 6 x 10 x 1 inches (15 x 25 x 2.5 cm) with
foil or greaseproof paper and oil lightly.   Set the oven to 400°F (200°C)
gas mark 6.
Separate the eggs, beat yolks and caster sugar together until pale and
mousse-like.   Melt the chocolate with water and coffee in a thick-bottomed
saucepan.   Cool slightly and add to the egg yolk mixture.   Whisk egg
whites until stiff but not dry.   Fold 1 tbs of egg white into the mixture
to loosen it, then fold in the remaining whites.   Spread evenly in the
lined tin and bake for 15 minutes, until firm to the touch.
Slide the cake mixture in the foil on to a cooling rack.   Cover immediately
with a damp tea towel and leave to cool.
When cool, spread with whipped cream and, using the foil, roll up.   Put
on to a plate and dust with icing sugar.

GÂTEAU DE CHOCOLAT AUX DIPLOMATES

3½ oz (90 g) chocolate
1 tbs instant coffee powder
3 eggs

2½ oz (60 g) ground almonds
5½ oz (160 g) butter, softened
9 oz (250 g) chestnut purée

Melt the chocolate in a bain-marie.   Add the coffee very gradually without
water.   Mix the egg yolks , the almonds, the butter and the chestnut purée.
Add to the chocolate mixture.   Beat the egg whites until very stiff and fold
them in.   Put the mixture into a mould lined with foil.   Do this the
evening before and leave in the fridge overnight.   Turn on to a pretty plate,
decorate as you wish, and serve with pouring cream and:
Chocolate Sauce: dissolve 6 oz (175 g) chocolate in 8 tbs milk and 4 tbs
strong black coffee, in a bain-marie.   Add 2-3 tbs of sherry, cool and use.

Madame la Comtesse de Beausaq, via Mrs. Alfred Friendly, Washington

Mousse de Karlsbad

6 eggs
1 pint (600 ml) double cream
knob of butter

1 tbs vanilla sugar (or to
  taste)
caster or demerara sugar

Separate the eggs.   Put the cream into a large saucepan and add the egg
yolks, butter and vanilla sugar.   Stir and beat over low heat until it
thickens, and be careful it does not 'catch'.   Remove from the heat at
the first sign of boiling and go on beating, off the heat until cool.
Meanwhile, whisk the egg whites stiff with a little extra vanilla sugar,
and fold into the custard cream, mixing gently into a frothy mousse.
Pour into a deep soufflé dish until almost full, then strew the top,
fairly thickly, with caster or demerara sugar, so that no mousse shows,
and smoothing it off, level with the brim.
Brown with a salamander, or flash under the grill, long enough for the
surface of the pudding to just melt, and turn colour and caramelize.
Then cool it at once.

NB Karlsbad Mousse is delicious if it is accompanied with a thick fruit
salad (as below) or prepared like it used to be in the Belgrade Embassy
in the days of that great cook - and friend - 'Tončika'.
She used a large soufflé dish and filled the bottom with a delicious
mixture of candied fruit: crystallized apricots and cherries, walnuts,
bananas, candied peaches, peeled white grapes, blanches almonds and large
seedless sultanas, then poured the mousse in on top and caramelized it.

H.E. Lady Peake

Thick Fruit Salad

6 oz (175 g) crystallized apricots, cut
  into pieces
3 oz (75 g) glacé cherries, halved
1 tbs diced candied orange
2 fresh bananas, sliced
14 oz (400 g) canned sliced peaches
  or pears, drained

small bunch seedless grapes,
  peeled
8 oz (225 g) lychees, or
  fruit chow-chow, drained
3-4 kiwi fruit, sliced
6 oz (175 g) skinned and blanched
  walnuts

Put everything together in a bowl.   Make a thin syrup by simmering 4 oz
(100 g) sugar in ½ pint (300 ml) water, until it is reduced to ¼ pint
(150 ml).   Add a little of the canned fruit juices and pour over the
fruit.   It should only wet, not drown it.

VERA'S GRANDMAMMA'S CAKE - A lunch-party gâteau

6 eggs, separated
6 tbs sugar
6 tbs ground walnuts (or hazelnuts)

1 tsp finely ground real coffee beans
apricot jam
½ pint (300 ml) whipping cream

Beat the egg yolks and sugar to a pale cream; add the nuts and coffee.   Fold in the egg whites beaten to a peak.
      Bake in a square tin in a moderate oven, 350°F (180°C) gas mark 4, for 15-20 minutes or until done.   Let it cool. Then cut the cake in half horizontally and put sieved apricot jam between the halves.   Cover the top with stiffly whipped cream and let it dribble down the sides.

H.E. Madame Velebit

ORANGE AND ALMOND CAKE

2 oz (50 g) fine breadcrumbs
juice of 3 oranges
grated rind of 1 orange
4 oz (100 g) ground almonds

4 eggs, separated
4 oz (100 g) caster sugar
¼ tsp salt
cream

Mix together the breadcrumbs, orange juice and rind and add the ground almonds.
      Beat the egg yolks well with sugar and salt and add them to the first mixture.   Fold in stiffly beaten egg whites and put into a greased cake tin.   Bake in a low oven, 300°F (150°C) gas mark 2 for 15 minutes or a shade longer.   Turn out when cool and chill.
      Just before serving decorate with whipped cream and orange slices, and hand a compôte of oranges in another dish with it.

ZORICA'S CHEESE CAKE

For the biscuit-crumb flan

6 oz (175 g) digestive biscuits, crushed
2 heaped tbs ground almonds

2 tbs caster sugar
$\frac{1}{4}$ lb (100 g) unsalted butter

Mix the biscuits with the ground almonds and sugar and work in the slightly melted butter.
Line a plain, greased flan tin which has a loose bottom, with this paste; pat it smooth.

For the filling

1 sachet ($\frac{1}{4}$ oz (10 g)) gelatine
2 eggs
$\frac{1}{4}$ lb (100 g) caster sugar

grated rind and juice of 1 lemon
$\frac{1}{2}$ pint (300 ml) cream
1 lb (500 g) Philadelphia cream cheese

Steep the gelatine in a cup with 4 tbs of cold water. Separate the eggs; whip the yolks and sugar until thick, adding the lemon juice and rind. In a blender, beat up half the cream with the cheese; add to it the egg and sugar mixture, and continue beating for a little. Dissolve the gelatine by holding the cup over hot water; partially whip the remaining cream and add both cream and gelatine to the mixture in the blender. Whip egg whites to a peak and fold these in with a metal spoon. Pour mixture into the prepared flan tin and leave overnight in the fridge.

To serve, turn out very carefully and dust the top with icing sugar.

NB Cheese cakes are traditional English sweet-meats, with countless regional variations, that have been eaten in this country since medieval times. They were introduced by early settlers to America, Canada and Australia, but for some reason their excellence has been forgotten in this country. Probably because most modern and commercial recipes are floury and stodgy? This one isn't.

Lady Glen

Four Quick Puddings

1. Iced Coffee Tazzas

Buy some good quality coffee ice cream.   Melt it a little and pile it into
pretty china coffee cups or small china teacups.   Smooth off the top.   Put
the cups in the fridge or deep freeze and to serve, just wipe the cups dry,
replace them on their saucers, and serve with coffee spoons and a jug of
single cream.   You can melt a bar of dark chocolate and dribble a little
over the top of each cup, or grind up a few coffee beans and sprinkle them
over the ice.

2. Fitz's Rapid Apples FOR 6

Peel, core and chop up about 5 sharp juicy Granny Smith's apples.   Pat dry
with kitchen paper and squeeze a little lemon juice over them to stop
discoloring.   Mix with ¼ pint (150 ml) sour cream and pile into glass
goblets.   Sprinkle over 3 tbs molasses sugar, then about 1 tbs old-fashioned
coffee sugar and serve very cold.

3. Sukie's Green Fruit Salad

Mix together in a bowl 1 white or green-fleshed ripe melon, scooped into
balls with a melon baller; a bunch of green grapes - muscatel if possible -
skinned and de-pipped; 2 ripe William pears, peeled and chopped, and
11 oz (300 g) canned lychees, drained and chopped.
If you don't have enough juice, make a little syrup by boiling the lychee
juice with sugar and water, and, when cold adding it to the fruit.   Then
spoon fruit and juice carefully into a glass serving bowl which you have
lined with 5 or 6 kiwi fruit, cut into thin rounds.   Decorate with a sprig
of scented geranium leaves, or a spoonful or two of fraises des bois.

4. Charlie's Green Grapes

Pare the rind from 2 oranges as finely as you can.   Make a syrup by boiling
20 lumps of sugar with ¼ pint (150 ml) water.   When the syrup is cold,
add ½ pint (300 ml) champagne and the orange rind.   Peel and remove the
pips from 1½ lb (700 g) green grapes, preferably muscatels.   Pour the syrup
over them and leave to cool for 2 hours.

CHERRY MERINGUE

Take one large tin of black cherries (about 14 oz (400 g)), if possible the Swiss kind in heavy syrup.

Pour into a soufflé dish and chill.   Fifteen minutes before the meal cover them with a good 1 inch (2.5 cm) of vanilla ice cream and cover this with a meringue mixture.

Put under a very hot grill for about 8 minutes to bake the meringue.

Lady Caroline Somerset

PEARS PORTUGUESE FASHION, WITH CURRANTS (1759)

3-4 pears
1 pint (600 ml) port
8 lumps of sugar

a stick of cinnamon
lemon peel
6 oz (175 g) currants

"Take three or four Williams or other good winter pears, pare them, cut them in two and take out the choke, boil them in water only half an hour, put them into a stew pan, pour in a pint of port wine with a lump of fine sugar, a stick of cinnamon, a bit of lemon peel, a spoonful of two of water and about five or six ounces of the best dry currants;   let them all stew together till your pears are very tender, dish them up and pour your currants over, but take out the cinnamon and peel".

AUTUMN FRUIT SALAD

6 fresh ripe William pears
6-8 fresh figs
1 avocado
$\frac{3}{4}$ pint (450 ml) water
3 oz (75 g) loaf, or crushed lump sugar

1 lemon
6 apples and their equal weight
   of quinces
1 small jar crab apple jelly
madeira or Van der Hum liqueur

Peel and slice the first three fruit and put them in a pretty china bowl. Make a light   syrup from $\frac{1}{2}$ pint (300 ml) of the water, sugar, and the juice and half the thin rind of the lemon.   When cold, pour over the fruit. Meanwhile, peel, core and slice the apples and quinces and poach them very slowly in the oven in a syrup made from the crab apple jelly, $\frac{1}{4}$ pint (150 ml) water and a large curl of thin lemon rind.   Let the apples cool in this syrup and then add them to the other fruit.   Flavour with madeira or Van der Hum liqueur - as preferred.   Chill well, and serve with a bowl of double cream, or better still, Devonshire cream.

THE CREGGANS INN
STRACHUR
ARGYLL PA27 8BX

A.A. ★ ★ ★ R.A.C.
CHAÎNE DES RÔTISSEURS
EGON RONAY

TELEPHONES:
STRACHUR 036.986.279 and 777
TELEX: 727396 ATT.CREGGANS

RACHEL'S VACHERIN BRESILIEN
Cordon Bleu Classic

Ingredients for Meringue

3 egg whites (4 if small)
2oz (28 gms) caster sugar
6oz (168 gms) soft brown sugar

Filling

½ pint (300 ml) double cream; 1 rounded teaspoon instant
coffee; 2-3 small ripe bananas; 3-4 pieces glacé ginger.

Decoration

3 tablespoons sifted icing sugar; 4 fl.oz (120 ml) cream,
whipped.

Set the oven at 140/275°, Gas Mark 1 and line two baking
sheets with Bakewell paper.
Beat the egg whites and caster sugar in a bowl until stiff
and then quickly fold in the sifted soft brown sugar with
a large metal spoon. Divide the mixture in two and spread
carefully in circles 8" in diameter or use a forcing bag
with a plain ½" tube and pipe the meringue in a spiral
pattern on the baking sheets.
Bake the meringue in the pre-heated oven for about 60-70
minutes or until it is dry and lightly coloured. Cool
on a wire rack and when almost cold, peel off the paper.
Flavour the cream with the coffee dissolved in a very little
water and sweeten lightly. Cut the glacé ginger into fine
shreds and slice the bananas. Fill the meringue rounds with
the coffee flavoured cream, ginger and bananas, making sure
the bananas are well coated with cream to prevent discolour-
ation. Dust the top of the vacherin with icing sugar and
decorate with rosettes of whipped cream.

Rachel Lund

Fromage Rose with Strawberries

I do not usually like fruit out of season but this is a delicious and easy pudding that can be made with frozen strawberries as well as with fresh ones.

1½ lb (700 g) frozen unsweetened or fresh strawberries
4-5 oz (100-150 g) caster sugar
juice of 2 oranges

2 tbs cointreau
1¼ lb (600 g) cream cheese
2 eggs, separated
a little white pepper

Divide the strawberries into two bowls. Sprinkle each bowl liberally with sugar, keeping a little in reserve, and pour the orange juice which you have mixed with half the cointreau over both.

Defrost slowly, if the strawberries are frozen, or leave them to marinate for 1-2 hours if they are fresh.

When they are soft beat half the strawberries to a squashy purée with a fork, or whirl them in a liquidiser. Soften the cream cheese with a fork and beat it into the strawberry purée, adding more sugar if you wish, and the rest of the cointreau. Mix in the beaten egg yolks, and lastly fold in the egg whites, which you have beaten to a peak.

Pour the mixture into a rinsed-out mould, or a soufflé dish, and put it in the fridge to firm up.

The second bowl of strawberries over which you now sprinkle a little pepper, to bring out their flavour, can be served either separately, as a compôte, or in a wide flat bowl surrounding the turned out fromage rose. Sablé or amaretti biscuits should accompany it.

Vegetables

ALEXIS BENOIT SOYER
1809–1858
Cook to the Duke of Sutherland,
the Marquis of Ailsa and the Reform Club

BETH'S BOSTON BAKED BEANS

1st stage, if using dried haricot beans*

Soak 1 lb (500 g) haricot beans for at least 2 hours or overnight.
Drain and put into a pan with an onion into which you stick
2 cloves, a carrot, a stick of celery and a bouquet of herbs.
Cover with cold water, bring to the boil and simmer very gently
for 1-2 hours, or even longer if beans are old.   Remove carrot
etc. and drain - but keep about 1 pint (600 ml) of the cooking
liquid.

2nd stage

Take a deep earthenware ovenproof pot and put in it:
1 layer of beans
1 layer of chopped onions
1 layer of bacon, cut in thick pieces

Sprinkle with a little Demerara sugar and dribble a big spoonful
of molasses (black treacle) over it.   Repeat the layers and the
sugar and molasses again.   Then pour on half the reserved liquid
that you have heated to simmering point and bake in a slow oven,
300°F (150°F) gas mark 2, for about 4 hours.   Look at it
occasionally and add a little more boiling bean water if it looks
like drying up too much.   You can also stir in a little more
bacon fat.   Salt the beans, if necessary, at the last minute,
before serving.

* Omit 1st stage if you are using tinned beans.

Mrs. P.S. Bush

MRS. BEMISS'S 'SNAPPER' BEANS

Melt 6 oz (175 g) mild grated cheese (Cheddar, Romano etc.) in
½ pint (300 ml) creamy béchamel sauce.   Cook together for 5-6
minutes, then pour over about 10 oz (275 g) (or a 2 pint (1.2
litre) measure) of just cooked and drained 'snapper' beans
(haricots verts, the continental kind).   Mix through and serve.

Mrs. FitzGerald Bemiss

HARICOTS VERTS WITH BACON AND ALMONDS

(By this I don't mean the flat runner beans that are sliced diagonally and too often eaten when middle-aged, but the rounded, stringless continental variety that you eat young and whole, merely topping and tailing to prepare. Americans call them 'snapper' beans.)

Throw the beans into boiling water, add salt at the last minute, just before serving, or it will toughen the beans. Cook until tender but still firm. Drain in a colander. In the hot pan you have cooked the beans in, melt 1 tbs of bacon fat, and fry crisp 2-3 chopped up rashers of streaky bacon and a handful of blanched almonds.

Return the beans and toss them in the hot fat until they colour a little and are well mixed with the bacon and almonds. The leftovers from this dish will make a delicious salad (Germans call it Bohnen-Salat) - you merely add a good vinaigrette dressing and some chopped chervil.

FRENCH BEANS À LA CREME, - great grandmother's recipe

½ lb (225 g) young French beans
3 egg yolks
3 tbs cream

2 oz (50 g) unsalted butter
1 tbs vinegar
salt

String and slice this amount of French beans, or as many as you may require, and boil them in a large quantity of water until they are tender, then drain them. Beat the egg yolks with the cream and the butter. When they are thoroughly mixed together pour into a saucepan and set it over the heat. When very hot, stir in the vinegar, then add the beans, and let it all simmer for 5-6 minutes; stir it constantly with a wooden spoon, salt it to taste and serve it up very hot.

This recipe can be used today with frozen French beans, and will make them much more interesting.

ITALIAN RED BEANS STEWED WITH MUSHROOMS

red beans
12 small onions/2 tbs butter
½ pint (300 ml) red wine

½ lb (225 g) mushrooms
salt and pepper
grated nutmeg

Cook as many red beans as you will want (if they are fresh start them cooking in boiling water, if dried, in cold, but in the latter case they should have been first soaked overnight). When done, take them out, but do not drain them, put them into a casserole, together with the onions, butter, red wine, mushrooms, salt and pepper and a little nutmeg. Simmer gently for 30 minutes and serve.

BRUSSELS SPROUTS, CHESTNUTS AND BACON

Choose as small and tight sprouts as possible.   Wash and
pick them over, removing all faded leaves etc.   Put them
into boiling water and cook them for 15 minutes.

Strain them into a colander;   throw a little cold water over
them, drain again thoroughly;   then put them into a saucepan
with a little piece of butter, salt and pepper, a grating of
nutmeg and a little stock (about 4 tbs).   Leave them by the
side of the hot plate to heat through.

Meanwhile, prick, boil, peel and boil again 12 chestnuts;
break them up when they are just soft and crumble them and
4 rashers of bacon that you have grilled crisp over the sprouts.

Served this way they are good enough to eat on their own.

POLISH BEETROOT AND APPLE

2-3 tbs butter
about 12 small beetroots
1 onion, grated
2-3 tbs molasses
juice of 1 lemon
salt
¼ pint (150 ml) decent red wine
2-3 apples, peeled and sliced
beurre manié

Melt the butter in a cast iron frying pan.   Add roughly
chopped or grated beetroot, onion and molasses.   Brown over
low heat, stirring constantly.

Add the lemon juice and salt.   Simmer covered for 2-2½ hours,
stirring occasionally.   Add wine and apples halfway through
cooking.   Before serving, stir in a walnut of beurre manié.

Serves 6-8.

CELERY FONDU

(This can also be served as a first course)

To make sufficient fondu for a small dinner you require 5 good long stalks, or a small head of celery.

When it is well washed and cleaned, chop the celery up finely and put it into a saucepan with enough cold water to cover it.   Put in a little salt, heat up and boil for 5 minutes.   Strain and put into another saucepan, add 1 pint (600 ml) milk, a bouquet garni, and cook it until it is tender enough to pass through a sieve.   Then add 1 oz (25 g) butter, 1 oz (25 g) very fine flour, and cook it until the purée becomes quite thick.   Add again a little salt, and cayenne pepper, if liked, and lemon juice.   Beat up the yolks of 3 eggs until they are quite like cream, add them to the purée, away from the heat, and then lastly fold in the whites of the 3 eggs after they have been whipped to a very stiff froth.

Pour the mixture either into ramekin dishes (only half-fill them) or into a soufflé dish, sprinkle some lightly browned breadcrumbs over, add a morsel of butter to keep them moist, and bake in a moderate oven, 350°F (180°C) gas mark 4, for about 15 minutes.

Leeks Shelton

Take some leeks and cut to the length required, leaving very little green on them.   Parboil them for about 20 minutes and drain well.   Put some grated cheese - Bel Paese or Cheddar - in a buttered fireproof dish, and then a layer of leeks and then again cheese, and season to taste.   Pour some cream over the leeks, and sprinkle with some more cheese.   Bake in a moderate oven, 350°F (180°C) gas mark 4, until a golden brown.   Serve very hot.

Purée of Onions

12 medium onions, sliced
¼ pint (150 ml) double cream
3 tbs sherry
salt and pepper
grated nutmeg
3 tbs butter

Preheat the oven to 350°F (180°C) gas mark 4.   Parboil the onions until tender but still firm, about 10 minutes.   Drain and turn into a greased earthenware baking dish.   Mix cream, sherry, salt, pepper and nutmeg and pour over the onions.

Dot with butter.   Cover and bake until the onions are tender, about 30 minutes.

Endives Meunière (Chicory Meunière)

Take the necessary quantity of chicory (the outer leaves having been removed and the chicory heads washed in cold water) and dispose them in a flat tin or braising pan.   Squeeze half a lemon over them, sprinkle with salt and cover them with water; they should be only just covered. Bring to the boil and keep them boiling, covered all the time with a buttered paper.   They take rather long to cook, about 30-45 minutes. At the end they should be quite soft and almost transparent.   Drain them well and keep them hot.   In a frying pan, melt a good piece of butter; when it has reached the foaming stage, put in the chicory, cook quickly, turning them so that they are pleasantly browned on both sides.   Then put in a serving dish, add salt and another squeeze of lemon and pour over them the butter from the pan.

CARROTS POULETTE

Scrape and cut young carrots into slices. Put them into boiling water
with a little salt and a little butter. When they are cooked drain
them. Whilst they are draining put into a saucepan a piece of butter
as big as a walnut (about ½ oz (15 g)) and 1 tbs flour. Mix well and
season with salt and pepper. Add about ¼ pint (150 ml) of good, ungreasy
stock.

When your sauce is well mixed and smooth, add the yolk of an egg mixed
with a little of the carrot juices, to thicken it. Then add ½ oz (15 g)
butter, in small pieces, a little at a time, and finally, a good squeeze
of lemon juice. Turn the carrots in the sauce, heat up and serve, with
chopped parsley sprinkled on top.

FEZ CARROTS

2½ lb (1.25 kg) young carrots

¼ lb (100 g) butter

½ onion

½ tsp grated nutmeg

4 tbs white wine

salt and pepper

¼ lb (100 g) seedless raisins or sultanas

2 tbs brown sugar

Peel the carrots and slice them into rounds about ¼ inch (5 mm) thick.
Put them in a saucepan with the butter. Add the shaved, paper-thin rings
of the onion, the nutmeg and the wine. Season and cover closely and
cook so gently that it only just simmers for about 40 minutes - 1 hour or
until the carrots are quite tender. Soak the raisins during this time,
drain and add to carrots, with the sugar, a few minutes before serving.
The liquid may reduce too fast, in which case you simply add more boiling
wine.

BRAISED CHICORY (ENDIVES) WITH BEEF MARROW

2 lb (1 kg) chicory
salt and pepper
juice of 1 lemon
3-4 slices beef marrow
a little consommé to poach marrow

2 oz (50 g) butter
¼ pint (150 ml) demi-glace,
  or rich brown gravy stock,
  fortified with some meat
  jelly

Wash and inspect the chicory.   Remove any damaged outer
leaves;   simmer for 15 minutes in boiling salted water.
Remove and drain by laying on top of a silk or nylon sieve,
or an enamel or plastic colander.   Then arrange the chicory
heads in a shallow entrée dish or a casserole with a lid.
Season with pepper and the lemon juice.   Pour over enough
demi-glace or rich gravy to cover the chicory.
    Cover the dish with buttered greaseproof paper, replace
the lid and cook slowly in the oven, 325°F (160°C) gas mark 3,
for 1 hour.   When it is brown and semi-braised, put the slices
of beef marrow (that you have poached in a little consommé) on
top of the chicory, spoon a little sauce over, and continue
cooking slowly for another 15 minutes.

Mrs. John Noble

SWEET BASIL JELLY

Make this when basil is plentiful.   It is useful for winter
sauces, looks pretty and makes a nice present for a friend.

2 oz (50 g) fresh basil leaves
8 fl oz (225 ml) vinegar
about 3 lb (1.5 kg) granulated
  sugar

8 fl oz (225 ml) bottled pectin
12 fl oz (350 ml) water
green food colouring or dark
  spinach juice

Mix the basil leaves with the vinegar, sugar and water.   Bring
to a full rolling boil and boil for 1 minute.   Strain off
the liquid and add to it the pectin and enough green colouring
to make it mint green or a little darker.   Pour into jars and
seal.   Makes about 8-9 ½ pint (300 ml) jars.

Genevieve Hyndman

GREEN PEPPERS BAKED IN OIL or PAPRIKE DOMACI

8-10 medium sized pale green young peppers
5-7 tbs good, strong olive oil
1 tbs coarse sea salt

Wipe and trim the peppers, cutting the stalks off as
short as possible, but do not cut open or deseed.   Pack
them tightly, stalk side down, into a shallow baking tin.
Spoon over them the olive oil and roll each one over in
it until they are well coated.   Sprinkle the salt over
them and bake in a moderate oven, 350°F (180°C) gas mark 4,
for about 25 minutes.   You can turn them over halfway
through so that both sides will colour.   Take them out of
the oven, and either eat them hot, or allow them to get
cold, and make them into a salad.

For this you pour the pan juices into a bowl and make a
French dressing with them, adding a little vinegar, salt
and pepper etc.   Then pour the dressing back on to the
peppers, and mix them up in it.

This makes one of the best salads in the world and it is
so quick and easy to prepare that I can't think why it is
not more often used.

Ruziča Napotnik

The next four delicacies can still be found growing wild in our woods and fields, and it is very rewarding to hunt for them. Cêpes and chanterelles are easily recognisable and are found in woods in September. Morels are found in birch woods in the spring but should be identified with caution. Field mushrooms, now rare, are found in July and late summer, and also need experience in identifying.

HOW TO COOK CÊPES A French husband's recipe

These large fleshy mushrooms are excellent as a side dish with roast beef. The first step is to scald them in boiling water for 5 minutes. Then place them on a cloth to drain. My wife does this the night before, to give them plenty of time to dry, and even so she sometimes finds in the morning that they are still moist, and has to press them between cloths.

If you are using canned cêpes instead of fresh ones, you can skip the scalding, but it is advisable all the same to take them out of the can the night before and let them drain. The cêpes should be cooked in peanut or walnut oil, not olive oil - about $\frac{1}{2}$ inch (1 cm) deep in a frying pan. Put in a large garlic clove for every 1 lb (500 g) cêpes. Brown 5 minutes on each side and then transfer to a deep earthenware cooking dish (or a cast iron pot), together with the oil and the garlic, adding more of the former if much has boiled away.

Season to taste with salt and pepper, add finely chopped parsley, (at least 3 tbs), and cook over a low heat for 1 hour, very slowly. Do not let the oil give more than an occasional bubble. If the cêpes are very large, then cook them for $1\frac{1}{2}$ hours. Then 10 minutes before serving, add more parsley. Serve hot from the stove in the oil.

HOW TO COOK CHANTERELLES

Wipe with a damp cloth or wash if very dirty. Dry well. Sauté in butter or peanut or walnut oil for 3-4 minutes with crushed garlic, as much as you like. Scatter chopped parsley over and add cream if you want a sauce.

HOW TO COOK MORELS

If they are fresh, cook them like chanterelles, but a little longer. If dried, scald them, and leave them in hot water, or appropriate light stock until they are well 'plumped out', then dry well, and proceed in the same way.

FIELD MUSHROOMS AND SOUR CREAM

1 lb (500 g) fresh mushrooms   ½ pint (300 ml) sour cream
1 small onion, sliced   1 tbs sherry
2 oz (50 g) margarine (not butter)   salt and pepper

Wipe the mushrooms with a damp cloth.   Trim the ends off their stalks.
Slice them vertically, through cap, stalks and all.

Sauté the onion in melted margarine until limp and dead.   Add the
mushrooms, cover the pan, and cook slowly for 5 minutes.   Add cream,
sherry and seasoning.   Enough for 6-8.

FOUR DAY SPINACH

This recipe, of unusual goodness, demonstrates the ability of spinach
to absorb butter.   I believe one could go on adding butter to it for
seven days, but by the end of four days it looks and tastes so good
that it has to be eaten.

3-4 lb (1.5-1.75 kg) spinach   grated nutmeg
1 lb (500 g) unsalted clarified butter   lemon juice
salt and pepper

Day 1: Cook the spinach: wash it in 4 waters, shake it dry, then cook
with no water in a pan with a lid until it is tender.   Chop it roughly
before reheating it with ¼ lb (100 g) of the butter.   Leave it to cool
in a clean basin, then store overnight in the refrigerator.

Day 2: Reheat the spinach again, stirring in another ¼ lb (100 g) butter.
Remove from the heat as soon as butter is absorbed, and the spinach
reaches boiling point.   Leave to cool.   Store in refrigerator.

Days 3 and 4: Repeat Day 2, but on the 4th day, do not leave it to
cool, but eat it.   You will have a rich, dark green purée, a cream or
sauce rather than a vegetable.   Serve it with boiled gammon, or a roast
joint of beef or veal, or charcoal-grilled steak, or a carré de porc.
Or eat it by itself, with snippets of toast.

Should there be any spinach left over, use it to stuff an omelette or
to make individual eggs Florentine.

Dalmatian Tomatoes and Aubergines

3 lb (1.5 kg) tomatoes	1 tbs chopped basil
salt and pepper	2 tbs chopped parsley
4-5 tbs olive oil (unrefined)	4 garlic cloves, crushed
4 tbs breadcrumbs	2 tbs grilled crumbled bacon
1 tsp chopped fresh thyme	and/or a little grated cheese
or oregano	

Cut the tomatoes in two and arrange them, cut side up, in a
shallow baking dish or roasting pan.   Salt and pepper them;
sprinkle half the olive oil over them, then mix the other
ingredients together in a bowl.   Put a teaspoonful of the
stuffing on top of each tomato half.   Sprinkle the rest of the
olive oil over them, and bake, uncovered in a moderate oven,
350°F (180°C) gas mark 4, for 30-40 minutes.

When they are cooked finish them off by browning under the grill,
and if you like cheese, sprinkle a little grated cheese over
the tomatoes before you do this.

You can cook aubergines in the same way, cutting them in two
lengthways, leaving their skins on, and sweating them for 1
hour before you prepare them.   They make a nice 'garniture'
arranged alternately with the tomatoes round a simple meat salad.

Quick Spanish Rice

1 tbs lard, or unrefined olive oil
2 bacon rashers, finely chopped
14 oz (400 g) rice
14 oz (400 g) canned Italian tomato sauce, or tomato soup
1 small celery stick, including leaves, chopped
salt

Melt the lard or heat the oil in a heavy pan; fry the bacon,
add the rice and other ingredients and cook for a few minutes.
Add about 1¼ pints (750 ml) of water and let boil fast until
almost dry.   Then put a lid on the pan and cook over a low
heat until done.   You can add a few red or green peppers to
this dish if you wish.   Pork fillets or lamb cutlets are very
nice arranged on top of it.

POMMES ANNA

2½ lb (1.25 kg) potatoes
salt and pepper
6 oz (175 g) butter

Peel and shape the potatoes into cylinders of roughly the same size, then
slice them thinly by hand or in a food processor. Dry the slices well,
salt and pepper them and place them in a round, well buttered tin or 'Anna'
mould, or in a small sauteuse. Arrange the bottom layer artistically
with the potato slices neatly overlapping, then build up with layers of
potato slices until the mould is well filled. Pour slightly browned
melted butter over the top and bake in a hot oven, 400°F (200°C) gas
mark 6, for about 40 minutes.

When the potatoes are done, soft in the middle and crispy brown on the
outside edges, press them down lightly and turn out carefully on to a round
serving dish. Before serving, glaze lightly by brushing with melted
butter. They turn out (like a cake) particularly well if the mould or
sauteuse is stood in a bain-marie in the oven, with hot water in the outer
pan.

CREAM AND CHEESE POTATOES

Peel and thinly slice 2 lb (1 kg) raw potatoes. Put them in a basin and
add salt, pepper, grated nutmeg, a beaten egg, 1 pint (600 ml) scalded
milk, and ¼ lb (100 g) of grated Gruyère cheese.

Mix these all together, put into an earthenware dish, rubbed with garlic,
and well buttered. Spread the surface with grated cheese, add several
nuts of butter, and cook in a moderate oven, 350°F (180°C) gas mark 4,
for 40-45 minutes. If you want to make it very rich and delicious, use
cream instead of milk.

POTATO PANCAKES

This is a very ordinary dish in Scotland, perhaps so humble that it is
beneath most cookery books' dignity to mention - and yet it is the perfect
accompaniment to cold venison or game. It looks well arranged in a row
on a large dish with a twin row of pease pudding patties or chopped cabbage
patties, cooked the same way.

Use leftover potato purée, or make some rather stiff, very smooth mashed
potatoes. When they are cold, shape them into flat round cakes or patties,
the size of a scone. Do it on a lightly floured marble or formica surface.
Season well, and transfer them carefully to a heavy frying pan in which you
have a little good, hot beef dripping. Cook them slowly, without moving,
until a golden brown skin has formed, then turn them over with a spatula
and brown the other side. Not too much dripping - the skin should be
crisp.

POMMES DE TERRE LORRAINE

Grate 1 lb (500 g) of fine big potatoes on the largest part of a
cheese grater. Drain over a nylon sieve. Mix with 2 eggs, well
beaten together with salt and pepper. Add 3-4 finely crushed
garlic cloves. Mix together well.
Heat some butter in a frying pan, add the potatoes to a depth of
about ½ inch (1 cm), level off and let each side of the potato cake
become golden, like a pancake. It will take about 20 minutes.

(If you want more, work with double quantities and have 2
frying pans going).

RUZICA'S ROAST POTATOES   Korčula

Every Sunday in Korčula we eat a delicious roast chicken,
surrounded by a special kind of roast potato that I have never
met with anywhere else. They are something between a chip, a
sautéed and a roast potato. This is how Ruzica cooks them.

The potatoes are peeled and cut lengthways in two, then each half
is cut into three or four quarter-moon shaped pieces. These are
dried on a cloth and then put into the already boiling fat and
olive oil round the chicken. More really hot olive oil is poured
over them and they continue cooking, with the chicken, for about
another 40 minutes or until they are crisp and golden outside and
floury and cooked inside. At the last moment they are sprinkled
with salt. The secret is to put them dry and raw into boiling oil.

Ruzica Napotnik

Mustard Rice Salad

8 oz (225 g) patna rice (long-grain)

1 pint (600 ml) chicken stock

8 fl oz (225 ml) salad oil

2 tbs vinegar

2 tbs prepared English mustard

salt and pepper

4 oz (100 g) olives, chopped

2 hard-boiled eggs, diced

3 celery sticks, sliced

4 oz (100 g) dill pickles

½ lb (225 g) chopped green pepper

1 small onion, minced

6 fl oz (175 ml) mayonnaise

chopped parsley

Cook the rice in the stock until the liquid is absorbed and the rice is 'al dente.' Blend together the oil, vinegar, mustard, salt and pepper. Pour over hot rice, toss and set aside to cool. Add remaining ingredients, toss gently and chill. Put a little chopped parsley on top.

Green Rice Salad

1 oz (25 g) butter, melted

about ¾ lb (350 g) cooked hot rice

2 oz (50 g) finely chopped parsley

3 celery sticks, chopped, or fennel

½ green pepper, deseeded and chopped

black pepper

Add butter to the hot rice, then with a fork mix with the other ingredients through it to distribute evenly. Dust with black pepper.

The Duchess of Portland

Beetroot à la Parisienne

beetroot
tarragon vinegar
anchovies
eggs
capers

gherkins
herbs
oil
vinegar
mustard

Cut up a cooked beetroot into thick round slices, hollowed
out in the middle so as to form a cup. Marinate these for
two hours in tarragon vinegar, then fill them with a mixture
of anchovies, hard-boiled eggs, capers, gherkins and herbs,
all chopped up and seasoned with oil, vinegar and mustard.
Keep them on ice and serve as cold as possible, as a side dish
or garnish to cold meat, or as a summer first course on its own.

Fried Beetroot

beetroot
1 tbs white wine
flour
cream
1 egg

salt and pepper
$\frac{1}{4}$ tsp ground cloves
breadcrumbs
chopped parsley
lemon

Cook a beetroot, peel it and cut it into long slices (lengthways
in the shape of cutlets), then dip these slices into a paste
made as follows: 1 tbs of white wine, very fine flour, cream,
a raw egg (but use rather more yolk than white), salt, pepper
and half a powdered clove. When you have dipped the slices
of beetroot into this paste, dust them over with breadcrumbs
a little flour and chopped parsley and fry them. Drain and
serve with slices of lemon, or with lemon juice.

Fried Salsify

Salsify

vinegar

4 tbs flour

1 tbs olive oil

pinch of salt

a little beer

2 egg whites

dripping

parsley

Scrape the salsify gently so as to strip them of the outside peel; only then cut them into pieces of equal size and throw them into water with a little vinegar to keep them from getting black. Boil them for about 45 minutes in salted water. Make a batter of the flour, olive oil, salt and a little beer. Beat up the whites of egg and pour them into the batter and stir gently. Drain the salsify on a cloth and put them in the batter. Take them out one by one and fry in dripping. Do not let them stick together. Serve with fried parsley.

ARTICHOKES AU GRATIN

1 lb (500 g) canned artichoke
  hearts, or fresh ones if available
butter
1 rounded tbs flour
½ pint (300 ml) hot milk
salt and pepper

1 tsp mustard
1 tsp vinegar
¼ lb (100 g) grated cheese,
  half Parmesan and half
  Gruyère ideally
¼ pint (150 ml) cream

Drain the artichoke hearts, dry them and sweat them for a
few minutes in butter until tender.   Put them in a shallow
ovenproof entrée dish, greased with butter.   Make a roux
with ½ oz (15 g) butter and the flour, cook it a little,
pour in the hot milk, and bring to boiling point, stirring
hard.   Simmer for 10 minutes, then cool a little, and add
the mustard and vinegar.   Put the pan back on the stove,
add most of the cheese, and cook for a few minutes more.
Then take off the heat and beat in the cream and pour the
sauce over the artichokes.   Sprinkle the rest of the cheese
over the top and dot with butter.   Bake at 325°F (160°C)
gas mark 3, for 20 minutes.   Put under a very hot grill
just before serving, to brown the top.

This dish makes an excellent first course.

Mrs. Rob MacPherson

RIZ À LA CRÉOLE

10 oz (300 g) Carolina rice
5 oz (150 g) butter

1 pint (600 ml) water
salt

Pour the rice into a heavy casserole with half the butter,
melted.   Add the water, season with salt, cover and cook
in a warm oven, 325°F (160°C) gas mark 3, for about 14-18
minutes, or until the grains are tender but al 'dente', and
have absorbed all the liquid.   Add the remaining butter
in small pieces.   Let it rest for at least 10 minutes in
a warm place.   Separate the grains by stirring with a fork
just before serving.

Index

Recipes

FIRST COURSE HOT

FIRST COURSE COLD

Index

Contributors

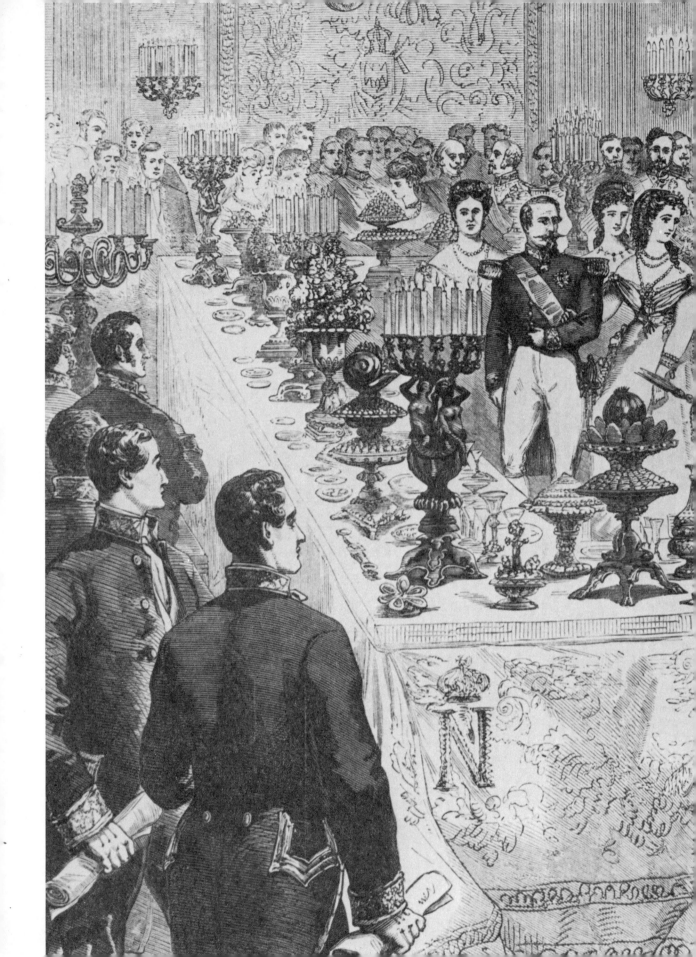